Mission Among the Blackfeet

Mission Among
the Blackfeet

by

Howard L. Harrod

NORMAN

UNIVERSITY OF OKLAHOMA PRESS

International Standard Book Number: 0–8061–0966–1

Library of Congress Catalog Card Number: 77–160494

Copyright 1971 by the University of Oklahoma Press, Publishing Division of the University. Composed and printed at Norman, Oklahoma, U.S.A., by the University of Oklahoma Press. First edition.

Mission Among the Blackfeet is Volume 112 in *The Civilization of the American Indian Series.*

Preface

Some of the motivation for this study began when I first became aware of racial and cultural differences. In the Oklahoma of my childhood borders between the black and white world were kept inviolable by the practice of segregation, and I remained ignorant of the black experience in American society. By contrast with blacks, Indians were not often segregated from the rest of the population. Indians and whites mingled in the public schools, the market place, the barbershop, the swimming pool—and even in the peculiar institution of adolescent dating. Intermarriage was not uncommon. Heirs of well-to-do Indians might also be graduates of a University and own a substantial portion of the community real estate. All this is not to say that prejudice and discrimination against Indians were absent from social practice. Along with blacks, some Indians felt the hatred of white eyes and the burden of white exploitation, but there was no impenetrable caste line. It was possible for Indians and whites to communicate. My interest in Indian lore and history was nurtured by such experiences.

Graduate study in religion gave me further opportunity to expand this interest and to focus it through disciplined exploration. Some of the attitudes resulting from my formal study are implicit in this work. For instance, from the sociology of religion I learned much. From Max Weber I learned the importance of religious ideas and values for motivating individual and collective behavior. From Emile Durkheim I learned the importance of social cohesion and the part which religion plays in man's corporate life. I also learned from Karl Mannheim's sociology of knowledge that man's mental products depend upon a shared, value-laden world view. On the philosophical-theological side, George H. Mead and H. Richard Niebuhr taught me to see in a deeper way the self and its products as social realities.

Through these several perspectives I came to understand the relationship between white and Indian as a series of confrontations between different social worlds, each with its own integrity and institutional forms. Seen in this way, Indian-white relations can be understood as the conflict between the two evaluations of the world and of the meaning of life. Since religious experience and its institutional expression is often the locus for such meanings and values, I thought that a study of the missionary movement might shed light upon the principles of the white world presented to the Indians. Likewise, I hoped that this way of seeing the subject might also lead to a deeper understanding of the meanings and values of the Indian world.

Since it is impossible to understand Indians generally, their cultures being so diverse, I decided to focus my questions upon a single tribe, the Blackfeet. There will be those who think that I have understood the white missionary activity better than I do the Blackfoot response. This may be true. I have tried to compensate for my non-Indianness by living on the Blackfeet Reservation in Montana during the summers of 1963 and 1969. In addition to talking with countless Indians and whites on the reservation, I immersed myself in both the published sources on the Blackfeet and the unpublished archival collections located in the Museum of the Plains Indian in Browning, Montana, and the Montana Historical Society in Helena.

In many ways the white world of the missionary was easier to reconstruct. In the case of both Protestant and Roman Catholic missionary enterprises, unpublished archival resources were available in the Oregon Province Archives of the Society of Jesus located at Gonzaga University in Spokane, Washington; in the Chancery Archives of the Diocese of Helena; in the Montana Conference Historical Collection located at Rocky Mountain College in Billings, Montana; and in documents preserved at the missions on the reservation.

On the basis of these several sorts of data I have built a narrative which aims at an explanation of the role of missionary institutions in representing the white world to the Blackfeet and the corresponding responses. The interpretations which I have given this history, as well as the assessment of what was fact, are matters of judgment. For these judgments I take full responsibility. I take particular responsibility for the method of the study. The nature of the questions dictated that I transgress the boundaries of several diverse disciplines: anthropology, history, sociology, and social psychology. I am sure that specialists in these areas will recognize the limitations of such a procedure. To my mind the benefits of the study are clear; it allows the rich complexity of human reality to be refracted through a multidimensional perspective. I have concluded that the outcome is worth the methodological risks.

I am dependent upon a number of persons in addition to the resources already mentioned: to Professor James M. Gustafson of Yale University, under whose tutelage my initial work on the Blackfeet was focused in a Ph.D. dissertation; to John C. Ewers of the Smithsonian Institution, who shared with me his detailed knowledge of the Blackfeet and who read more than one draft of the manuscript; to the Reverend James E. Bell, former United Methodist missionary among the Blackfeet, without whose cooperation this study could never have been completed; to Father Egon Mallman, S.J., who kindly shared with me his experience of over three decades among the Blackfeet; to Professor Carroll Bourg, who read the manuscript and made a number of helpful suggestions; to Doug King, who checked the footnotes and held me to a standard of excellence in matters of detail; and to Harlan Beckley for assistance in making the index. In addition, I should like to acknowledge the assistance of the University Research

Council of Vanderbilt University which made possible my return to the Blackfeet in the summer of 1969.

HOWARD L. HARROD

The Divinity School
Vanderbilt University
February 1, 1971

Contents

Illustrations

Maps

Abbreviations

BAA—Blackfeet Agency Archives, Museum of the Plains Indian, Browning, Montana.

BMC—Browning Methodist Church Files, Browning, Montana.

CHC—Montana Conference Historical Collection, Rocky Mountain College, Billings, Montana.

CA—Chancery Archives, Diocese of Helena, Helena, Montana.

DNM—Official Files of the Division of National Missions of the Board of Missions of the Methodist Church, Philadelphia, Pennsylvania.

JA—Oregon Province Archives of the Society of Jesus, Crosby Library, Gonzaga University, Spokane, Washington.

MHS—Montana Historical Society, Helena, Montana.

PS—University of Puget Sound, Tacoma, Washington.

Introduction:

Indian Missions and Social Change

Christian missions among American Indians have long stimulated the popular religious imagination. During the seventeenth, eighteenth, and nineteenth centuries white Christians eagerly read exotic tracts describing the civilizing and Christianizing of the "savages," although most of these readers had never seen a living Indian and would never travel to Indian country. One of the consequences of this romantic portrayal was a sentimental view of Indian missions which still hinders a realistic grasp of their history and often obscures a clear understanding of their present state.

Seen from a more realistic perspective, the missionary movement and the missionary were integral in the relations between Indian and white on this continent, one short chapter in the history of the vast process of white migration and settlement which formed a nation and at the same time displaced the Indian, leaving him subordinate to an alien culture. When Indian missions are thus conceived, the missionary takes his place alongside other important persons: the fur trader, the Indian agent, the soldier, and the white settler.

Though complexly motivated at the personal level, each of these individuals represented institutions embodying the purposes of the wider society in relation to Indians. The fur trader may have been personally attracted by lucrative pelts in Indian country or by wanderlust or by the lure of Indian ways. But he was also conditioned by the economic demands of eastern markets and by the policies of the trading company for which he worked. Institutionally, the Indian agent was responsible for implementing the policies of the United States government in its various relationships with Indians. Privately, the agent was often a good man, but in many cases he failed to have the best interests of Indians clearly in view. The soldier, whatever his individual motives, was the enforcer of government policy. Regardless of his personal attitude toward Indians, the white settler ultimately found his interests in conflict with those of the Indians. With a hungry eye on Indian land, he put continual pressure on the American government to solve once and for all the "Indian Problem."

Alongside these diverse representatives of major western institutions stood the missionary. Through him, Indians were introduced to the white man's religion. Although the missionary's motives were usually theological, concerned with the conversion of the Indian to Christianity, the consequences of his missionary action were deeply shaped by unique historical contexts. Investigation into particular historical situations reveals that the role of the missionary and of the church he represented was fraught with ambiguous consequences for Indians. In some situations the missionary and the mission church were among the several forces which destroyed and disintegrated Indian life. In other situations the missionary enterprise worked along with other forces to integrate and humanize Indian life. Most of the time, both creative and destructive outcomes were bound together in a tragic historical whole. In hardly any case was the impact of Christian missions neutral in its effect upon Indian life.

Since it is impossible to generalize about either Indians or Indian missions as a whole, even a limited understanding of the impact of the missionary enterprise must begin with a focus upon particular tribes. One such tribe, the Blackfeet, now living on reservations in the state of Montana and in Alberta, Canada, provides a microcosm in which to compare missionary activity because both Protestants and Roman Catholics have been among the Blackfeet for many years.[1]

Historically, the Blackfeet were composed of three tribal subdivisions which were politically independent but culturally and linguistically homogeneous: the Pikuni or Piegan, the Kainah or Blood, and the Siksika or the Northern Blackfeet.[2] The entire tribe's relationship with white society falls into two broadly distinguishable periods. First, there was a time of relative political, economic, cultural, and religious autonomy for the Blackfeet, lasting roughly from the early decades of the 1700's to the late 1870's. From the beginning of white influences through the fur trade in the eighteenth century until about 1850, Blackfoot life and institutions were expansive and flourishing. After 1850 Blackfoot life moved slowly from autonomy toward dependence as more destructive aspects of white culture continually undermined tribal life. With the disappearance of the buffalo in the late 1870's, the Blackfeet's food supply was destroyed, their economic life collapsed, and they became completely dependent upon a white society operating through the soldier and the Indian agent. The second period of Blackfoot life began with the destruction of vast portions of traditional tribal culture and continues to the present.

1 This work is limited to a consideration of missionary institutions in the United States. Comparisons with Canada would be illuminating because government and church policies have been quite different from those in this country. However, tribal and missionary history in Canada is so complex that an adequate comparison is beyond the scope of a single volume.

2 Browning, the headquarters of the reservation in Montana, contains predominantly Indians of Piegan descent. The reserves in Alberta, Canada, are divided according to the three subgroups. The headquarters of these reserves are Cardston, Brocket, and Gleichen, all in Alberta. On these reserves are located the Bloods, the Piegans, and the Northern Blackfeet, respectively. Throughout this book the term "Blackfeet" will be used generically to refer to the entire tribe. When it is necessary to refer specifically to the subdivisions, the terms "Piegan," "Blood," and "Northern Blackfeet" will be used. The official designation of the reservation in Montana is the "Blackfeet Reservation." In all other cases the proper noun will be used in normal grammatical fashion. Bibliographical material on the Blackfeet may be found, among other places, in George P. Murdock, *Ethnographic Bibliography of North America*, 138–42. See also George Bird Grinnell, "Early Blackfoot History," *The American Anthropologist*, Vol. V (1892), 153–64, for a discussion of myths pertaining to the origin of the names of the Blackfoot subdivisions. One of the most readable and authoritative works on these Indians is *The Blackfeet* by John C. Ewers, senior ethnologist of the Museum of History and Technology, Smithsonian Institution.

Missionary activities are significantly illuminated by the distinction between autonomy and dependence.[3] During the period of greatest tribal autonomy the Blackfeet accepted some aspects of white culture, but usually on their own terms. Christianity was no exception, and therefore missionaries found it difficult to advance beliefs and practices which were in direct conflict with traditional tribal culture.[4] They were unable to conquer Blackfoot religion. Despite their efforts, both Protestant and Roman Catholic missionaries often found themselves viewed as medicine men and their religion interpreted as a new Power which was useful in war and other tribal activities.

As Blackfoot autonomy gradually eroded away, the position of the missionary changed. Before the collapse of the Blackfoot economy missionaries had little power to influence Indian behavior; after the Blackfeet became dependent upon the government for food, the efforts of the missionaries were reinforced by the agent, the soldier, and the white settler. There was open co-operation between the government and the missionary in coercive attempts to transform Indian life from supposed savagery to what was believed to be a civilized state.

Even though Protestant and Catholic missions had differing impacts upon the Blackfeet, both churches have shared a similar role as social institutions[5] representing white culture. And both the Roman Catholic and the Protestant missionaries have thus been partly representative of this culture's policies. Furthermore, even though missionaries were partly aware of the consequences of their acts, many of their activities produced consequences

[3] A similar distinction is used by Robert F. Berkhofer, Jr., in *Salvation and the Savage* to analyze Protestant missions among a number of tribes. The distinction recalls that between "directed" and "non-directed" culture contact situations. In non-directed situations Indians possess social autonomy, while in directed situations they are in the hands of a dominant society. See Ralph Linton, ed., *Acculturation in Seven American Indian Tribes*, 501 f., and the formulations of Edward H. Spicer, ed., *Perspectives in American Indian Culture Change*, 517–43.

[4] Practices which were accepted were usually incorporated into traditional society without much basic change in the social system. See Spicer, *Perspectives in . . . Change*, 530.

[5] Recent books which have influenced my thought about the social character of the church are David O. Moberg, *The Church as a Social Institution*, and James M. Gustafson, *Treasure in Earthen Vessels: The Church as a Human Community*. The influences of Max Weber's *The Protestant Ethic and the Spirit of Capitalism* and Emile Durkheim's *The Elementary Forms of the Religious Life* are obvious.

which were either unknown or unanticipated by them.[6] Unanticipated consequences of actions are as important in an analysis as consciously intended results.

In the course of a given historical situation, religion may serve as an innovative, a conservative, or even a destructive force in human affairs. Furthermore, the impact of religion upon traditional societies may produce more than one of these effects upon different parts of the society or at different points in time. This is a complex and multidimensional view of religion, but it is required if Indian missions are to be adequately understood. For instance, missionaries may introduce innovations in ritual and ethics which are ultimately destructive for Indian life. At the same time, participation in missionary institutions may provide a needed center of social order and identity for Indians undergoing rapid social change—a conservative, stabilizing function. And in some cases, mission churches may become creative nuclei around which Indian life is innovatively reorganized. Among the Blackfeet, Christian missions have been both destructive and conservative. Although there have been creative episodes, the emergence of Christianity as a force for renewal of the tribe remains only a future possibility.

[6] The sociological distinction between anticipated and unanticipated consequences is made by Robert K. Merton in *Social Theory and Social Structure*, 60 ff.

PART I

*Traditional Culture
and
Early Christian Missions*

CHAPTER

I

Buffalo Days

Little more than a century ago the Blackfeet were masters of the northern plains. In 1850 they controlled a vast area bounded on the west by the Rocky Mountains, on the north by the Saskatchewan River, on the south by the Missouri River, and on the east by the mouth of the Milk River in the present state of Montana.[1] So great was their military power in the 1840's that westward migrations of Americans prudently followed the Oregon Trail far to the south of Blackfoot country.[2]

Christian missionaries who sought the souls of the Blackfeet and who made the first dangerous journeys into the land of the great mountains and endless plains, confronted a people with a vigorous culture and a proud history. Blackfeet born during the first decade of the nineteenth century came to maturity when

[1] Clark Wissler, *Indians of the United States*, 87. Wissler's definition placed the eastern boundary at the point where the Yellowstone River empties into the Missouri. John C. Ewers has indicated that the eastern boundary should actually be the mouth of the Milk River. See his "The Horse in Blackfoot Indian Culture," B.A.E. *Bull. 159*, 121.

[2] Ewers, *Blackfeet*, 205. A decade before, in the 1830's, the hostility of the Blackfeet was evident in their ruthless attacks on trappers. For instances of the fear trappers had of the Blackfeet, see *The Journal of John Work*, William S. Lewis and Paul C. Phillips, eds., 96–97, 107, 127. Work, a chief trader for Hudson's Bay Company, was in Blackfoot country in 1831 and 1832.

their culture was at its zenith. They had a firm place in the world, for vital economic, political, social, and religious institutions provided them with meaningful activities from birth until death. Even though these institutions had already been modified by the horses, tools, and weapons of the white man, in 1850 the Blackfeet were still in control of their own destiny.[3]

Blackfoot economic life deeply conditioned all other aspects of the tribe's existence. Extremes of temperature and short growing seasons made their homeland unsuited for agriculture. However, buffalo blackened the plains at mid-century, providing food for many nomadic tribes. For the Blackfeet, the buffalo was the source of life. Their social organization centered on the character and movements of this great mammal. Economic and political institutions reflected the necessities of the hunt, and social and religious institutions celebrated the buffalo by teaching the values associated with the hunt. These institutions gave men and women order and meaning in life.

For the Blackfoot man, the central economic activity was hunting. To be a man was to be a hunter. Thus by the time a boy reached the age of ten, he was encouraged to accompany the men of the tribe on the hunt. Mounted on his favorite colt, he rode with his elders, imitating their hunting techniques. By the time he had reached his teens, a young man had sufficient experience to perform his fundamental economic function.[4] He had also been taught one of the major social values—generosity—a personal virtue that was instilled and reinforced by the group. Poor families, as well as the aged and the families without an able hunter, were totally dependent upon the generosity of success-

---

[3] The period of greatest cultural vigor for the Blackfeet falls between the time of their acquisition of horses and the final extermination of the buffalo. If horses were acquired within the second quarter of the eighteenth century, and if the late 1870's was the period of the disappearance of buffalo, then the "high culture" period comprises about a century and a half. This period reached its peak about 1850. For an excellent summary of the scholarly debate on the acquisition of horses, see Ewers, "Horse," B.A.E. Bull., 15–19. Ewers believes that the Blackfeet were probably originally forest dwellers, having migrated west to the plains. Before they acquired horses, they probably used dogs as beasts of burden. Their culture in 1850 was thus the product of a long evolutionary process. See his Blackfeet, 18, for an imaginative summary of their life in the prehorse period, and Grinnell, "History," The American Anthropologist, Vol. V (April, 1892), 153–64, for a discussion of evidence pertaining to their origins.

[4] Ewers, Blackfeet, 80.

ful hunters. Blackfoot society condemned the stingy man and rewarded the generous one with social status and political power.[5] Such rewards encouraged most young men to overcome their fears or their selfishness and to emulate the generous hunters.

Blackfoot women were responsible for preparing the product of the hunt. From an early age, each young girl was taught the skills which would make her an attractive wife: the dressing of buffalo hides, the making of clothing and lodges, and the preparation of food.[6] Even though her life was hard and she became old before many years passed, the Blackfoot woman created a home for the Blackfoot man that was both sustaining and fulfilling.

At the height of tribal culture, Blackfoot political institutions were formed by the nature of the hunting economy. Political organization had to be small enough to make sustenance possible and large enough to make the hunt successful. For this purpose the primary political unit was the band.[7] Before 1850 bands were probably composed of blood relatives, but after mid-century membership was quite fluid and loosely defined. Each band had a special name which marked it off from others and gave it a character all its own.

Political leadership was centered in the band chief. In addition to generosity, the major qualification for this office was the demonstration of bravery. Without an impressive war record, as well as a history of philanthropy, no man could hope to become a band chief.[8] As defender of the social order, the band chief was responsible for preserving peace in the group and for arbitrating conflicts which arose in the course of daily camp life. In Blackfoot society the band chief was assisted in his task by the social pressure of ridicule, which was used to control mild cases of misconduct. Often the shamed offender was driven to heroic deeds on the warpath to regain his position in the community.[9]

5 Ewers, "Horse," B.A.E. Bull., 163.

6 Ewers, Blackfeet, 102–103.

7 Clark Wissler, "The Social Life of the Blackfoot Indians," *Anthropological Papers of the American Museum of Natural History* (hereafter cited as *Anthropological Papers Am. Mus. Nat. Hist.*), Vol. VII, Part 1 (1911), 22ff.

8 George Bird Grinnell, *Blackfoot Lodge Tales*, 219.

9 Wissler, "Social Life," *Anthropological Papers Am. Mus. Nat. Hist.*, Vol. VII, Part 1 (1911), 23–24.

The rhythm of life for the band involved four discernible periods: the season of the winter camp, the spring hunting and root-gathering season, the summer hunting and sun dance season, and the fall hunting and berry-gathering season.[10] The entire Blackfoot tribe had unified political existence only during the summer hunt and sun dance season; during the rest of the year members separated into the smaller hunting bands, each under the leadership of its chief. When they came together as a group, the Blackfeet were led by a tribal chief, a political office which tended to be hereditary.[11] Except during the summer camp, the tribal chief had no extensive political power, and even then he served as chairman of a tribal council composed of band chiefs. This council arrived at its decisions through discussion and consensus, each chief being heard before a decision was reached. In this way traditional Blackfoot society discouraged the development of great inequalities of power, especially political control by a single person.[12]

Blackfoot social institutions enabled members of the tribe to find a sense of personal identity and meaning in life. Among the more important dimensions of this social organization were the age-graded men's societies, the pattern of warfare, the form of marriage, and the family. Blackfoot social life can be understood through a sympathetic and imaginative view of these institutions.

Age-graded men's societies were probably limited to five of the plains tribes: the Hidatsas, Mandans, Arapahos, Gros Ventres, and Blackfeet.[13] According to the observations of the German scientist and explorer, Maximilian, Prince of Wied, there were seven such societies among the Blackfeet. During the months of August and September, 1833, when Maximilian stayed at Fort McKenzie on the north banks of the Missouri River, he recorded the names of the societies he observed: the Mosquitoes,

---

[10] Ewers, "Horse," B.A.E. Bull., 123–24.

[11] Wissler, "Social Life," Anthropological Papers Am. Mus. Nat. Hist., Vol. VII, Part 1 (1911), 25; Ewers, "Horse," B.A.E. Bull., 248–49.

[12] Wissler, "Social Life," Anthropological Papers Am. Mus. Nat. Hist., Vol. VII, Part 1 (1911), 25; Ewers, Blackfeet, 97.

[13] Robert H. Lowie, "Plains Indian Age–Societies: Historical and Comparative Summary," Anthropological Papers Am. Mus. Nat. Hist., Vol. XI, Part 13 (1916), 919.

the Dogs, the Prairie Dogs, the Ravens, the Buffalo with Thin Horns, the Soldiers, and the Buffalo Bulls.[14] These societies, known collectively as the All Comrades, were related by a principle of progressive membership. Every four years a man could sell his membership to a younger man and purchase membership for himself in the next appropriate society.[15] Looking at the system as a whole, a young man could expect to enter the societies by purchasing membership in the Mosquitoes and then progress through the various groups until the purchase of his membership in the Buffalo Bulls. From youth to old age the lives of most men were ordered and given meaning through such social participation.[16] Not all could participate, to be sure, for a certain amount of wealth was necessary in order to buy membership. But like points on a compass, the societies gave most Blackfoot men a sense of their location in the stages along life's way.

The men's societies also acted as a kind of tribal police. During the march to the sun dance encampment they protected the front, flanks, and rear of the tribe. At night they preserved order in the camp.[17] Furthermore, they disciplined the selfish in the interest of successful tribal hunting. Selfishness could not be tolerated, especially during the summer hunt. This hunt had to

---

[14] *Travels in the Interior of North America*, 255–56. The number of societies varied according to the subdivision of the Blackfeet and the time of the observation. Thus Wissler, who began his field work in 1903, listed ten societies among the Piegans, nine among the Bloods, and fourteen among the Northern Blackfeet. See Wissler, "Societies and Dance Associations of the Blackfoot Indians," *Anthropological Papers Am. Mus. Nat. Hist.*, Vol. XI, Part 4 (1913), 369. See also Rev. John Maclean's list based upon observations among the Bloods in 1892, "Social Organization of the Blackfoot Indians," *Transactions, Canadian Institute*, Vol. IV (1892–93), 255, as well as Grinnell, *Tales*, 220–22, for a list of Piegan societies. A discussion of the mythical origins of a number of the societies can be found in Clark Wissler and D. C. Duvall, "Mythology of the Blackfoot Indians," *Anthropological Papers Am. Mus. Nat. Hist.*, Vol. II, Part 1 (1908), 105–107.

[15] Wissler, "Societies," *Anthropological Papers Am. Mus. Nat. Hist.*, Vol. XI, Part 4 (1913), 425.

[16] A women's society, the Matoki, existed among the Bloods and Northern Blackfeet but was apparently unknown among the Piegans. Women belonging to this society built a ceremonial lodge prior to the performance of the annual sun dance. The lodge resembled a buffalo corral, and the ritual revolved around the ceremonial driving of buffalo into the corral. See Wissler, "Societies," *Anthropological Papers Am. Mus. Nat. Hist.*, Vol. XI, Part 4 (1913), 430–35, and Walter McClintock, *The Old North Trail*, 450–52.

[17] Wissler, "Societies," *Anthropological Papers Am. Mus. Nat. Hist.*, Vol. XI, Part 4 (1913), 370; cf. Maximilian, *Travels*, 255.

provide the whole tribe with meat, skins for new lodges, and a supply of ceremonial buffalo tongues to be used in the sun dance. The societies disciplined men who would not co-operate in the summer hunt by stripping them of their clothing or depriving them of other property.[18]

Maximilian observed that the men's societies also helped to preserve the moral order of the community. In traditional Blackfoot society one of the most highly valued virtues for women was marital fidelity. Failure to uphold this standard threatened the moral integrity of the entire group, but harsh punishment by the men's societies usually discouraged widespread laxity. Any woman who was tempted knew that if she was discovered, her nose could be cut off, she might be publicly molested, and she would surely be ostracized from the group. In extreme cases she might be put to death for her transgression. Though harsh, such punishment meted out by the men's societies gave the Blackfeet a feeling that justice was satisfied and the integrity of the group preserved.[19]

Another important activity for men during this period was warfare. Before the Blackfeet had made their territory secure, war was a tribal affair, depending for its success upon numbers in the field and strategy during battle.[20] This early type of warfare was primarily motivated by the impulse to defend and expand tribal hunting grounds. However, there were important secondary benefits for Blackfoot men as well: prestige, wives, and booty.

By the middle of the nineteenth century, with Blackfoot hunting territory secure, the small raiding party overshadowed all other types of warfare. The spoils of the raiding party were horses, the primary standard of value in the Blackfoot economy. Raiding for horses brought the successful man the status and wealth necessary to participate in other aspects of his society. Some observers believe that the emergence of the small war party may have been an important factor in stimulating the development of individualism.[21]

18 Ewers, "Horse," B.A.E. *Bull.*, 163–64.
19 Maximilian, *Travels*, 256–57.
20 For a striking description of early Blackfoot warfare, see David Thompson, *David Thompson's Narrative of His Explorations in Western America, 1784–1812*, Ch. XXII, 326ff.

For men, raiding for horses was a zesty way to acquire a sense of achievement. The lure of the warrior role, of course, was based largely upon the virtue of bravery. So important was this virtue that when a boy was born, his father held him up to the sun and prayed: "O Sun! Make this boy strong and brave. May he die in battle rather than from old age or sickness."[22] From a very early age boys imitated the bravest warriors of the tribe in their play and their games. Thus it was not surprising that few young men could resist the social pressure to make war. Ambition in Blackfoot society had few outlets, but the road to glory on the warpath was taken by all but the sick, the cowardly, or the rich. In war the young men could prove their bravery, and with their booty they could demonstrate their generosity. Upon the men successful in war, the Blackfeet conferred prestige, honor, and a place in the decision-making councils of the tribe.

While the men's societies and warfare were important male activities, marriage and the family were the primary social institutions. During the 1850's polygamy was the normal pattern in marriage.[23] Early observers of Blackfoot marriage customs conjectured that polygamy might have been stimulated and expanded by a surplus of women created by heavy war losses.[24] Other interpreters argued that polygamy was further expanded by the fur trade.[25] Since dressing the buffalo hides was women's work, it is clear that the more wives a man had, the more lucrative was his economic return.

The marriage ceremony was very simple, centering in an exchange of gifts. One scholar holds that marriage was defined by the idea of purchase and that divorce was a refund of the purchase price.[26] Whatever the interpretation, marriage was a per-

21 Oscar Lewis, *The Effects of White Contact Upon Blackfoot Culture*, 59; see also pp. 46–59 for Lewis' account of the changes in Blackfoot warfare because of the influence of the fur trade.

22 Ewers, "Horse," B.A.E. *Bull.*, 214.

23 The form of marriage seems to have varied according to social class. The wealthy and the middle class families were usually polygamous, while the poor were generally monogamous. Ewers, "Horse," B.A.E. *Bull.*, 250.

24 John Maclean, *Canadian Savage Folk*, 62.

25 Lewis, *White Contact*, 38–40.

26 Wissler, "Social Life," *Anthropological Papers Am. Mus. Nat. Hist.*, Vol. VII, Part 1 (1911), 14. Ewer's informants denied that the idea of bride purchase was really descriptive of Blackfoot marriage customs, although they admitted that an exchange of property did take place. See Ewers, *Blackfeet*, 99.

manent and relatively dependable relationship in the 1850's. Divorce was uncommon. From the man's point of view, the chief grounds for divorce were laziness or adultery. On the point of the husband's faithfulness, the Blackfoot woman had to live with a double standard. Indeed, it was a mark of status for young men to amass a number of sexual conquests, and it was a coup of the first order to seduce a married woman. Thus the Blackfoot man entered marriage with an outlook quite different from the woman's. And while neglect or common cruelty might be grounds for a woman to leave her husband, she would never do so simply on the evidence of his unfaithfulness.

Within the context of the polygamous family, the lore of the tribe was presented to the children.[27] There they learned the social roles which they had to perform as adults; there they were taught the skills necessary for full participation in their society. In the family they assimilated a life style and a set of feelings appropriate to Blackfoot culture in 1850. Individual and group identity emerged in and was reinforced by the family structure. Central parts of this identity were an intense group loyalty, a co-operative life style, and a deep sense of kinship. These feelings were expressed in patterns of mutual obligations which affected not only the relationship among members of the family but also the relationship among families. Apparently some feelings of mutual obligation have extended into the present. According to one modern Blackfoot informant, "We feel like we are one big family. We feel like we want to help one another at all times."[28]

Economic, political, and social institutions were only a part of the total group life of the Blackfeet in 1850, and an understanding of the activities and cultural values preserved and imparted by these institutions is only a partial understanding. For the Blackfeet lived in a world permeated with meanings that can be fully grasped only through an interpretation of their religious institutions. This aspect of their life persisted long

[27] See Wissler, "Social Life," *Anthropological Papers Am. Mus. Nat. Hist.*, Vol. VII, Part 1 (1911), 29ff.; Ewers, "Horse," B.A.E. *Bull.*, 214–15; Grinnell, *Tales*, 188ff. These sources contain excellent accounts of the details of child-rearing practices during the high culture period.

[28] Mrs. Mae Williamson, personal interview, September, 1963.

after conquest and the disintegration of their political, economic, and social institutions. Modified survivals of their ancient religion remain even today.

A rich and imaginative view of life and the world permeated the lush mythology common among the Blackfeet in 1850. Although many of their legends were shared by other tribes, a unique impress was placed upon myths by both individuals and the group. Stories about the origin of the world and men, the beginning of the Blackfeet as a people, and the source of their important religious practices were told and retold in each generation. In the fluid oral tradition, mythology was continually reshaped and received new meanings that often reflected the personality of the narrator.

All Blackfeet knew that creation of the world was an act of Napi, the Old Man. Some said that creation took place one day when Old Man was sitting on top of a high mountain, with a group of animals, contemplating the waters of a great flood which surrounded the mountain on all sides. Curious about the depth of the water, Old Man sent several animals to see if they could reach the bottom and bring up some earth. First an Otter, then a Beaver, and finally a Duck tried desperately to touch the bottom, but the water was too deep and they all were drowned. When the Duck's body at last floated to the surface, Old Man noticed that a small piece of earth clung to one foot. He took the earth, made three symbolic feints toward the water, and dropped it on the fourth movement. After a while the little piece of earth grew large and became the world; the Sky People sent rain, and plants and living things began to grow and move on the dry land.

Later, Old Man and his companion, Old Woman, had to decide what to do about life and death among men. Old Man suggested that he throw a buffalo chip on the water. If it floated, people would die for four days; if it sank, people would die forever. Old Woman, being of a contentious nature, could not agree. She proposed throwing a rock into the water. If it floated, people would die for four days; if it sank, they would die forever. She threw the rock into the water and it immediately sank out of sight. Old Woman was happy with this arrangement until she had a daughter who died. In her sorrow, she said to Old Man, "Let us have our say over again." "No," he answered, "we fixed it once."[29]

Stories of the daring deeds and foibles of Napi abound in the mythology of the Blackfeet.[30] These tales often related Old Man's crude sexual exploits. Thus, even though the creation of the world was attributed to him, Old Man was the butt of much lusty humor. Such inconsistency was a pervasive quality in Blackfoot religious thought. The apparent contradiction between Old Man as creator and Old Man as prankster did not occur to the Blackfoot mind. Indeed, the fickle character of life and death, expressed in the agreement between Old Man and Old Woman, indicates the wry humor which the Blackfeet injected into the most serious of matters.

Basic also to the Blackfoot understanding of the world was a belief in Power which could communicate itself to men.[31] Ultimately symbolized by the sun, this supernatural force irrupted into the world in many surprising ways. Animals, rocks, and even natural events could contain the manifestation of Power. Communications of Power usually took place in a dream, in which an animal or a natural phenomenon, such as thunder, transferred Power to men. Probably a distinction was made between the Power symbolized by the sun and its concrete manifestation in animal or other forms. Even among contemporary Blackfeet this distinction is made—although it is usually mixed with Christian influences: "It is not the little bird or the little weasel or the little animal that . . . you are praying to. There is a

[29] Wissler and Duvall, "Mythology," *Anthropological Papers Am. Mus. Nat. Hist.*, Vol. II, Part 1 (1908), 21. The preceding story is based on Wissler and Duvall's myths No. 1 and No. 3, *ibid.*, 19–21.

[30] See Wissler and Duvall, "Mythology," *Anthropological Papers Am. Mus. Nat. Hist.*, Vol. II, Part 1 (1908), 19–39, for a typical collection of Napi stories. On September 10, 1963, in Browning, Montana, I recorded a Napi story told by a full-blood Piegan, Mrs. Albert Wells. This story was a variant of the one recorded by Wissler and Duvall under the title, "Old Man Roasts Squirrels in Hot Ashes," *ibid.*, 25–27. It is also interesting to note that one of the local bars in Browning is called the Napi Bar, indicating something of Old Man's proclivities and character as described in traditional mythology.

[31] The conception of Power or *mana* has been observed, of course, among many tribes on this continent as well as in other parts of the world. For a representative discussion, see Gerardus van der Leeuw, *Religion in Essence and Manifestation*, 2nd. ed., 23–28.

greater Spirit beyond that gave this little animal the power for an intercession."[32]

In addition to this basic belief in Power, the Blackfeet populated the sacred world with spirits of various kinds. There were earth spirits, sky spirits, water spirits, and underwater spirits, as well as spirits which inhabited animals and human beings. Under special conditions individuals could communicate with this host of beings in the sacred world. There was no attempt to reduce the confusing array of supernatural agents by a systematic explanation. In the Blackfoot world it was not strange that animals spoke to men, that thunder became a person, that rocks could sing, or that the beaver was powerful.

This did not mean that the Blackfeet lacked technological or "scientific" knowledge—that they were hopelessly imbedded in dreams and magic. For alongside Power emanating from the sacred world was the profane world. In this world the Blackfeet possessed a great deal of practical knowledge about horse breeding, hunting, weapons, and tools. Many of these activities might be enhanced by experiences of Power, but it also took skill and technique to make men good horsemen and hunters.[33]

In relation to the sacred world, individuals were rarely passive. Rather than waiting for a communication of Power, young men actively sought the experience.[34] The quest for Power usually followed a conventional pattern, beginning when the young man went out alone to a deserted spot. There he implored the inhabitants of the sacred world to grant him some of their Power. He fasted until he fell asleep exhausted. Then the dream might come. Usually, in the dream an animal appeared to reveal sacred objects to the young man, to instruct him in their proper

[32] Mrs. Mae Williamson, personal interview, September, 1963.

[33] This discussion follows a distinction developed by Malinowski and Durkheim: the sacred order is that dimension of reality believed to be controlled by supernatural powers. Human action in this realm is prescribed in ritual and taboo. By contrast, the profane world can be mastered by rational knowledge. See Bronislaw Malinowski, *Magic, Science, and Religion*, 17, and Durkheim, *Religious Life*, 243. In the Blackfoot world the sacred and the profane were interpenetrating rather than separate realms.

[34] The vision quest was a widespread phenomenon among the Plains tribes. See Erik H. Erikson, *Childhood and Society*, 150 ff., for a discussion of this experience among the Sioux.

use, and to teach him the appropriate songs, taboos, and face paints. Returning to camp, the young man began the process of gathering ritual objects into a medicine bundle. The songs and other knowledge associated with the bundle remained the personal possession of the individual until he was willing to transfer the bundle and its Power to another.

In Blackfoot society, the medicine man was a special person whose knowledge and charisma enabled him to orient individuals properly to the sacred world. Thus, when a young man had a dream of Power, he went to the medicine man, who—after a proper payment—helped him to gather the articles prescribed by the dream.

Besides the medicine men, there were also men to whom Power was granted for specific purposes. These individuals were the "doctors" of the tribe during buffalo days. Medicine experiences conferred Power to avoid pregnancy, to make hair grow long, to prevent death by lightning, to stop bleeding, to handle hot stones, to extract bullets and objects from the throat, to make bullets pass through the body, to cure disorders of the bowels, cramps, rheumatism, and sore throats, and, finally, to make and administer love potions.[35]

Because hunting and warfare were especially dangerous pursuits, men sought the blessing of the sacred world to enhance their luck and their chances of success. For this purpose the Blackfeet had a variety of personal charms, medicines, and small bundles containing special sacred objects. Often composed only of the skin of a bird wrapped in a cloth, these tiny bundles were taken on dangerous journeys, on hunting expeditions, and into battle. The bundle originated in the individual owner's dream experience, although he was free to sell his bundle to another person.

Because their supply of food was often short, the Blackfeet sought Power to help them find buffalo. One of the most interesting ways to obtain Power was through the *iniskim*, or buffalo

[35] Wissler, "Ceremonial Bundles of the Blackfoot Indians," *Anthropological Papers Am. Mus. Nat. Hist.*, Vol. VII, Part 2 (1912), 71 ff. One of my informants, Albert Wells, was believed to possess such powers. The source of his Power, according to his interpretation, was Jesus Christ. This demonstrates an interesting mixture of traditional culture forms and Christian content.

rock.[36] A Piegan version of the origin of buffalo rocks said that a woman went out one day to search for berries when her people were near starvation and unable to locate buffalo. As she moved among the berry bushes, she heard a strange noise, as if someone was softly singing. Soon the words became clear to her:

> *Yonder woman, you must take me.*
> *I am powerful.*
> *Yonder woman, you must take me,*
> *You must hear me.*
> *Where I sit is powerful.*[37]

As she walked toward the singing, she saw the *iniskim* nestled in a broken log on a bed of buffalo hair and sagegrass. She took the buffalo rock from its resting place, and, after it had taught her certain songs and ritual, she returned to her people. She told her husband of the buffalo rock and promised to transfer the songs and the Power to him so that all the people would have good luck on the hunt.

Besides the small personal bundles and charms, there were large and important bundles which were transferred many times and became traditional in Blackfoot society. Although these bundles were all individually owned, their benefits were shared by the entire tribe. Probably the most ancient of all the bundles was the Beaver Bundle. The Blood version of the Beaver medicine said that it began when a man and his wife were camping on the shore of a small lake. Because the man was a good hunter, his wife spent many days alone in the lodge while her husband was away. One day a Beaver came out of the lake and made love to the man's wife. This went on for some time without the husband's knowledge until the day the man returned to the lodge but could not find his wife anywhere. When he saw her tracks going into the water, he realized what had happened. He continued his hunting as usual, and after four days the woman came up out of the water. In due time she gave birth to a beaver. In-

[36] I purchased a buffalo rock from Clarence Butterfly in 1963. Although he was willing to sell me the stone, he would not sell the songs and the ritual associated with its use. Thus he retained possession of the *iniskim's* power.

[37] Wissler and Duvall, "Mythology," *Anthropological Papers Am. Mus. Nat. Hist.*, Vol. II, Part 1 (1908), 85.

stead of becoming angry, the man grew fond of the little beaver and was kind to it. Pleased, the Beaver-father decided to share some of his Power with the man, and so he came out of the water. After rites of purification and smoking, the Beaver taught the man all the songs that belonged to the Beaver medicine and showed him certain animal and bird skins, which the man gathered into a bundle. This was the origin of the Beaver Bundle.[38]

Another important bundle was the Medicine Pipe Bundle. As late as 1903 at least seventeen of these bundles were distributed among the Blackfeet in the United States and Canada.[39] Some seventy songs associated with this bundle had to be sung in proper order to complete a successful transfer. The opening of all Medicine Pipe bundles followed a general pattern. After the bundle was unwrapped, there followed songs and dances for each object, with periods of rest and a pause for food during the course of the ceremony. Historically, there were four occasions when the Pipe Bundle could be opened: to mark the sound of the first thunder in the spring, to renew the tobacco in the bundle, to transfer the bundle to a new owner, or to fulfill a vow. The myth describing the origin of this bundle relates that it was given to man by Thunder and had to be opened at least once a year at the time of the first thunder.[40] During this opening the bundle was carried outside, prayers were addressed to Thunder, and intercessions were made for the tribe.

The supreme expression of religious and tribal unity among the Blackfeet was the sun dance. As a religious ceremony, the sun dance gathered up important parts of individual life and gave them ritual expression. The central figure in the sun dance was a woman who had made a vow during a personal crisis or illness to purchase the Natoas Bundle.[41] Even though purchase

[38] Ibid., 75–76.

[39] Wissler, "Bundles," Anthropological Papers Am. Mus. Nat. Hist., Vol. II, Part 2 (1912), 136ff. On September 15, 1963, in Browning, I observed the opening of a Medicine Pipe Bundle. The medicine man was Dan Bull Plume, and one of the drummers for this occasion was Fish Wolf Robe, both of whom have since died.

[40] Wissler and Duvall, "Mythology," Anthropological Papers Am. Mus. Nat. Hist., Vol. II, Part 1 (1908), 89–90.

[41] See Clark Wissler, "The Sun Dance of the Blackfoot Indians," Anthropological Papers Am. Mus. Nat. Hist., Vol. XVI, Part 3 (1918), 223–70. My discussion follows Wissler's main outline. I observed a sun dance on the Rocky Boy's Reser-

of the bundle was costly, there was a feeling in the tribe that an annual sun dance was necessary for the good of the group. Thus social pressure forced even the most reluctant woman to perform her sacred role.

To purchase the Natoas Bundle, the medicine woman had to be industrious, truthful, and—above all—faithful to her marriage vows. She symbolized perfection in womanhood and served as a model for the young girls in the tribe. During the sun dance, fathers took their daughters to the medicine lodge to point out the sacred woman, saying:

> There is a good woman. She has built this Medicine Lodge, and is greatly honored and respected by all the people. Once she was a girl just like you; and you, if you are good and live a pure life, may some day be as great as she is now. Remember this, and try to live a worthy life.[42]

One of the central acts in the sun dance was the ritual preparation and distribution of buffalo tongues. Associated with this sacramental act was another celebration of womanly virtue, a ceremony in which certain women ritually sliced the tongues. At this time they might make accusations of improper sexual advances, naming the man involved. The man could then challenge the woman, creating a situation of extreme psychological tension. Such tension was viewed as necessary for tribal health, and women were assisted in their ordeal by an appeal to the Sun before they sliced the tongues: "Sun," they confessed, "I have been true to my husband ever since I have been with him and all my life. Help me, for what I say is true. I will skin this tongue without cutting a hole in it or cutting my fingers."[43]

For men the sun dance was a time to celebrate the virtue of bravery. There young boys heard of the warrior ideal as they listened to the older men recount their coups. If they were especially fortunate, they might see a young man engage in the ulti-

vation in Montana during the summer of 1960. Although this reservation is the home of the Chippewas and the Crees, many elements of the sun dance were similar to those described by Wissler.

42 Grinnell, *Tales*, 191.

43 Wissler, "Sun Dance," *Anthropological Papers Am. Mus. Nat. Hist.*, Vol. XVI, Part 3 (1918), 236.

mate expression of bravery—the self-torture ceremony.[44] Before the ceremony, attendants painted the participant and made deep incisions in his breasts and back. Then they attached wooden skewers to rawhide ropes and passed the skewers through the incisions in his breasts. Sometimes the attendants also attached a shield to each skewer before it was driven through the incisions in his back. Finally, they took the long rawhide ropes attached to the breast skewers and tied them high up on the center pole of the sacred lodge. After embracing the pole, the man began his orgiastic dance. With the man's every movement, blood flowed freely from his chest and back. Onlookers commented gravely upon the quality of his suffering. Usually before pain or loss of blood overcame the dancer, the skewers ripped through his flesh, freeing him from the ordeal. Attendants bore him away to treat his wounds with herbs, and the ceremony was complete. Anyone who engaged in this great ritual of bravery earned a place of high tribal honor. And, although he often died soon after his self-torture, the dancer became a model of courage for all to emulate.

After the yearly ritual the tribe again broke up into hunting bands that went their separate ways. Old friendships had been strengthened, the spirit world had been invoked, and life had been renewed. The Blackfeet had no doubt that when the yearly cycle was complete, they would return again. They knew little of the white man, even though they had already tasted his liquor, traded for his guns, and died from his diseases. In 1850, they could not possibly understand the extent of his power, which pulsated from a growing industrial base, sending waves of settlers surging inexorably toward Blackfoot country. As far as the tribe could see, the land was theirs. And upon that land ten thousand buffalo moved in a single day, the thunder of their mighty hoofs drowning out rumors of the white man's iron horse and his other wonders. In the shadow of the Rocky Mountains their forefathers had roamed and hunted, fought and died. Surely they would do the same.

[44] For an excellent description of the self-torture ceremony, see John C. Ewers, "Self-Torture in the Blood Indian Sun Dance," *Journal of the Washington Academy of Sciences*, Vol. XXXVIII, No. 5 (1948), 166–73.

White Man's Medicine

After the War of 1812, rising tides of American nationalism combined with the acquisition of huge territories. In 1845 Texas was annexed as was the Oregon Territory the following year. Through the Mexican Cession in 1848, the United States acquired Arizona, California, Nevada, and Utah, as well as portions of Colorado, New Mexico, and Wyoming. Then, almost 30,000 square miles were added by the Gadsden Purchase of 1853. Land attracted wave after wave of restless settlers who soon dotted the new territories with small but bustling communities. The settlers' ceaseless activity and their individualism took deep root in the spirit of the American West.

Between 1812 and 1850 Blackfoot country was penetrated by a few adventuresome white men. But on the whole, currents which affected the rest of the country were absent from the northern plains. There, space and time were still dominated by the rhythms of the buffalo and the movements of nomadic tribes across the prairies. "The Blackfeet say they are a great and powerful people, but the whites are few and feeble."[1] This statement,

---

[1] U.S., Department of the Interior, *Annual Report of the Commissioner of Indian Affairs* (hereafter cited as U.S., *Report*, followed by the appropriate year), 1859, 119.

reported in 1859 by Agent Vaughn, clearly reveals the sense of freedom and autonomy prevailing among the Blackfeet at mid-century. It was a perception about life based upon evidence available for all to see. In response to stories about the white man's power, the Blackfeet reasoned, "If the white men are so numerous, why is it that the same ones come back to the country year after year?"[2] Only a handful of the small number of white trappers, fur traders, and missionaries hardy enough to remain in Indian country were familiar to them.

Even though the Blackfoot sense of reality did not consciously include the idea of dependence, their lives nevertheless had been deeply shaped by contact with the white man, especially during the course of the fur trade. And a part of the strength and vigor of their institutions arose from social changes introduced by the fur trade itself. At the most basic material level, Blackfoot life had been improved by the metal tools, cooking utensils, and weapons provided by the traders. Glittering metal fleshing tools were much more efficient than the crude stone blades women had formerly used to prepare buffalo hides. Iron kettles replaced the primitive clay pots which broke quickly and were left to litter the plains after each move to a new campsite. Iron arrowheads, as well as the white man's guns, also had revolutionary effects upon Blackfoot warfare and hunting.[3] For a while it seemed that life was easier and better, despite the obsolescence of many traditional Blackfoot crafts.

The institutional structure of Blackfoot society was also changed by the fur trade. Traditional economic, political, social, and religious institutions were modified and often strengthened by innovations introduced by the traders. For example, an economic transformation took place with the change from producing only for tribal needs to producing for trade, a market which was dynamically related to the demands of white society east of the Mississippi.[4] For the Blackfeet, increased wealth made possible the purchase of trade goods in greater quantities and for a time increased the affluence of the entire tribe.

2 *Ibid.*

3 See John C. Ewers, "The North West Trade Gun," *Alberta Historical Review,* Vol. IV, No. 2 (Spring, 1956), 3–9.

4 Lewis, *White Culture,* 34.

The political authority of Blackfoot chiefs was enhanced as long as the fur companies dealt with them as the sole representatives of the tribe. Clearly, when a chief was agent for the entire tribe, his authority and power were great. Unfortunately, the policies of the companies were directly dependent upon the extent of competition for Indian products. As competition increased, policies were changed, with the result that companies increasingly by-passed the traditional authorities to deal directly with the younger hunters. It was not surprising that tribal elders had difficulty controlling the passions engendered by this practice. Alexander Henry, an employee of the Northwest Company, commented on this problem: "It is lamentable that the natives in general . . . have lost that respect they formerly had for their chiefs." That this situation was bad for business was clear when he added, "The consequences are now serious to us, as the natives have been taught to despise the counsels of their elders, have acquired every vice, and been guilty of every crime known to savages."[5] Henry's remarks foreshadow some of the more destructive consequences of Blackfoot relations with the white man.

Social organization, especially the family and the age-graded men's societies, changed under the influence of the fur trade. The young and expansive hide-dressing industry which developed had definite affinities with polygamy. The more wives a man possessed, the more hides he could prepare for market.[6] In addition to a significant increase of polygamous marriages, the age-graded men's societies increased both in number and importance. Intertribal relations fostered in the camps around trading posts modified many of the older societies and introduced among the Blackfeet new societies. Furthermore, while the societies were formerly devices of social order, by 1850 they also served as means of achieving upward social mobility in Blackfoot society.[7]

5 Alexander Henry and David Thompson, *New Light on the Early History of the Greater Northwest: The Manuscript Journals of Alexander Henry and David Thompson*, Vol. II, 550. See also Harold A. Innis, *The Fur Trade in Canada*, 270 ff., for an excellent discussion of the competitive effect of the fur trade upon Indian culture.

6 Lewis, *White Contact*, 38.

7 *Ibid.*, 41–42.

Religious institutions also gained new functions in response to the fur trade. For example, the economic importance of medicine bundle transfers grew. Bundle ceremonies had always included an exchange of property, but as the Blackfeet became more affluent, the economic importance of bundle ownership grew rapidly. During the fur trading period, bundle transfers were more frequent, and by 1850 this commercialism was at its height in Blackfoot society.[8] Thus, while it is true that religious ceremonies such as the sun dance continued, changes in the economic base of the society made their mark upon every major institution, including religion.

The strength of Blackfoot institutions at mid-century, combined with the relatively small number of white men in the area, made the task of the Christian missionary formidable indeed. But even a cursory reading of history indicates that while men were driven by lust for power, gold, land, and discovery, men were also lured into the wilderness in search of the treasure of Indian souls. These often strange and complicated men were compelled to spread their religion among the Indians. There were also Indians who, for equally complex reasons, received the white man's medicine and then felt compelled to teach it to others. An examination of the spread of early Christian missions will reveal how important the strong Blackfoot institutions were in shaping the missionaries' success or failure, as well as how selectively the Blackfoot appropriated this new medicine.

The tortuous path along which Roman Catholic Christianity traveled into the camps of the Blackfeet began among the Iroquois. Through the leadership of Ignace La Mousse, an outstanding Iroquois Indian with powerful charismatic gifts, the seeds of Roman Catholicism were carried into the northwestern part of what is now Montana, and ultimately into Blackfoot country. Between 1812 and 1820 a band of Christian Iroquois under the leadership of La Mousse left the Mission of Caughnawaga on the St. Lawrence River and migrated toward the Northwest. Finally, in the Bitterroot Valley east of the Rocky Mountains, they settled among the Flathead Indians, the traditional enemies of the Blackfeet. La Mousse taught the Flatheads such rituals of

8 *Ibid.*, 42.

Roman Catholicism as the sign of the cross and a few simple symbolic movements. While the personal motives of Ignace La Mousse were never entirely clear, it is thought that he continually pressed the Flathead councils to send a deputation to the east to ask for a Black Robe to instruct them in the true faith.[9]

The Indian request for Black Robes came in the form of three deputations to St. Louis—one in 1831, another in 1835, and a third in 1839.[10] No one really knew what these Indians thought about the white man's medicine they had come so far to obtain because they had to communicate through sign language since they could not speak English. However, both Protestant and Catholic interpretations of these visits reveal the deep missionary passions of churchmen in the nineteenth century.

Methodists learned of the Flathead request through a letter written on January 19, 1833, by William Walker, a Wyandotte Indian interpreter, and published in the *Christian Advocate and Journal* on March 1, 1833. Response was not long in coming from Dr. Wilbur Fisk, President of Wesleyan University in Middletown, Connecticut. Dr. Fisk wrote an appeal for missionaries which was published on March 22, 1833, in the *Christian Advocate and Journal*. The intensity of his missionary zeal is indicated in the language of his appeal:

> Let two suitable men unencumbered with families, and possessing the spirit of martyrs, throw themselves into the

9 L. B. Palladino, S.J., *Indian and White in the Northwest*, 2nd. ed., 8–9. Palladino assigns the diffusion of Christianity among the Iroquois to the ministry of Father Isaac Jogues, a French Jesuit missionary in the seventeenth century. See Martin J. Scott, S.J., *Isaac Jogues Missioner and Martyr*. Palladino also surmises that the first white contact with the Flatheads may have occurred during exploration by the de la Verendryes from 1740 to 1743. Palladino says that on this trip the explorers came as far as the southeast corner of Montana. See Palladino, *Northwest*, 2–3. In his *History of the Catholic Church in Western Canada*, A. G. Morice says the de la Verendryes party came to the southwestern corner of Montana, in which case they probably came into contact with the Blackfeet. See Morice, *Western Canada*, Vol. I, 37. In any case, Lewis and Clark were the first white men to pass directly through Flathead country.

10 There is some confusion concerning the dates and number of expeditions. I have accepted Palladino's interpretation of the evidence. According to him, three expeditions actually reached St. Louis: 1831, 1835, and 1839. Another delegation left Flathead country in 1837, but the Indians were killed by the Sioux before reaching St. Louis. See Palladino, *Northwest*, 9–10; 25–28. Cf. Ewers, *Blackfeet*, 186–87.

nation. Live with them—learn their language—preach
Christ to them, and, as the way opens, introduce schools,
agriculture, and the arts of civilized life.[11]

In 1834, as a consequence of this appeal, the Methodist
church[12] dispatched Rev. Jason Lee with his nephew, Rev. Daniel
Lee, and three laymen to establish a mission among the Flatheads. Instead of settling among the Flatheads, however, the
Lees founded their mission in Oregon on the east side of the
Willamette River about sixty miles above its junction with the
Columbia River. Evidently the Lees became convinced that a
mission located in Flathead country would be too dangerous.
Whatever the reasons, the outcome of their decision delayed the
spread of Protestant Christianity into the vicinity of Blackfoot
country.[13]

With the exception of Rev. Robert T. Rundle's brief Methodist mission in 1840 at Fort Edmonton in what is now Alberta,
Canada, Protestants did not reach Blackfoot country until 1856.[14]
In that year the Presbyterian Board of Missions sent Rev. Elkanah Mackey and his wife to Fort Benton, where the Blackfeet were apparently receptive toward Short Coat Medicine
Men.[15] After consultation with the tribal council concerning
the efficacy of Protestant medicine, one of the Blackfoot chiefs
said to the missionary:

We are satisfied that white men are *our* friends, if they
were not they would not go to the trouble of sending us so
many valuable presents every year. We desire them to come

[11] Wilbur Fisk Proclamation, *Christian Advocate and Journal*, March 22, 1833,
Vol. VII, 118. Cited in Cornelius J. Brosnan, *Jason Lee, Prophet of the New Oregon*,
11–12. See also Brosnan, 1–16, for a fuller treatment of the Methodist response.

[12] Except in specified cases the term "Methodist church" will be used to refer
to this denomination. At present, however, the official designation is The United
Methodist Church.

[13] See Brosnan, *Jason Lee*, Ch. IV, for a description of the founding of the
Willamette Valley Mission.

[14] Ewers, *Blackfeet*, 194–95. Cf. Palladino, *Northwest*, 20–24, for a Catholic interpretation. According to Palladino, another Protestant, W. H. Gray, unsuccessfully attempted to establish a mission among the Flatheads.

[15] In their concrete mode of expression Blackfeet distinguished between the
Long Robes (Catholics) and the Short Coats (Protestants) who came among them
as missionaries.

and teach us about the Great Spirit and tell us plenty of good things.[16]

Hardly a month had passed, however, before the young missionary encountered serious difficulties. Learning that she was pregnant, Mrs. Mackey became apprehensive because there were no other white women at Fort Benton. Although the Indians treated her with kindness and respect—mixed with curiosity— she remained in a "most distressing state of nervous derangement."[17] Thus, after much soul-searching the Mackeys, who had felt a special call to become Indian missionaries, concluded that they were now called to return to the East. Obviously, a married clergy was ill suited to missionary activity in the Northwest— the climate was too severe, the white population too sparse, and the land too lonely to sustain any but the most hardy.

Though never put into practice, Presbyterian policy was chiefly concerned with civilizing the savages. The Presbyterian Board of Foreign Missions contemplated a program of civilization that had two primary dimensions, education and agriculture. Walter Lowrie, the secretary of the board, was convinced that the work patterns and values of Western society had to be instilled in the Blackfeet: "No permanent benefit will result from any agency for the good of this people, unless they are taught the absolute necessity of supporting themselves, by the cultivation of the soil. The mission farm will bring that fully before them."[18]

In the area of education Lowrie envisioned the construction of a boarding school among the Blackfeet. He estimated that the establishment of the project would cost about $10,000, of which the government was asked to pay three-fourths. Lowrie further

16 Guy S. Klett, "Missionary Endeavors of the Presbyterian Church Among the Blackfeet Indians in the 1850's," *Journal of the Department of History of the Presbyterian Church in the U.S.A.*, Vol. XIX, No. 8 (December, 1941), 343. The letters of Mackey, as well as those of other officials responsible for missions in the Presbyterian church in the 1850's are preserved in this collection.

17 Private letter of E. D. Mackey, November 5, 1856. Klett, "Endeavors," *Journal of the Department of History of the Presbyterian Church in the U.S.A.*, Vol. XIX, No. 8 (December, 1941), 338–39.

18 Walter Lowrie to the Commissioner of Indian Affairs, February 16, 1857. Klett, "Endeavors," *Journal of the Department of History of the Presbyterian Church in the U.S.A.*, Vol. XIX, No. 8 (December, 1941), 350.

estimated that about $6,500 would be needed annually to maintain the school. These overtures foreshadowed later co-operation between church and state. However, at this time when the plan was submitted by the Presbyterians to Commissioner Manypenny, he made no response and turned the matter over to his successor for a decision. In 1859—after receiving no answer to his request of 1857—Lowrie concluded sadly, "In these circumstance[s] we have reluctantly concluded to give up this mission, at least for the present."[19] It would be well into the twentieth century before Presbyterians returned to the Blackfeet.

Among Roman Catholics, shortages of missionary personnel prevented any immediate response to the Flathead visits of 1831, 1835, and 1839. There were no Black Robes available. But in 1837, the Catholic bishops of the United States, assembled in the First Plenary Council of Baltimore, assigned missionary work among the Indians to the Jesuits.[20] This important decision gave responsibility for Indian missions to a group with an iron discipline, a vast fund of missionary experience, and a strong organizational structure upon which to mount the missionary campaign. Moreover, the Jesuits were unencumbered with family responsibilities, were usually excellent linguists, and were hardy enough to withstand the rigors of the Northwest. However, even among the Jesuits resources were extremely limited, and thus success in the mission was dependent upon the imagination and initiative of creative individuals.

One such individual was Father Pierre Jean De Smet. Almost singlehandedly, he scraped together money and material to make the Flathead mission a reality.

Born in 1801 in Termonde, a small town in Belgium, De Smet was to become one of the most vigorous of all the pioneer mis-

---

[19] Walter Lowrie to Alexander Culbertson, April 19, 1859. Klett, "Endeavors," *Journal of the Department of History of the Presbyterian Church in the U.S.A.,* Vol. XIX, No. 8 (December, 1941), 352.

[20] Palladino, *Northwest,* 30. Evidently 1837 was the date of the final decision in a long process. Chittenden and Richardson report that on October 27, 1833, the Second Provincial Society of Baltimore petitioned Rome requesting that Indian missions be assigned to the Jesuits. On July 26, 1834, Rome acted formally. See Hiram Martin Chittenden and Alfred Talbot Richardson, *Life, Letters, and Travels of Father Pierre-Jean De Smet,* Vol. I, 8.

sionaries. Although he was often plagued by poor health, his enormous physical stamina enabled him to make nineteen Atlantic crossings, including one voyage around Cape Horn and two by way of Panama, on missionary and other official business. His voluminous correspondence and other writings still provide one of the richest sources on early western history.[21]

On March 27, 1840, Father De Smet left St. Louis by boat to survey the missionary possibilities in the Northwest. He first traveled to Westport, now Kansas City, where he joined an American Fur Company expedition.[22] On June 30, a party of Flathead warriors met De Smet at Green River. Leaving the American Fur caravan, he journeyed with the warriors for about eight days until he reached the main delegation of the Flatheads camped in the Pierre Hole valley on the Idaho-Wyoming border. The Flatheads and a number of Nez Perces, Pend d'Oreilles, and Kalispels, had come eight hundred miles from their homeland to meet with the Black Robe Medicine Man. The sight of these Indians, some sixteen hundred in all, was sufficient to convince Father De Smet of the missionary possibilities in the Northwest.

It was on his return to St. Louis in August that De Smet made contact with a band of Blackfeet. The traditional hostility of these Indians was apparently subdued by the sight of De Smet with his long black gown, his crucifix, and his commanding presence. After explaining through an interpreter that he could communicate with the Great Spirit, De Smet was invited to smoke. Then, to his surprise, twelve warriors carried the large buffalo robe upon which he was sitting into the main camp. From his description of Indian reactions, it is evident that they identified him as a great medicine man possessed of strange powers. The Blackfoot chief was so impressed that he sent his son and two

21 It is not the purpose of this study to provide an extensive analysis of De Smet's life and his important activities among other tribes. For more complete coverage, consult E. Laveille, S.J., *The Life of Father De Smet, S.J.*; Chittenden and Richardson, *De Smet*, Vols. I–IV; and Gilbert J. Garraghan, S.J., *The Jesuits of the Middle United States*, Vol. III, Ch. XXX. For an analysis of De Smet's activities as a mediator and peacemaker during the Indian wars, consult Robert Ignatius Burns, S.J., *The Jesuits and the Indian Wars of the Northwest*, especially pp. 329–40, 349–53, and 360–61.

22 Palladino, *Northwest*, 31 ff.

other young boys with De Smet to Fort Pierre to learn more about the Christian faith, as well as to give the priest protection from other hostiles.[23]

When De Smet described his first experience among the Blackfeet in a letter the next year, he evidently wished to establish in the minds of his superiors the need for missions. His interpretation of Blackfoot behavior reveals his desire to show the Indians' readiness for the true faith.

> It was on this occasion, that, whilst I said grace, I was astonished to see that they struck the earth with one hand and raised the other towards heaven, to signify that the earth produces nothing but evil, whilst all that is good comes from above. From all this you will easily conclude that the harvest is great, whilst the laborers are few.[24]

Obviously, the Blackfoot belief in powerful earth and sky spirits must have motivated their symbolic gestures, although it is understandable that De Smet interpreted these signs within his own cultural and religious point of view.

The next spring, after hurried trips to New Orleans, Philadelphia, and several other cities in search of funds for the mission, De Smet left St. Louis for the Rocky Mountains. He was accompanied by Fathers Nicolas Point and Gregory Mengarini, who had just arrived from Rome, as well as three lay brothers—William Claessens, a Belgian blacksmith; Charles Huet, a carpenter from the same country; and Joseph Specht, a German tinner. Father Point was to become the first missionary to live among the Blackfeet for an extended period of time.[25]

As the priests passed through the country, they were attracted by the splendor and mystery of the mountains. In one memorable description of the peaks, De Smet wrote, "They are nothing but rocks heaped upon rocks; you think you have before your eyes the ruins of a whole world, covered with the eternal snows as with a shroud."[26] After an exhausting journey, the party finally

23 Reuben Gold Thwaites (ed.), *Early Western Travels: 1748–1846*, Vol. XXVII, 152f.

24 *Ibid.*, 285.

25 Point had been stationed at Westport before he joined De Smet. *Catalogus Vice Provinciae Missourianae, Societatis Jesu, 1841*, 58.

26 Chittenden and Richardson, *De Smet*, Vol. I, 214–15.

reached the spot some twenty-eight miles south of Missoula in the Bitterroot Valley where they established the mission. They named the mission St. Mary's, and from this center they began their vigorous activity. Because the objects of their ministry were nomadic buffalo hunters, the priests were forced to sacrifice stability for proximity by accompanying the Flatheads on the hunt. The dangers of this practice were great, to be sure, but the priests considered their presence necessary to give continuity to religious instruction, to administer the sacraments to the sick or dying, and to provide moral restraint and a mediating presence on common hunting grounds where conflicts among different tribes so often broke out.[27]

Even though reports of their success during the first year contain elements of hyperbole, the priests were extremely busy. They had to build shelter, secure food, and begin to communicate the elements of their religious life to the Flatheads. Father De Smet began by having the Lord's Prayer, the Ten Commandments, the Hail Mary, and other liturgical portions of Catholic Christianity translated into the Flathead language.[28] Father Mengarini, who was to remain for a decade among the Flatheads, began a serious study of their language which ultimately resulted in the publication of his *Selish Grammar* in 1861.[29]

The first Christmas at St. Mary's was a memorable one for De Smet. He began masses at seven in the morning and did not finish until after five in the afternoon.[30] And it was on this Christmas in 1841 that he baptized the first Blackfeet, an old chief named Nicolas and his family.[31] This Blackfoot family probably belonged to a powerful and independent band, the Small Robes band of the Piegans. Prior to 1846, they camped by themselves, followed their own policies, and called whom they would enemy or friend. Thus, while most of the Blackfoot bands were hostile toward the Flatheads, the Small Robes maintained regular trading relations with them in the Bitterroot Valley.

27 See Palladino, *Northwest*, 51–53 for typical instances of the dangers entailed in accompanying Indians on the hunt.
28 *Ibid.*, 45–46.
29 *Ibid.*, 78–79.
30 Thwaites, *Western Travels*, Vol. XXXVII, 318.
31 *Ibid.*, 318, 351.

Through Nicolas, other Blackfeet learned of the powerful medicine which they thought the Black Robes were willing to dispense without cost to those who would accept the rite of baptism.[32]

The Small Robes were also important because they interpreted Black Robe religion as war medicine. Their experiences among the Flatheads reinforced their view that Christianity was the most powerful war medicine of all. This band of the Blackfeet probably was living among the Flatheads in 1846 and witnessed a striking victory of the Flatheads over the Crows. Their interpretation of the victory is significant.

> While the battle lasted, we [the Blackfeet] saw their old men, their women and children, on their knees, imploring the aid of heaven; the Flatheads did not lose a single man— one only fell, a young Nez Perce, and another mortally wounded. *But the Nez Perce did not pray.* We prayed morning and evening with the Flatheads, and heard the instructions of the chiefs.[33]

They were so overwhelmed that they allowed Father De Smet to baptize eighty of their children.

Encouraged by the baptisms among the Small Robes, De Smet and Point set out in search of the main body of Blackfeet on August 16, 1846. Their purpose was twofold. First, the priests hoped to establish peace between warring Flatheads and Blackfeet. Marauding Indians made conversion even more difficult than it already was. Second, De Smet hoped to establish sufficient rapport with the Blackfeet so that he could leave Point in charge of developing a permanent mission among them. On their journey the priests encountered a group of friendly Blackfeet in the Upper Yellowstone Valley, and they were soon joined there by groups of Flatheads and Nez Perces. They moved from this location to Fort Lewis, where a formal peace was concluded.[34]

De Smet left Fort Lewis on September 28, after five weeks among the Blackfeet, while Father Point remained in charge of

[32] Ewers, *Blackfeet*, 187. See also Ewers, "Identification and History of the Small Robes Band of the Piegan Indians," *Journal of the Washington Academy of Sciences*, Vol. XXXVI, No. 12 (1946).
[33] Chittenden and Richardson, *De Smet*, Vol. II, 579. My emphasis.
[34] Gilbert J. Garraghan, S. J., *Chapters in Frontier History*, 143.

the missionary task. This pattern clearly illustrates that De Smet's talents and energies were more organizational and promotional than missionary in the sense of living among the Indians. Actually, he never remained long in any one place, and in contrast with other Jesuits of this period, he failed to become really competent in Indian languages. When he left Fort Lewis in September, 1846, he went precisely for the purpose of seeking funds to support the new mission.

A letter De Smet had written to a London supporter the year before, in 1845, illustrates his skill as a propagandist. His keen sense for the dramatic and his feeling for what would appeal to the imagination demonstrates his proclivity for fund raising:

> I am now on my way and on the eve of penetrating among the numerous and barbarous Blackfeet nations East of the Rocky Mountains. They have never been visited as yet, and there exists an hereditary war between them and our Christian tribes, which, with the grace of God, I will endeavor to put a stop to.[35]

Then, in an appeal to missionary passions in his reader, De Smet concluded dramatically.

> They are the most treacherous and wily set of savages among all the nations of the American desert, in whose words no reliance can be placed. However, the Lord keeps the hearts of all men in his hand, he may change them as he pleases. I put all my trust in him, and in the holy prayers of so many thousands of Christians, who daily beseech their heavenly Father, in behalf of these benighted tribes. Should my life be spared, this winter, I hope, I shall announce the glad tidings of salvation to most, if not all of the Blackfeet.[36]

To such descriptions of heroic efforts and spiritual conquests, performed in the face of overwhelming dangers, Christian hearts warmed and Christian coffers opened to support De Smet's labors.

The contrast between the style of De Smet the administrator

[35] P. J. De Smet to Rev. Jenkins of London, England, October 30, 1845. This letter is preserved intact in De Smet's microscopic script in the Jesuit Archives, Crosby Library, Spokane, Washington.
[36] *Ibid.*

and Nicolas Point was striking. In comparison with the former's difficulties with Indian language, the French-speaking Point was an excellent linguist. Furthermore, his arsenal of communications skills included an extremely sensitive and imaginative mind, an ability to enter into some of the central meanings of Blackfoot culture, and considerable artistic talent. Left in charge of the Blackfeet, he immediately went to work, baptizing twenty-two children the day after De Smet's departure from Fort Lewis.

Point's method of instruction depended as much on his artistic talents as on his linguistic abilities. He had come to believe, "The savages learned more quickly through their eyes than through their ears, whereupon I made a great effort to speak to them through pictures."[37] Using his prolific talents, Point seemed determined to paint the Blackfeet into the kingdom of heaven. He drew representations of the great events of Christian history and then diligently sought to explain the pictures to the Indians. Instruction using more traditional methods was not neglected, however. And in this area, Point's technique was direct and simple:

> Every day after Mass I teach the children their prayers; every evening the men recall them to one another mutually; at six o'clock in the evening these recite their prayers in common in my room, after which I give them an instruction; then comes the turn of the women.[38]

During his brief ministry among the Blackfeet, Point baptized 330 boys and 295 girls, but only 4 men and 22 women.[39] The reason for his lack of progress among the adults apparently stemmed from two causes. First, Point was convinced that with-

[37] Nicolas Point, *Wilderness Kingdom* (tr. by Joseph P. Donnelly). 12. This volume contains, in addition to Point's artistic products, the text of four out of the six volumes of his journals which are preserved in the archives of the College Sainte-Marie in Montreal. For an example of Point's sensitivity and powers of description, see Nicolas Point, "A Journey in a Barge on the Missouri from the Fort of the Blackfeet [Lewis] to that of the Assiniboines [Union]," *Mid-America*, Vol. XIII (1930–31), 236–54.

[38] Garraghan, *Chapters*, 149.

[39] *Registre des baptimes et Mariages administres sur la terre des Pieds-noirs Par le P. N. Point missionair S.J. Depuis le 29 Septembre 1846 Jusqua 1847*. Microfilm, JA. The original of this document is in Rome.

out a permanent mission, nomadic adults could not possibly develop either moral dispositions or knowledge sufficient for continuing the Christian life.[40] Second, he was continually frustrated by the Blackfoot persistence in interpreting Christianity as powerful war medicine. Writing to Father De Smet, Point described his frustrations with this situation:

> I could have baptized a great number of adults; they even seemed to desire it ardently, but these desires were not yet sufficiently imbued with the true principles of religion. *I could not content myself with the persuasion generally existing among the savages, that when they have received baptism they can conquer any enemy whatsoever.*[41]

He then went on to attribute the Blackfoot attitude to their relationship with the Flatheads.

> The courage and the happiness of the Flatheads have inspired them with this belief. This explains why some wretches, who seek only to kill their neighbors, were the first to petition for baptism.[42]

Frustration with the Indian response to baptism was only one part of a wider frustration with Indian resistance to missionary policies. These policies entailed not only baptism but also the acceptance of Western views of work, agriculture, and marriage. The radical changes sought by the Jesuits were bound to be resisted by the Indians, especially since their own culture was vital and their life satisfying.

In developing his ministry among the Flatheads, Father De Smet turned to Jesuit work in Paraguay as a model for his missionary policy. The central motif in this policy was the establishment of a kind of "Jesuit culture" which was then superimposed upon the natives. Thus, among the Flatheads and later among the Blackfeet, De Smet hoped to establish "on a small scale, the order and regularity which once distinguished our missions in Paraguay."[43]

[40] Garraghan, *Chapters*, 149.
[41] Chittenden and Richardson, *De Smet*, Vol. III, 952–53. My emphasis. Cf. A. M. Jung, *Jesuit Missions Among the American Tribes of the Rocky Mountain Indians*, 25.
[42] Chittenden and Richardson, *De Smet*, Vol. III, 953.
[43] *Ibid.*, Vol. I, 317.

The first change the padres sought was a shift from a nomadic to an agricultural way of life. In this respect, they shared the aims which the Presbyterians set forth but were never able to carry out among the Blackfeet. However, the Jesuits were concerned not only with the civilizing power of self-support through agriculture but also with the suppression of war. They believed that with the cessation of hunting the Flatheads would cease to be drawn into traditional war activities, especially since war making often took place on the common hunting grounds. If these hostilities disappeared, the Jesuits believed that the total war complex would then cease to function.[44] Naturally, the acceptance of agriculture meant instilling values and behavior patterns quite different from those of traditional Indian culture. One of the most important of the virtues Father De Smet sought to inculcate was the "love of work."[45] But Flathead culture, like Blackfoot culture, had a shape which did not easily conform to such an ideology. Theirs was a nomadic hunting economy which was not congenial to sedentary pursuits.

As the priests planted the first seeds to demonstrate the superiority of agriculture, the Indians watched with a mixture of curiosity and disbelief. But when young plants appeared they seemed to be somewhat impressed. However, they accepted only those vegetables similar to their wild varieties, such as potatoes, corn, peas, beans, turnips, and carrots. They refused to accept "greens and especially disliked onions. The latter made their eyes water, while they thought the former good only for horses."[46] On one occasion, when the missionaries found carrots and onions were gone from their garden, they noticed the next morning that while more carrots were missing, the onions had been neatly replaced in their rows.[47] Even though the Jesuits persisted in their attempts to introduce the Indians to agriculture and related pursuits through such innovations as a sawmill and a grain mill,[48] the Flatheads made no widespread response. There was much optimism concerning the ease with which Indians could

[44] *Ibid.*, 366.
[45] For De Smet's discussion of principles to guide missionaries, see *ibid.*, 328–30.
[46] Palladino, *Northwest*, 47.
[47] *Ibid.*
[48] Chittenden and Richardson, *De Smet*, Vol. II, 570–71.

be made into civilized agrarians, but Alexander Culbertson's sound analysis of the Blackfeet in 1853 applied equally to the Flatheads:

As to Agricultural operations they are not to be thought of as long as Game is abundant. Indians will not work unless their necessities compel them—it is beneath their dignity— and it is evident the day is far off when the Blackfeet will turn the Sword into the Ploughshare and make the wilderness bud and blossom like the Rose.[49]

Among both the Flatheads and the Blackfeet, Jesuits made a direct attack on the institution of marriage. Father De Smet enunciated the general principle that "there are no valid marriages among the savages of these countries . . . because they have never known well in what its essence and obligation consisted."[50] For the priests, valid marriage, even among the unbaptized, was based upon right intention, which required that the persons bind themselves together for life. Since they could daily observe Indians failing to observe this principle, they concluded that there was no right intent in polygamy and that therefore all the marriages were invalid.[51]

In dealing with polygamous households, the priests tried to persuade husbands to choose one mate from among their several wives. After the choice was made, the Indians were supposed to present themselves to the priests so that their marriage could be legitimated by the church.[52] Naturally, the Indians found the new ways of the Jesuits very difficult, but they initially worked out an acceptable response. They gave up those wives to whom fewer children had been born and retained the wife with the greatest number of children. Despite cultural conflicts, Father De Smet reported in 1846 that polygamy was completely abolished among his "converted Indians." He did not say, however, what percentage of the total Flathead population was converted.[53]

49 Alexander Culbertson to Isaac I. Stevens, ca. 1853, Indian Office Records. Cited by Ewers, *Blackfeet*, 214.
50 Chittenden and Richardson, *De Smet*, Vol. I, 332.
51 See Palladino, *Northwest*, 48, for a later softening of the Jesuit view of polygamy.
52 Chittenden and Richardson, *De Smet*, Vol. I, 41.
53 *Ibid.*, Vol. II, 572.

And there is evidence of defections to older marriage patterns after an initially positive response to the Jesuit attempt to abolish polygamy.[54]

Between 1841 and 1850 the tiny mission at St. Mary's struggled against almost overwhelming odds. The longer the priests remained among the Indians, the more resistance they met to their attempts to change important life patterns and institutions. The priests' contact with the Blackfeet during this period was sporadic and, despite Father Point's baptisms, insignificant in its influence on Indian life. Finally, in 1844, Point was ordered by his superiors in France to work with the missions in Canadian territory north of the International Line. (That it was fully three years before the message reached him is concrete evidence of the missionaries' isolation.) After little more than a year among the Blackfeet, Father Point left for his new assignment.[55] Blackfoot culture was then at its zenith, and although the Small Robes had convinced some Indians of the power of Black Robe medicine, all significant attempts to modify traditional life had failed.

Among the Flatheads, likewise, Jesuit activity grew increasingly burdensome. The conflict between Jesuit expectations and Indian values became so acute that in 1850 the Jesuit mission was leased to Major John Owen, an independent trader. St. Mary's remained closed for sixteen years, and the Flatheads returned to the ways of their fathers. The Blackfeet, of course, had never really departed from those ways.[56]

It is apparent from available evidence that Indians' interest in Black Robe religion was largely defined by their own cultural needs. Since the meanings of religion are generally closely associated with the major cultural values of a civilization, this fact was not peculiar to the Indians. The Black Robes were moti-

54 *Ibid.*, Vol. I, 335.

55 William N. Bischoff, *The Jesuits in Old Oregon*, 86; see Palladino, *Northwest*, 61.

56 Palladino attributes the closing of St. Mary's to the evil influence of several whites who stopped at the mission during the winter of 1849–1850. Through their influence, says Palladino, they led the "docile" Indians astray. Palladino, *Northwest*, 64–65. Schaeffer's interpretation is perhaps more accurate. He attributes the Flathead rejection of the Jesuits to cultural conflict. See Claude Schaeffer, "The First Jesuit Mission to the Flathead, 1840–1850: A Study in Culture Conflicts," *The Pacific Northwest Quarterly*, Vol. XXVIII, No. 3 (July, 1937).

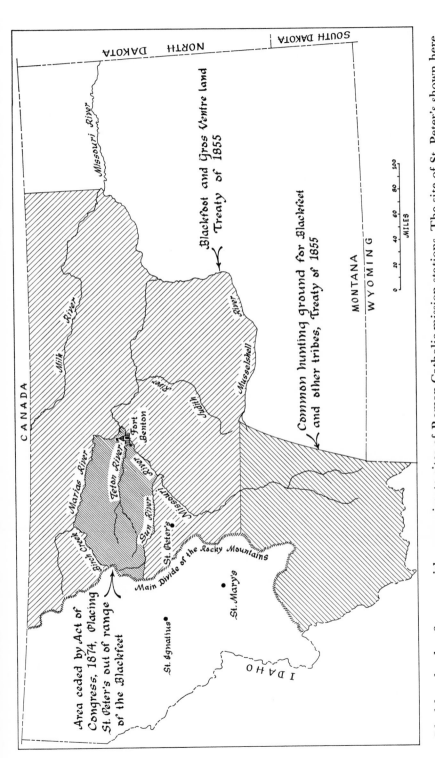

Blackfoot lands, 1855–74, with approximate sites of Roman Catholic mission stations. The site of St. Peter's shown here is the fourth location of this mission. It was west of the present town of Cascade, Montana, and the ruins are still visible. Based on a map in John C. Ewers, *The Blackfeet.*

vated by a missionary impulse rooted deep within Christianity but also were influenced by the cultural values of the nineteenth century and the ethos of the Jesuit order. Thus, the padres were compelled not only to Christianize but also to civilize the Indians. From the Indian point of view, the prayers and liturgical elements of Christianity were interpreted as acts similar to those of their traditional religion, especially when religion was appealed to in times of danger. The identification of Christianity as powerful war medicine, and by implication the identification of the Black Robes as powerful medicine men, was probably inevitable under the circumstances.

The cultural and political autonomy of the Flatheads and Blackfeet before and up to 1850 is perhaps the largest single factor in determining which portions of Catholic Christianity they appropriated. The priests really had no power to coerce, and their personal influence was limited by what the Indians were willing to accept on their own terms. The penetration of Christianity into the center of Indian life and thought was impossible. And from the point of view of the grand missionary intention, there was very little success. Baptism, despite its importance to the missionaries, had little actual effect upon the inner or outer world of the Indian.

It was the destruction of the Indian world between 1850 and 1900 that made possible further penetration by the white man's medicine. Even then, the collapse of economic, political, and social institutions did not always mean the destruction of Indian religious institutions or the values and meanings associated with them. This part of the Indian world was tenacious and often resisted the combined pressures of the soldier, the agent, and the missionary.

CHAPTER

III

The Last Buffalo

The destruction of the Blackfoot world came neither all at once nor as the simple consequence of a single cause. Like every historical phenomenon, the collapse of Blackfoot society was the consequence of a complex interaction of events. And although the Blackfeet struggled desperately to preserve their world, too many events were beyond their control. For a time, contact with Western civilization had an innovative and expansive influence upon traditional Blackfoot institutions, but the positive effects were eventually overshadowed by more ominous processes. White diseases took a grisly toll on the plains, as did the expanding liquor traffic; white conquest of tribes along the frontier proceeded apace; and the buffalo were systematically exterminated by both white and Indian hunters. While these processes affected all of the plains tribes, it was their peculiar combination, as well as the telescoping of their impact into a brief time span, that struck a hammer blow at Blackfoot life. Thus, the historical configuration of disease, liquor, conquest, and starvation must be understood specifically as it related to the Blackfeet. For it is this particular web of historical events which formed the context for the next period of Protestant and Catholic missions.

There were three great smallpox epidemics among the Blackfeet—the first in 1781, the second in 1837, and a third in 1869–70. The tribe was able to survive the first two onslaughts mainly because their traditional institutions were still strong, but the combination of disease with liquor prevented any such vigorous recovery after 1870.

The Blackfeet contracted smallpox from their enemies, the Shoshonis, in the epidemic of 1781. Saukamappee, a contemporary Indian observer, graphically described the scene of a Blackfoot attack on the Shoshonis in what is now Alberta, Canada.[1]

> We attacked the Tents, and with our sharp flat daggers and knives, cut through the tents and entered for the fight; but our war whoop instantly stopt, our eyes were appalled with terror; there was no one to fight with but the dead and the dying, each a mass of corruption.[2]

Stripping the camp of plunder, the Blackfeet went their way, only to fall prey to the disease several days later. Before the fever spent itself, about one-third of the population had died. In their maddened state, those who were camped by a river rushed into the water and perished. And according to Saukamappee, the survivors suffered tremendous psychic trauma: "When at length it left us, and we moved about to find our people, it was no longer with the song and the dance; but with tears, shrieks, and howlings of despair for those who would never return to us."[3]

A harsh struggle for survival followed, for during the epidemic the buffalo had moved away from the Blackfoot camp. Desperate for food, the Blackfeet made many offerings of feathers, sweet grasses, and leaves to the good spirits in the hope of receiving power to find buffalo. Despite their great suffering, the tribe's institutions were vigorous enough to enable the Blackfeet to recover within about three years, at which time they turned on the Shoshonis and drove them west of the Rocky Mountains and out of the Blackfoot hunting grounds.

In 1837 a second great smallpox epidemic, this time in the

---

[1] Thompson, *Narrative*, 336f. It is impossible to evaluate the accuracy of Thompson's translations of Indian descriptions, although there is no reason to doubt their substance.

[2] *Ibid.*, 336.

[3] *Ibid.*, 337.

United States, struck the Blackfeet. Infected clothing had been put aboard an American Fur Company boat bound for Blackfoot country, and the disease eventually spread to all the upper Missouri tribes. As a consequence, almost six thousand members of the tribe died. Their culture was strong enough, even in the light of such losses, to possess amazing powers of recovery. It was estimated that the Blackfeet had regained all but about one-third of their lost population just seventeen years after the epidemic of 1837.[4] Contemporary observers emphasized, however, the destructive effects of the epidemic upon Blackfoot kinship structures. Whole families were wiped out by the disease, and knowledge of family relationship was often lost to those who survived. Furthermore, the epidemic seemed to be followed by a slow physical decline among members of the tribe.[5]

Like its predecessors, the epidemic of 1869–70 decimated the tribe. However, this time the smallpox had a much more destructive effect upon the Blackfeet because it was combined with the liquor traffic in a marriage of events that finally placed intolerable strains upon traditional Blackfoot institutions. More and more unhealthy forms of personal and social decay had begun to appear, with the result that the third epidemic dealt the Blackfeet a stunning blow. The death of their traditional life came only after white conquest and starvation, of course, but liquor and disease interacted to prepare the Blackfeet for destruction.

The spread of liquor was especially devastating to Blackfoot society because there were no traditional social controls to protect individuals from the effects of the powerful "white man's water." As with smallpox, the Blackfeet had little immunity to liquor, and their desire for it became almost insatiable. The consequences for tribal life and the individual personality were observed by Father De Smet as early as 1839, long before the final smallpox epidemic.

> Under the influence of liquor their passions lead them into the grossest excesses, beginning with songs of joy and

4 Edwin T. Denig, *Indian Tribes of the Upper Missouri*, 625.
5 "The Bradley Manuscript," *Contributions* to the Historical Society of Montana, Vol. III, 232–33.

ending with howls and screams. Disputes and quarrels follow, then stabbing and head-smashing; finally, murder is the crowning crime of these abominable orgies. The ground is strewn with the dead, and the living are horribly mutilated.[6]

Certainly these conflicts often involved relatives and friends, a circumstance which further weakened the tribal structure and ultimately produced widespread social disorder.

Competition among the great fur interests in the United States and Canada, as well as the uncontrolled activities of independent trappers, made liquor a standard trade item despite its effects upon the Indians. By 1843, competition between the American Fur Company and the powerful Fox, Livingston, and Company was so keen in Blackfoot country that the field employees pressed St. Louis for more liquor. Writing to St. Louis in January, one of the American Fur employees indicated that their rivals had a good supply of liquor. "Under these circumstances," he said, "we must lose the Blackfeet and Assiniboine trade next year *unless we have liquor.*"[7] Needless to say, this demand from the field was met with a generous supply—despite the law of 1833–34 which prohibited liquor in Indian country.

A number of "whisky forts" were constructed in Blackfoot country north of the International Line.[8] By 1874 more than twelve had been completed, the largest and most notorious of which were Fort Whoop-Up, Fort Standoff, and Fort Slide-Out. Though colorfully named and managed by energetic, enterprising men, the forts spread death among the Blackfeet. Just a year after the tribe had been decimated by the smallpox epidemic of 1869–70, eighty-eight Northern Blackfeet were killed in fights during drunken sprees.[9] Two years later, thirty-two Piegans died under similar circumstances in the United States;[10] and in the

[6] Father De Smet to Mr. Charles Van Mossevelde, September 18, 1839. Cited in Laveille, *Father De Smet,* 92.

[7] Honore Picotte to Pierre Chouteau, Jr., January 4, 1843. Cited in Hiram Martin Chittenden, *The American Fur Trade of the Far West,* Vol. I, 31. Emphasis in the original.

[8] Ewers, *Blackfeet,* 256ff.

[9] Charles M. MacInnes, *In the Shadow of the Rockies.* Cited by Ewers, *Blackfeet,* 258.

[10] U.S., *Report,* 1873, 252. Cited by Ewers, *Blackfeet,* 258.

winter of 1873–74, forty-two Northern Blackfeet died from causes directly traceable to liquor.[11] In 1873 the Blackfoot agent in the United States estimated that 25 per cent of the Indians under his jurisdiction had died between 1867 and 1873 as a result of the liquor traffic.[12] Although many of the reports of this period are based only on informed estimates, they do indicate the harvest of individual and social chaos reaped as a result of the liquor traffic.

It was Father Constantine Scollen, however, who perceived the tragic connection between the liquor traffic and the smallpox epidemic of 1870. When he first met the Blackfeet in Canada in 1861, he saw them as "a proud, haughty, numerous people . . . having a regular politico-religious organization."[13] After 1870, however, the Blackfeet had lost more than half their population, and their social organization was in deep decay. "In fact," Scollen observed, "they have been utterly demoralized as a people."[14] In explaining the social factors involved in Blackfoot disorganization, he gave considerable weight to the combination of liquor and disease:

> Surviving relatives [of the epidemic of 1870] went more and more for the use of alcohol; they endeavoured to drown their grief in the poisonous beverage. They sold their robes and their horses by the hundred for it, and now they began killing one another, so that in a short time they were divided into several small parties, afraid to meet.[15]

Just four years after the epidemic of 1870 the Blackfeet were a severely damaged people. Said Scollen:

> In the summer of 1874, I was traveling amongst the Blackfeet. It was painful for me to see the state of poverty to which they had been reduced. Formerly they had been the most

[11] John McDougall, *On Western Trails in the Early Seventies.* Cited by Ewers, *Blackfeet,* 258.

[12] U.S., *Report,* 1873, 252. Cited by Ewers, *Blackfeet,* 258–59.

[13] Constantine Scollen to the Governor of Manitoba, September 8, 1876. Reproduced in Alexander Morris, *The Treaties of Canada with the Indians of Manitoba and the North-West Territories,* 247–49.

[14] *Ibid.*

[15] *Ibid.*

opulent Indians in the country, and now they were clothed in rags, without horses and without guns.[16]

Liquor and disease had struck a devastating blow to Blackfoot life and institutions. Even so, they might have been able to survive this experience, but in 1870 a violent conquest brought an end to this possibility—at least for the Blackfeet in the United States.[17]

In Montana the decade and a half between 1855 and 1870 was marked by increasing hostility between Indians and whites. Complex factors contributed to depredations on both sides, but the most significant contours stand out clearly. National priorities at this time were defined by involvement in a bloody Civil War. The administration of Indian affairs naturally took second place, even in the minds of responsible officials. Moreover, because of a number of venal officials in the field, the Blackfeet suffered their share of exploitation.[18] Under these conditions, the liquor flowing freely around such centers as Fort Benton added to the climate of violence building up in both Indians and whites.[19] Then, in the summer of 1862 when gold was discovered in Blackfoot country, white passions surged in anticipation of easy riches. The prospectors invading the country increased the Blackfoot hatred of whites and confirmed their fears of white designs upon their land. In 1865 the government contributed to this suspicion by negotiating a treaty with the Blackfeet which was never ratified by Congress. When the annuities promised in the treaty failed to arrive, the Blackfeet concluded that the whites had lied.[20]

In retrospect, it is clear that social order and civil justice were rare in Blackfoot country during the 1860's. National political and legal institutions were operative only east of the Mississippi.

---

16 *Ibid.*

17 Among the Blackfeet in Canada, white conquest took a different shape, leading to a smoother transition from autonomy to dependence. A review of the major factors reveals the large part which wise administration by the Canadian government played in this process. For an example of the quality of law enforcement, see Sir Cecil E. Denny, *The Law Marches West*, 118–19.

18 See U.S., *Report*, 1864, 293–98 for examples.

19 U.S., *Report*, 1868, 204–205. For examples of the lawless character of many of the whites, see U.S., *Report*, 1867, 255–56. See also Gov. Smith to Agent Wright, September 18, 1867 (MHS), regarding depredations.

20 Ewers, *Blackfeet*, 239–40.

The United States government was unable to articulate and enforce consistent policies in the vast territories of the West. Furthermore, there were few representatives of law and the institutions of civilization. Agent Reed, commenting on this point in 1863, said:

> . . . from Fort Randall to Fort Benton, a distance of some eighteen hundred miles . . . there was . . . not a single military post, nor civil officer of any kind, not an officer or soldier of the army, indeed no authority or government of any kind, except singly and alone, one or two Indian agents.[21]

Under these conditions the answer of the United States to the problem of hostile Indians was harsh repression. This policy often amounted to extermination, as the Blackfeet discovered in the winter of 1870.

In 1869 it was reported that 56 white men had been murdered and over 1,000 horses stolen by the Blackfeet.[22] After a respected citizen of Montana, Malcolm Clark, was murdered, the United States considered the Blackfeet to be in a state of war. The response of the federal troops was both swift and horribly effective. General Sheridan planned to attack the Blackfeet during heavy snow, the time when they would least expect a battle. Colonel E. M. Baker was dispatched from Fort Shaw on this mission. General Philip de Trobriand, the commander of Fort Shaw, had given orders that Baker should attack only Mountain Chief's band, among whom the murderers of Malcolm Clark were supposed to be hidden. On January 23, 1870, Baker and his men struck. They killed 173 Indians and captured 140 women and children. Even though many of the Indians were still suffering from smallpox, their lodges were burned and the captives turned loose in sub-zero weather.[23]

---

21 U.S., *Report*, 1863, 164. Agent Reed wrote this report from his home in Epworth, Iowa—a great distance from Blackfoot country.

22 The loss of horses was expensive for business interests in Montana. For instance, C. C. Huntley filed a claim in 1866 against the Blackfeet for the loss of $2,200 in horses. "Brief of Evidence in Case of C. C. Huntley Claim Against Piegan's (Blackfeet Indians) for Depredations in 1866" (BAA).

23 For an account of the Baker massacre, see Ralph K. Andrist, *The Long Death*, 171. Cf. Ewers, *Blackfeet*, 246–53. The Baker episode is partially obscured by controversy, and the full account should be consulted. For the military point

Although the quality of military action was excessively harsh, involving the slaughter of 53 women and children,[24] Baker's action was doubly tragic for the band of Blackfeet he attacked was not that of Mountain Chief but rather a friendly band under the leadership of Chief Heavy Runner. This military action had such a telling effect upon the Blackfeet that nearly a decade after the massacre, Indians who had once been masters of the plains ran panic-stricken for cover at the appearance of a United States soldier.[25]

The final blow to the autonomy of the Blackfeet came in the fourth element of their experience—the disappearance of the buffalo and the tribe's ensuing starvation. The Blackfeet emerged a broken people, unable to recover their past and dependent upon their conquerors for the preservation of their very lives.

By the late 1870's the seemingly inexhaustible supply of buffalo was disappearing from the plains. In 1878 the agent for the Piegan in Montana, John Young, informed Washington that the Blackfeet themselves were beginning to realize that "Buffalo will within a limited time fail and that it is necessary to prepare some other means of support."[26] At this time, the only other alternative was the government ration house which was already strained by the appearance of increasing numbers of hungry Blackfeet. In January of 1881 there were 605 Indians camped near the agency; in 1882 the number had risen to almost 2,000; by 1883 there were about 3,000 Blackfeet dependent on government rations.[27] In February of 1883 Young desperately wrote to Wash-

---

of view, see *Record of Engagements with Hostile Indians Within the Military Division of the Missouri from 1868 to 1882*. This volume also contains an interesting letter from Alexander Culbertson in which he points out that the Bloods and Northern Blackfeet were not involved in the hostilities; only the Piegans felt the full brunt of white power and thus were involved in traditional military resistance. See Alexander Culbertson to Commissioner, September 2, 1869, *ibid.*, 4.

24 National Archives, Records of the Washington Superintendency of Indian Affairs, telegram from Colonel Baker to General Sherman, March 27, 1870 (BAA).

25 Letter from Piegan chiefs to the Commissioner of Indian Affairs, October 23, 1878 (BAA). Cited also by Helen B. West, "Starvation Winter of the Blackfeet," *Montana*, Vol. IX, No. 1 (January, 1959), 7.

26 West, "Starvation," *Montana*, Vol. IX, No. 1 (January, 1959), 6. As early as 1847 Father De Smet realized too many Indians were dependent upon too few buffalo. See Thwaites, *Western Travels*, Vol. XXIX, 365.

27 Ewers, *Blackfeet*, 290.

ington that unless something was done soon, there would be widespread starvation. Washington was singularly unresponsive, as is indicated by the commissioner's reply:

> Referring to your letter . . . that the balance to be delivered will not be enough to prevent suffering and the destruction of the stock herd, you are advised of the fact that the total appropriation made by Congress for the Indians belonging to your agency has already been exhausted . . . and as it is not in the power of this Department to make any further provisions for their support . . . nothing further can be done.[28]

Nothing further was done. When Young's replacement, Agent Allen, reached Montana in the middle of March, 1884, he found miserable, starving Blackfeet huddling about the ration house. Between September, 1883, and March, 1884, nearly six hundred Blackfeet starved to death. Some families were almost exterminated. For instance, six out of fourteen died in Running Crane's family and six out of nine in Little Bull's family. Allen's report of the grisly details in 1884 leaves little to the imagination:

> The little children seemed to have suffered most; they were so emaciated that it did not seem possible for them to live long and many of them have since passed away . . . so great was their destitution that the Indians stripped the bark from the saplings that grow along the creeks and ate the inner portions to appease their gnawing hunger.[29]

Even after Allen's arrival, rations were minimal, amounting to little more than two pounds of beef and two pounds of flour per week for adults; children received half this amount.[30] Blackfeet scratched in the ground in an attempt to grow potatoes, but to no avail. Deaths continued to average at least one a day, and a contemporary observer indicates the macabre quality of the reservation under these circumstances: "They still prefer to dispose of their bodies by tying them in trees or placing them on

[28] West, "Starvation," *Montana*, Vol. IX, No. 1 (January, 1959), 8.
[29] U.S., *Report*, 1884, 150–51.
[30] Reported by David Urquhart, Jr. on August 20, 1884. *Newspaper Files*, Vol. I, 27–29 (CA).

the surface of the ground on high places, and the hills and ridges around the Agency are dotted with these ghostly objects."[31]

The same observer reported that desperation had reached such levels in the Blackfoot councils that Indians were raising the question of "whether it would not be better for them to take the field and be killed rather than to die by degrees of starvation."[32] Reduced to such powerlessness, the Blackfeet were prey to both the white and the Indian raiders who attacked their remaining horse herds. In their terror, the Blackfeet gathered about the agency, paralyzed and completely unable to resist these intrusions or to defend themselves.[33]

The bitter winter of 1883–84 marked the end of the Black-feet as an independent people. Afterwards, Blackfoot life was never the same again—indeed, it could never be the same again. Many of the old values and ancient traditions survived disease, liquor, conquest, and starvation. But the vital institutions de-veloped during the high culture period were forever destroyed. Since the Blackfeet could not return to their old world, although many tried, they were forced to make some adjustments to the institutions and cultural values of white society. The nature of the adjustments and the quality of the dialogue between the white and Indian societies ushered in a close co-operation be-tween government and church as, together, they continued the grand task of civilizing and Christianizing the Blackfeet.

[31] *Ibid.*
[32] *Ibid.*
[33] Agent Allen to the Commissioner of Indian Affairs, June 4, 1884 (BAA). Cited by West, "Starvation," *Montana,* Vol. IX, No. 1 (January, 1959), 18.

PART II

Catholic Missions
and
Forced Acculturation

IV

Conflicts with the Powers of Darkness

The historical context out of which the Blackfeet emerged a broken people included not only disease, liquor, conquest, and starvation but also the activities of determined Roman Catholic missionaries. Since Protestants did not establish permanent missions among the Blackfeet until 1893, they escaped some of the more frustrating and destructive elements of the historical situation with which the priests had to cope. An examination of Catholic missionary action set against the dark background of the collapsing Blackfoot world reveals that the instabilities, turmoil, and conflict of the period were at times reflected in, occasionally influenced by, and often influential upon missionary activity.

The priests' interpretation of this confusing twilight period was naturally shaped by their theological view of their place in the scheme of things. They felt they were involved in a world created by God but fallen under the power of Satan. Thus, the essential conflict in human history, although it appeared in many forms, was the great cosmic struggle between God and the Powers of Darkness. As participants in the struggle they had, from their point of view, established a spiritual beachhead among the Blackfeet, for the baptisms performed by De Smet and Point had effectively deprived Satan of a small part of his flock. They could interpret their situation in this way mainly because baptism had such power within Roman Catholic theology, conferring "an 'indelible character' upon the person baptized, a divine seal to which the person may indeed prove unfaithful but which he cannot undo."[1]

Those Blackfeet marked by baptism had been rescued from the Powers of Darkness, but baptism was only the first step toward the Christian maturity of full incorporation into the institution which bore divine grace to men in her sacraments—the church. Thus, after baptism came instruction in the faith and confirmation; then penance, regular attendance at mass, and reception of the Eucharist; Christian marriage; and finally, in this life, extreme unction and Christian burial. In the next life came the ultimate reward of eternal life in heaven. The goal of assimilating the Blackfeet into the church also meant that the missionaries had to engage in further conflicts with the Powers of Darkness. While they clearly defined some of these Powers as demonic, they only dimly perceived that others were historical forces appearing in satanic forms.

Of the latter, the unsettled times limited what could be done. Many factors, of course, were beyond the control of the missionaries. Despite the fact that the priests were persistent, competent, and motivated by a powerful religious ideology, they often were the subjects rather than the masters of these broader historical processes. Furthermore, certain historical forces were often overlooked by the missionaries while they focused upon what they considered to be Satan's real stronghold—the remainder of Blackfoot culture. And as they came into cultural conflict with the Indians, the missionaries themselves sometimes became unwitting allies of the forces undermining the Blackfoot world.

In order to wage their battle against the Powers of Darkness, the priests first had to create an institutional base of operations. The St. Peter's Mission was to be such a base, and the frustrations involved in its founding reflected the general instability of the period when the Blackfeet were passing from relative autonomy

1 Jaroslav Pelikan, *The Riddle of Roman Catholicism*, 112.

through cultural trauma to political and economic dependency.

Between the time of Point's departure for Canada in 1847 and 1859 there were no Roman Catholic missionaries among the Blackfeet. In 1857, however, Agent Vaughn encouraged the priests to establish a missionary station. Writing to Father De Smet on May 20, Vaughn optimistically stated, "Catholic missionaries have always succeeded in gaining the Indians' hearts, in controlling their brutal outbreaks and ameliorating their condition in every respect."[2] Finally, in April, 1859, Father Congiato, the general superior of Indian missions in that part of the Northwest, dispatched to the Blackfeet Father A. Hoecken and Brother Magri. After spending the summer locating a site for the mission, they finally chose a spot on the Teton River close to the present town of Choteau, where Father Imoda joined them in October. That winter they began catechism classes among the children and plunged into the study of the Blackfoot language.[3]

In March of the following year, however, the mission's location was changed to the banks of the Sun River about eight miles above what was to become Fort Shaw. On August 9, 1860, Father Congiato abruptly ordered the missionaries to stop their work, and it was not until the next year, 1861, that Fathers Giorda and Imoda and Brother Francis De Knock were assigned to the Blackfeet. After wintering in Fort Benton, in the spring of 1862 they were joined by Brother Lucian D'Agostino and by Father Menetrey a short time later. They finally established a third mission site on the banks of the Missouri River about six miles above the mouth of the Sun River.[4] Unfortunately, their attempts to cultivate the land met with little success because they lacked a necessary seven-mile irrigation ditch.

Thus a fourth location was chosen, this time a site about two miles east of Bird Tail Rock, where St. Peter's was relocated on April 27, 1866.[5] Obviously, these missionaries merited Agent

---

2 Chittenden and Richardson, *De Smet*, Vol. IV, 1317. Cited by Ewers, *Blackfeet*, 229.

3 Palladino, *Northwest*, 192–93.

4 *Ibid.*, 193–94. After two months of operation they reported the baptism of 134 Blackfoot children. See Bischoff, *Old Oregon*, 86–87.

5 Palladino, *Northwest*, 210; cf. "The Bradley Manuscript," Book A, 125–27 (MHS).

Vaughn's opinion that they were the only ones "who have shown sufficient zeal, patience and industry to carry out any extensive measure the government may entertain towards the civilization of the Indians."[6]

No amount of zeal, patience, and industry, however, could enable the priests to master the external historical processes which surrounded them. Between 1865 and 1869, the years leading up to the Baker campaign on the Marias, the Blackfeet fought with desperation born of the realization that their way of life was in mortal danger. Indeed, they seemed to be "bent on exterminating every white man found in the country."[7] On the road to Fort Benton, among other places, the Blackfeet made white men pay in blood for invading Indian lands and threatening the tribe's way of life. Under these conditions the missionaries had to withdraw and wait until the Indians had been brought to their knees. In fact, the Jesuit hierarchy closed St. Peter's Mission on the same day it was relocated east of Bird Tail Rock and ordered the missionaries to St. Ignatius west of the Rocky Mountains. For eight years, from 1866 until 1874, St. Peter's was attached to the Mission of Helena. During this time, only occasional visits were made to the Blackfeet.

Then, in the spring of 1874 the mission was reopened under the leadership of Father Imoda.[8] Once again the missionaries faced a problem with their location. Old Agency, the government headquarters on the Teton River since 1868, had been closed. Furthermore, an act on April 15, 1874, moved the southern boundary of the Blackfeet Reservation to Birch Creek. This left St. Peter's about sixty miles outside the reservation boundaries and in the middle of an area which was prime for white settlement.

In 1875 Agent Wood established a new agency on Badger Creek in a location about fifty miles north of Old Agency and about fourteen miles from Birch Creek. With the center of Blackfoot population moved so far from St. Peter's and with the site for the new agency now clear, Fathers Imoda, Prando, and Rappa-

[6] U.S. *Report*, 1860, 83–84.
[7] Palladino, *Northwest*, 204.
[8] *Ibid.*, 210–14.

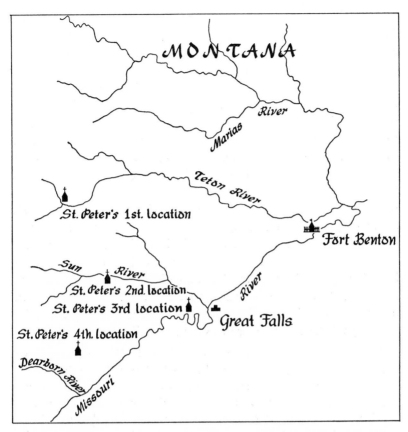

The four locations of St. Peter's Mission. First location, 1859, near present Choteau. Second location, 1860, near Fort Shaw. Third location, 1862, near Ulm. Fourth location, 1866, near Bird Tail Rock. Based on a map in L. B. Palladino, S.J., *Indian and White in the Northwest.*

gliosi[9] camped among the Blackfeet seeking an opportunity to establish another mission closer to the tribe. Finally, in 1881 Father Peter Prando built a new mission station on the south bank of Birch Creek just outside the southern boundary of the reservation.[10]

[9] Rappagliosi, the son of aristocratic parents, was born in Rome. After only four years at St. Peter's, he died on February 7, 1878. See *Memorie Del P. Pilippo Rappagliosi*, which contains a brief biography and a number of letters written at St. Peter's.

[10] Bischoff, *Old Oregon*, 90, 100.

Even though the permanent establishment of St. Peter's was fraught with difficulties, the priests worked with what they had and with as many Blackfeet as they could. In their efforts they had the co-operation not only of Agent Vaughn but also of Agent Upson who, in 1864, informed the commissioner of Indian affairs: "I propose either to aid the present Jesuit Mission here in the education of the children of the nation or procure a teacher to open a school at the farm."[11] Upson was referring to the third site of St. Peter's, located approximately fifteen miles south of the government farm on the Sun River. He indicated that Father Giorda had appealed for help and that he was favorably impressed with the priest's activities. Of Giorda, Upson said, "He speaks English poorly, but I am informed is well educated and an excellent linguist and speaks the Blackfoot language fluently."[12]

Both Upson and Giorda were frustrated in their intentions by existing conditions. For Giorda, whisky traders were a special problem. While he was camping among the Small Robes Band on the Teton River in December, 1863, whisky traders invaded the camp. The results were tragic yet familiar:

> Almost every evening one would see Indians running to and fro through the camps, bottle in hand, hallooing like wild beasts; Sometimes they would fight one with the other; Now a drunk man would unmercifully knock the poor wife, who was crying because the husband had stolen her more valuable property to buy liquor. Now was a herd of boys and girls running after those madmen to laugh at their folly, and at their tumbling at every step. Now these poor creatures were seen lying in the snow, or in some lodge throwing out the white water.[13]

Not only was the liquor traffic destructive of human relationships, but it was also disastrous for Giorda's attempts at religious instruction:

> I had started up a little school in two lodges, and three times a day I was there teaching [a] good many young boys

11 Agent Upson to Commissioner Dole, January 19, 1864 (BAA).
12 Ibid.
13 Father Giorda to Agent Upson, January 22, 1864 (BAA). Letters from the period from 1873 to 1875 also indicate that whisky trading continued on Birch Creek and Badger Creek as well as on the Marias and Teton Rivers.

and females eager after religious instruction . . . But drunkards would steal in among the little flock and put everything out of order. So that I have been obliged to stop our meetings. Then the little ones would call on me, Black Gown, why do you no more ring your bell to call us for prayer? I am sick at heart, I was obliged to answer: You see the drunkards do not allow us to worship the Lord in any decent way. Pray by yourselves in your lodges, and pray for your fathers.[14]

Giorda's sensitivity in reading the signs of the times was impressive for he saw that the whisky traders were rapidly impoverishing the Blackfeet, both physically and culturally. He also correctly foresaw the options open to the government as well as the consequences which could follow the trends apparent in then current events:

What will these Indians do when they shall . . . be robbed of their best horses? They shall starve, and starve their children and women. When starving, what will they do? Will they begin to farm? They will be too lazy . . . for it. What will they do? They will be at war with the whites . . . Then a war with the whites will bring on the destruction of these Indians, or draw them to the low stage of savage and brutal existence. They will like ghosts linger about the towns of the whites and tell our children to what wretched existence they had been reduced by the white man . . . Can their destruction be prevented? Will it be?[15]

By the end of the winter in 1883, Giorda's prophetic questions were answered—in the negative.

Shifting mission sites, whisky traders, white settlers lusting for gold, irresponsible officials, and the spread of white diseases could have been interpreted as the activities of hosts in the nether regions. But not many of the early Catholic missionaries had much to say about Satan in relation to such problems; perhaps liquor and drunkenness were not so much demonic to them as representative of all too human weaknesses. However, Blackfoot tribal culture was another matter, for in it the Jesuits saw Satan

14 *Ibid.*
15 *Ibid.*

firmly entrenched. Therefore, they launched a concerted attack upon polygamy, Blackfoot religion, and other "superstitions." One of the cleverest and most sensitive priests was Father Peter Prando. Because he employed not only his considerable linguistic skills but also creative guile, many times the Devil found himself hoodwinked rather than overcome by a frontal attack.

Part of Prando's method involved employing to his own advantage what he knew about Blackfoot culture and attitudes. For example, after Prando moved to the Birch Creek location in 1881, it was necessary for him to be away from the Blackfeet for some time. He was concerned that the Indians would be alienated from him when he returned. Knowing the importance which Blackfeet attached to pipes and smoking, Prando decided upon a brilliant stratagem. In Helena he purchased an enormous pipe with a stem over three feet long. It was so long that someone had to help him light it, and it required a prodigious amount of tobacco—an expensive item—to fill it properly. It was worth the expense and trouble, for Prando reasoned: "As soon as the Indians see me, they'll gather around me, and comment on my big pipe, and grow envious with the desire of getting a puff from it. As soon as I let them have their smoke, we'll all be friends again."[16]

Prando obtained sufficient tobacco for the pipe from Colonel Calson at Fort Shaw. He had come to the fort to give a sermon and casually mentioned to the colonel—who was a good Catholic —his need for tobacco to cement relations between the Blackfeet and the church. Leaving the fort with ten pounds of tobacco, he proceeded immediately to the Blackfoot camps. When he encountered the Indians, he fired up his pipe, giving no occasion for discussion of his absence. If Prando's analysis is correct, his scheme must have been a great success: "The greatest admiration was depicted in their countenances as they watched the volumes of smoke, clouding the air."[17] He repeated his smoking ritual in several camps and gave each person a small present of tobacco. His final act was to present the pipe and a good deal of the

---

[16] *Woodstock Letters* (hereafter cited as *W.L.*), Vol. XII. No. 3 (1833), 306. These rich documents were published for private use by the Jesuits and therefore have had a limited circulation.

[17] *Ibid.*, 307.

tobacco to White Calf, the great chief of the Blackfeet. This gift was such a success that Prando's absence did not cause alienation —even though White Calf was naturally concerned because several of his people had died unbaptized while the priest was away.

Upon his return to the Blackfeet, Father Prando began his daily work, essentially an attempt to dispel traditional religious ideas and practices and to replace them with the truths of Roman Catholic Christianity. Teaching was his primary method and, from his perspective, his most important activity: "To give instructions and to teach catechism, are the principal occupations of a missionary."[18] His teaching was far from ordinary, however, for he again employed the full measure of his creative energies. The Blackfeet were impressed by his knowledge of their language,[19] and he used this competence, along with his sensitive grasp of their culture, to impress upon them the true religion: "There is a vein of romance in the nature of these savages that accounts for their great love of song, and which greatly aids me in teaching them prayers and the truths of religion."[20] On the basis of this insight Prando composed a chant against polygamy which he claimed had a great deal of effect upon Indian behavior.[21]

Prando also perceived that in order to change a deeply rooted practice like polygamy he would have to influence the chiefs and head men. If he could make them monogamous, then he might convert others—perhaps the entire group. Thus, he concentrated first of all on Chief White Calf. Prando set as a prime condition for the chief's baptism that he give up three of his four wives. After giving serious and protracted consideration to the matter, White Calf finally agreed. Flushed with success, Prando told the Indians who had assembled for the baptism:

This whole tribe is as yet shrouded in darkness. But light

---

[18] *Ibid.*

[19] *W.L.*, Vol. XII, No. 1 (1883), 36. Prando left a number of works which clearly demonstrate his linguistic abilities. See Herbert J. Landar, *Taxonomic Bibliography of North American Indian Languages* (JA). This bibliography is unpublished as yet but is in computer print-out form. For general evidence of Jesuit language work, see Wilfred P. Schoenberg, *Jesuit Mission Presses in the Pacific Northwest.*

[20] *W.L.*, Vol. XII, No. 3 (1883), 326.

[21] *Ibid.*, 311.

has now begun to dawn upon you. To-day I baptize your chief, White Calf, and his wife.[22]

Then, he dramatically directed his attention to the chief:

Chief, I pour the water of holy baptism upon your head, and God purifies your soul. Your soul, on this day, is as bright as the sun, and as beautiful as heaven's inhabitants, and as you are properly married to-day, you have become God's friend, for *God hates polygamy, and shall condemn all polygamists to everlasting fire.* [23]

Prando then left the Blackfeet to ponder his words and recrossed Birch Creek to his little log hut. As usual, his sense of timing was excellent. His intentions were also very clear, as his report of White Calf's baptism to his superior, Father Cataldo, indicates.

I was happy with my victory over the powers of darkness, for if, as it ordinarily happens, subjects follow the example of their chief, I had reason to hope that all the Indians would soon abandon polygamy.[24]

His hopes were strengthened not long thereafter when he baptized three more polygamists, two of whom were band chiefs.[25]

The complicated ritual involved in the sun dance presented Prando with a greater problem than polygamy; the evil of polygamy was readily apparent, but Satan was more subtle in the sun dance. Like the snake in the Garden of Eden, he twisted in and out of the maze of prayers, dances, social activities, and ritual sacrifices which made up the sun dance. At first, therefore, Father Prando was cautious and observant. He was able to grasp an amazing amount of detail and, what is more important, many of the meanings which the sun dance held for the Blackfeet. But at this stage he was content to bide his time: "I had only lately come among them, and there had not yet been time enough to instruct them sufficiently; and as besides, they thought that they were rendering solemn honor to the Great Spirit, prudence counseled me not to oppose their action."[26]

22 *Ibid.*, 310.
23 *Ibid.* My emphasis.
24 *Ibid.*
25 *Ibid.*, 310–11.
26 *W.L.*, Vol. XII, No. 1 (1883), 39.

After he had been among the Indians for a while, however, the priest began to make a distinction between those elements of the sun dance which were essentially social and thus harmless, and those elements which, from his point of view, were religious and thus idolatrous. Sharing with many priests of his time a fear of superstition, he believed that the Powers of Darkness had their primal strength in these parts of the tribal religious festival.

After White Calf's baptism, Prando used every opportunity, especially his talks with the chief, to express his negative views about the sun dance. Once White Calf became a Christian, he came to the priest to find out what parts of the sun dance were good and what parts were evil. Prando's answer clearly reflects his position: "I explained to him that they might without any harm sink the posts and erect their lodge, beat the drums, dance beseeming dances, and have their speeches; but that they were not allowed to utter evil prayers, nor to offer anything whatever to the sun."[27] White Calf agreed, but those who attended the ceremonies were not so co-operative.

The ceremonies surrounding the buffalo tongues proved to be especially resistant to Prando's ideas. Of course, by touching these rituals, he was striking near the center of the traditional meaning of the sun dance. Resistance was thus predictable. Prando was particularly offended when the Indians refused to allow him to enter the hut where the buffalo tongues were being prepared: "I said to myself that some evil was surely going on within, else how explain their refusing to allow me to be present."[28] This experience led him to harden his position and to express stronger disapproval of the sun dance. On this occasion he even told the Indians that the medicine lodge itself was responsible for evil among them and spiced his analysis with several specific examples. Then, after saying good-by to the small children and silently leaving the adults, he galloped out of the camp with his habit flowing magnificently behind him. This bit of drama had its effect, as he knew it would, for the next day White Calf sent a messenger to ask if the priest intended to take the white man's medicine away from the tribe. "I answered," said Prando, "that

27 *W.L.*, Vol. XII, No. 3 (1883), 322.
28 *Ibid.*, 324.

if the savages intended to obey the law of God, I would never abandon them; but if they wished to set up [themselves] for teachers and dictate to me how God was to be honored, I would certainly leave them."[29] Again Father Prando's intuitive grasp of Indian culture and personality, combined with his sense of timing, made an impact upon those Blackfeet who were under White Calf's leadership. The rest were free to reject his authority —and most of them probably did.

In addition to his attacks upon polygamy and the sun dance, Prando sought to displace what he felt were pernicious practices surrounding death and sickness. By attempting to change this part of Blackfoot life, Prando was not only challenging a tension laden area of human experience but also the well-established practice of using medicine bundles and the status of doctors and medicine men. His method of dealing with expressions of grief at the death of a family member, as well as his changes in the practices surrounding traditional burial, are consistent with his other activities. In this instance, Prando's sense for the dramatic was especially marked. He decided to establish a cemetery and thus end the practice of burial in trees or in lodges. He constructed a cross twenty feet high which he intended to place upon the hill he had chosen as the site for the cemetery. On Sunday morning, Prando passionately addressed the Indians:

> We have made a cross, a great cross. It was on a cross that Jesus Christ died, in order that he might be our Saviour. He bore His cross to the top of a mountain. On his shoulders He sustained its load. And now the great chief and I will bear this cross upon our shoulders, and God will look down upon us and will be pleased. He will bless our camp. When we die, we shall be buried upon that hill, and at the end of the world, we shall rise up again. The earth in which we will plant this cross will be sacred to the dead, and they who die unbaptized, shall have no burial in this ground.[30]

Then Prando and an old chief named Robear bore the cross up the mountain. Although this event must have impressed those who saw it, there is little evidence that traditional burial prac-

29 *Ibid.*
30 *Ibid.*, 308.

tices ceased or were even significantly modified—except in the case of the baptized Indians.

Illness was in many ways more difficult to deal with than were death and burial practices. According to Prando, it was in sickness that humans were weakest, that "all the powers of darkness are leagued against the poor savage."[31] He threatened, cajoled, and pointed out the evil of their ways, but his tactics did not keep some Blackfeet from identifying Prando himself as one of the possible causes of their trouble. As was true with other aspects of their traditional culture, the Blackfeet retained many of their charms and medicines, and while some members of the tribe accepted the benefits of the white man's medicine, many more were unwilling to give up their ancient ways.

Though he sought to replace the Blackfoot world view and religious tradition with what he considered the true religion, Prando nonetheless made interpretations of events which were strikingly similar to interpretations made by Blackfeet. For instance, as he left the Indian camp on the day of his altercation about the ceremony of the buffalo tongues, Prando was almost swept off his horse while crossing a river. After he reached the other side of the stream, he attributed his deliverance to "a special providence of heaven, for the left hand pocket of my habit, in which there was a little statue of St. Joseph, remained perfectly dry; while the other was soaking wet."[32] Thus, while Prando sought to convert the Blackfeet to a better way, some of the more perceptive Indians remained unable to see any great distinction between the Black Robe's medicine and their own.

The only distinction which the Indians recognized—a practical one—was the occasional superiority of the priest's medicine in producing beneficial results for individuals or groups. For instance, one band attributed their good fortune during the year to the medicine of baptism: "Black Robe, after your departure, the children fell sick, and in the other camps more than a hundred of them have died: but here we have not lost even one, *because they were baptized by you.*"[33] These Indians, who were

[31] *Ibid.*, 320.
[32] *Ibid.*, 325.
[33] *W.L.*, Vol. XII, No. 1 (1883), 34. My emphasis.

members of White Calf's camp, had come to believe—as had the Small Robes several decades earlier—that baptism could be powerful medicine. Again, Prando's own view of these matters was strikingly similar to that of the Indians: "I am fully persuaded that the preservation of all these children in the camp of the head chief is due to a special Providence: for if they had died, superstition might have influenced him to attribute it to the Sacrament, and as a consequence, he would have become angry with the missionary and expelled him from the tribe."[34] However, Prando's attitudes are clearly understandable when set within the context of his belief that he was participating in the cosmic struggle between God and the Devil.

Above all, Prando depended primarily upon argument and reason rather than coercion. He trusted that Blackfoot leaders had the good sense to see the truth of his point of view. Thus, when White Calf affirmed that he believed God had created the world and that everything in it was good, Prando asked why God, if good, had created bears, snakes, and so many other creatures which were harmful to man. White Calf's answer to the conundrum was utterly unconvincing—even to the Indians who were listening. And as he had so many times before, the missionary allowed the chief and the others an opportunity to ponder the problem. "I promised to give him the true explanation on another day, when I should speak of the fall of the first man, his rebellion against God, and the consequent uprising of the brute creation against him."[35] Although Prando had a dualistic view of the world, he was skillful enough in his relations with the Blackfeet that they usually would grant him a second hearing.

Peter Prando's missionary activities show the action, sustained and systematic, of a man who felt a powerful religious commitment. As he confronted Indian culture, he was firm at the points where he concluded that his own religious principles were in jeopardy, but he was always sensitive and often accommodating to many Blackfoot cultural values. As his religious ideas were put into practice, they were always expressed in the context of a basic commitment to the Blackfeet themselves. Prando might

34 *Ibid.*
35 *Ibid.*, 38.

have felt pity, anger, and frustration many times, but there was none of the deep ethnocentric hostility shown by some later Catholic missionaries.[36] Although Prando was embedded in the ideas and practices of his age and was thoroughly committed to his religious point of view, he moved with sensitivity and passion among a people who, broken and poverty-stricken though they were, still possessed sufficient cultural vigor to select the things they considered good and to resist the things they considered bad in Catholicism.

In the final analysis, however, Blackfoot culture won the larger battle, for polygamy continued on the reservation for many years after Prando announced that he had "orders from the Son of God to take the sword and, going among those who had many wives, to separate them."[37] As late as 1893, the agent for the Blackfeet reported a total of thirty-five polygamous households, although considering the size of the reservation and the nature of communications, there were probably more which were not known.[38] Likewise, the sun dance continued into the twentieth century, even though it was increasingly transformed by white contact. Furthermore, the huts of the full bloods continued to be filled with bundles and other ritual paraphernalia which were employed in times of crisis just as they had been since before the oldest Blackfeet could remember. To an unbiased observer it may have appeared that Prando's God had failed, but Prando and his associates never capitulated to despair, for they were infused with the belief that signs of victory were all about them. Being men of their own time, they could not grasp what men in later times could see with greater clarity—that the confrontation between Blackfoot religion and Roman Catholic Christianity was a complex mixture of resistance, accommodation, and assimilation rather than a simple conversion of Indians to white man's medicine. And, as always, the sides influenced each other and thus were inevitably transformed into something new. What the priests could not possibly grasp were the unintentional consequences of their activities, for their attacks on traditional cul-

[36] See Ch. VII.
[37] Bischoff, *Old Oregon*, 101.
[38] U.S., *Report*, 1893, 699.

ture tended to weaken Blackfoot life even further and in a tragic way contributed to the historical forces which were destroying the Indian world.

A Temporary Protestant Establishment

The hardy Jesuits who came after De Smet and Point endured the rigors of nature, the dangers associated with Indian society, and the wiles of the Devil. But they were not at all prepared to deal with the mysteries of shifting government policies. If the priests were aware of the past, they should have known that Americans in colonial days dealt with Indians under the principles of international law, treating each tribe as a sovereign nation.[1] With population growth and increasing pressure from settlers who wanted Indian lands, the government decided to remove Indians beyond the Mississippi and to give them the lands of the unlimited West "forever." However, as pressures increased and Manifest Destiny dictated white settlement of the land from the Atlantic to the Pacific, hostile uncivilized Indians again became a source of national concern. Out of this conflict between Indians and whites emerged the dark period during which the government seemed bent upon exterminating the more warlike tribes.[2] The Blackfeet felt the effects of this policy in the Baker episode of 1870.

[1] For an excellent study of the development of early Indian policy see Francis Paul Prucha, *American Indian Policy in the Formative Years.*

[2] During the period of the so-called "Indian Wars," De Smet and other Jesuits played an important role in attempting to mediate conflicts, but this subject is

Ironically, just a few months after the military suppression of hostile Blackfeet, President Ulysses S. Grant inaugurated a new national policy toward Indians. Instead of fighting Indians, he declared, the government would feed them; and instead of exterminating Indians, the government would seek to lead them into the ways of peace. Known popularly as the Peace Policy, the new approach included an attempt to upgrade the quality of personnel in the Indian service. Until 1870, low salaries and harsh working conditions had not attracted large numbers of qualified men. Indeed, there had been too many cases of close association between Indian agents and whisky traders, as well as other incidents which detracted from an office already held in low esteem. Grant proposed to upgrade the job by having Indian agents chosen from candidates who were recommended by the churches. In this way the president hoped to infuse the Indian service with what he believed to be the superior moral authority of the church.

As a part of the Peace Policy, tribes were parceled out to the various denominations, which then were responsible for recommending qualified agents as well as for beginning missionary activities. Tribes were divided without much consideration for previous missionary work, and despite the fact that Jesuits had worked with the Blackfeet for more than a quarter of a century, this tribe— as well as agencies in California, Washington Territory, Oregon, Idaho, and Michigan—was allocated to the Methodist church.[3] Thus, almost a decade and a half after the abortive Presbyterian attempt to establish a mission among the Blackfeet, the Methodists were placed in a formal relationship with these Indians—even though they had never sent a Methodist missionary to the tribe.

For a time, a kind of Protestant establishment among the

---

beyond the scope of the present study. See Burns, *Indian Wars,* for an authoritative account.

[3] U.S., *Report,* 1875, 172. In addition to the Blackfeet, the Methodists were assigned the Crow and Fort Peck Reservations in Montana. See Wade Crawford Barclay, *History of Methodist Missions: The Methodist Episcopal Church, 1845–1939,* Vol. III, 327n., for a list of Methodist agents in 1877. See also R. L. Whitner, "The Methodist Episcopal Church and Grant's Peace Policy: A Study of the Methodist Agencies, 1870–1882."

Blackfeet was created since the agents who were appointed were also Methodist ministers. They began informal missionary activities which later led to the establishment of a permanent Methodist mission. Furthermore, since the agent was a Protestant minister, the Jesuits understandably felt extremely threatened. Indeed, on the Blackfeet Reservation the Peace Policy was responsible for engendering Protestant-Catholic tensions, some of which have continued until the present.

In explaining the way the new policy would work, President Grant made it clear that, in addition to reforms in administration, he expected denominations to assist the government in the grand task of civilizing and Christianizing the savages. The way these lofty goals actually worked out on the Blackfeet Reservation can be seen in the work of John Young, a Methodist-approved agent whose tenure spanned the difficult and tragic period from 1876 through the starvation winter of 1883.[4] Not only was Young branded as one of the villains in that macabre winter, but he was also viewed by Catholics as one of Satan's henchmen. He precipitated especially serious conflicts with Fathers Prando and Imoda.

Young was a Methodist minister and a member of the Oregon Conference. Furthermore, the way he performed his task as agent gave important clues to the shape of later Methodist activity with the tribe.[5] Some of the traditions which still live on the reservation in the present Methodist church were begun by Young. For instance, Young established a precedent for Methodist philanthropy when he held his special service on Christmas Day in 1876. In preparation for this occasion Young went to the trading post to purchase "Candies, Raisins, nuts, etc. and some paper bags, and . . . made up one for each child with an assortment."[6]

After the opening of the service, Young gave a short narrative of the:

---

[4] Two agents before Young, Richard F. May (1874–75) and John S. Wood (1875–76), may have been recommended by the Methodists.

[5] Barclay, *Methodist Missions*, 327n. The Methodist agents were usually ministers who were responsible to their Conferences, although their primary responsibility was to the government.

[6] John Young to Clinton B. Fisk, December 30, 1876 (BAA).

> . . . Coming of the "Babe of Bethlehem" and why the day
> was annually held thro. the world by Christians as one of
> joy, good will, bestowing gifts, etc. and impressing the lesson
> that as the Great Spirit had shown his abounding love to us,
> we ought to manifest our gratitude by loving each other.[7]

Then came the part of the occasion in which the agent obviously
took special delight:

> At the conclusion each child was called forward and given
> one of our parcels. These Indian children love Sweets, as
> well as white ones. And it would have done your heart good
> to have seen their black eyes twinkle with joy at the . . .
> gifts.[8]

At this time Young was assisted at the agency by another
Methodist minister, Hugh Duncan. Duncan apparently had
taken up temporary residence on the reservation at the suggestion of Francis Asbury Riggin, the presiding elder of the Helena
District.[9] Despite the Methodist church's lack of a consistent
missionary policy at this time, Young and Duncan attempted to
develop and support various sorts of religious activities among
the Blackfeet. They were often short of funds because they
relied wholly upon fluctuating local support. During the entire
period from 1870 to 1883, the Methodist church appropriated no
money for missionary activities on the reservation. Young himself contributed twenty-five dollars, and a tiny group of white
Protestants contributed an additional twenty-five dollars toward
educational and missionary work among the Blackfeet.[10]

Even though activities on the reservation fell somewhat short
of President Grant's stated goals, Young was enthusiastic over
the program and described the meeting of the first Sunday school
in glowing terms.

> We had the School room full, the children on the seats,
> and the old men and squaws, many of the latter with their

---

[7] *Ibid.*

[8] *Ibid.*

[9] F. A. Riggin to John Young, December 16, 1876 (BAA). Presiding elders are
now called district superintendents.

[10] *Annual Reports* of the Missionary Society of the Methodist Episcopal Church,
1870–1883.

papooses on their backs, squatted on the floor wherever they could find room.[11]

These Indians must have noted the sincerity of the agent, even though they probably did not share his sense of the occasion's gravity. However, they listened attentively as the Short Coats demonstrated their medicine.

> We had singing, prayer and reading the Scriptures. A brief explanation of what was read. And . . . as this was the first S. School ever held here, a Short Statement of the object and importance of this mode of instruction to the young . . . We concluded with Singing and the repetition of the Lord's Prayer all kneeling.[12]

A careful and sympathetic examination of Young's correspondence reveals that he was a man who possessed genuine concern for his "children," the Blackfeet. Also, Riggin, the administrative official responsible for the church's activities, was concerned with the quality of agents and other agency personnel. Writing to Young, Riggin emphasized:

> You will doubtless have seen the necessity of a change in the administration of affairs so far as some of the employees are concerned if the Methodist Church be honored by the Blackfeet Agency. Bro. Duncan alone of all at the agency is a member of our church. He went down with me and I hope you will retain him. Religious services should be had every Sabbath and as he is a Christian minister he can aid you. I hope you will gather round you as many Christian Men as you can. Montana can afford you better men than Squaw-Men for the positions of the Agency.[13]

During this period, however, the Methodist church had insufficient personnel to implement any policies it might have had. The serious shortage of ministers naturally led to a concentration of the available resources upon the white population. The Rocky Mountain Conference was created in 1872, but only four ministers were present at the first district conference in 1874. In 1879

[11] Young to Fisk (BAA).
[12] *Ibid.*
[13] Riggin to Young (BAA).

the number remained at four—sufficient evidence that the church had too few clergy to minister to the white population, much less to undertake extensive work among the Blackfeet.[14]

This conclusion was reached by William Wesley Van Orsdel, the young Methodist preacher from Pennsylvania who is credited with being the father of Montana Methodism. He began preaching among the Blackfeet in 1872 and established good relationships with the Indians. But he soon concluded that his primary ministry should be among the white settlers in Montana. Thus, he spent the remainder of his long life founding Methodist churches throughout the state. Although he was inducted into the Blackfoot tribe, his ministry was not as significant for the Blackfeet as were the Jesuit and the later Methodist efforts.[15]

Despite the shortage of Methodist ministers in Montana, some church officials still believed that vigorous missionary institutions ought to be developed on the reservation. The commissioner of Indian affairs quoted one of these officials in his correspondence with Young in 1879. The enthusiasm of this church official was not matched by reservation realities, although he did express what he believed to be the perspective of the Missionary Society of the Methodist Church:

> . . . we conclude that our [church] should at once go forward in the matter—judiciously using the means the Govt. appropriates and supplement them with funds from the church. Please give me such information as to number of teachers we ought to provide for and such other details as may enable our committee to promptly undertake this work.[16]

The Methodists could not translate such high ideals into institutional reality. Neither Duncan nor Young were able to establish permanent Methodist missions for while their work was apparently motivated by sincere concern for the Blackfeet,

14 See Edward L. Mills, *Plains, Peaks and Pioneers: Eighty Years of Methodism in Montana,* 51–53.

15 For a fine summary of the growth of Montana Methodism and Van Orsdel's place in this history, see Barclay, *Methodist Missions,* 254–58. More extended treatments are Stella W. Brummitt, *Brother Van,* and Robert W. Lind, *From the Ground Up.* Van Orsdel's papers and journals are collected in the Methodist Historical Archives, Rocky Mountain College, Billings, Montana.

16 Commissioner Hoyt to John Young, October 1, 1879 (BAA).

it could not be supported by the church. Thus, although the Methodists had formal responsibility for the Blackfeet, the commissioner of Indian affairs as late as 1882 wrote to the Indian Bureau of the Women's Home Missionary Society of the Methodist Church, "The denomination from which these Indians [Blackfeet] have a right to expect Missionary help has, until the present time, failed to meet its responsibilities, and repeated appeals to it have been disregarded."[17]

The Jesuits could not disregard Young, however. As far as they were concerned, both he and the Methodist church were poaching on Catholic territory. The priests had the early baptisms by De Smet and Point, as well as the baptisms recorded at St. Peter's—some 2,732 by 1879[18]—as clear evidence of their rights in the situation. Young, for his part, could not ignore the Jesuits and came to regard them as trespassers on the reservation and serious challengers of his authority. Under these conditions, the Protestant and Catholic conflicts which broke out created animosity and bitterness which are still remembered.

In order to understand the intensity and depth of these conflicts, it is well to realize that Young was a vigorous and dedicated man who had very clear ideas about what he wanted to do. These ideas were rooted in a substratum of values and religious commitments which made him act with passion and conviction. However, passion and conviction were equally characteristic of Roman Catholic missionaries, even though their theological perspectives were totally different from those of Young. Lured from as far away as Europe by the strong missionary impulses of the nineteenth century, the Jesuits were not about to surrender to Young —or even to the United States government—without a fight. The ensuing conflict pitted well-matched adversaries against each other.

If Catholic missionaries had to be men dedicated enough to endure physical and psychological deprivation, so did early Blackfoot agents. When John Young arrived at the new agency on Badger Creek in mid-December, 1876, he found about three-

---

[17] Cited by Barclay, *Methodist Missions*, 350.
[18] Palladino, *Northwest*, 223. Of course, not all of the baptisms at St. Peter's were Blackfeet.

fourths of the tribe engaged in the winter hunt. Only the aged and the children were camped around the agency. (Part of these people formed Young's tiny congregation on Christmas Day.) Hearing of his arrival, a number of chiefs returned briefly to satisfy their curiosity concerning their new "father" and to pay their respects before returning to the hunt.[19]

The agency buildings were certainly not impressive. They were still under construction, and their location on Badger Creek was a source of mystery and an irritation to Young.

> Why they were ever placed here, no one has as yet been able to tell me. Convenience, farming or grazing facilities, even defense, *all* appear to have been ignored. I don't believe a more unsuitable place in every respect could be selected on the reservation.[20]

He also was introduced to the peculiarities and hazards of the Montana winters. The cold was not extreme, but the winds were especially intense: "The winds which come down thru this valley are regular tornados. Sweep out the Snow, and make me a little uncertain whether the buildings will long remain behind."[21] Yet he endured these rigors for seven long and difficult years.

The attitudes which led to bitter religious conflict were partially rooted in the agent's general bias against Catholics, which many Protestants of his time shared. The conflict was also partially a result of his optimistic belief that the nomadic Blackfeet could be transformed into useful farmers with relative ease, for he felt: "With a proper number of instructions and efficient educational facilities, with the necessary Agricultural implements and domestic Animals . . . I do not doubt that in a few years they might become entirely self supporting."[22] Young believed that the church and the school were the primary instruments through which this social transformation would occur. And after two years among the Blackfeet he authoritatively reported to the commissioner of Indian affairs: "From my knowl-

19 Young to Fisk (BAA).
20 *Ibid.* Emphasis in the original.
21 *Ibid.*
22 John Young to Commissioner Hoyt, September (date faded), 1878 (BAA).

edge of, and intercourse with, these Indians, I am fully persuaded that the *Gospel* and the *School* are the instruments through which the Civilization and Christianization of the Indian may be accomplished."[23] It was precisely at these points, the gospel and the school, that the Roman Catholic missionaries proved to be so threatening to Young.

On the educational front, St. Peter's, even though it was now located outside the reservation, was the logical place for Blackfoot children to attend school—at least to the Roman Catholic missionary mind. Because the priests considered the Blackfeet as primarily Catholic in religious persuasion, it was natural to expect them to attend Catholic schools. Furthermore, at the most practical level, St. Peter's had to attract enough children to justify its existence since its missionary functions had been impaired by the restriction of the reservation boundary. Therefore, Father Imoda, who was in charge of St. Peter's, actively sought children for his school from the surrounding tribes. One such visit to the Blackfeet in the spring of 1880 precipitated an ugly conflict with Young.

The controversy revolved around the charge that Father Imoda had "enticed" or otherwise "abducted" three Blackfoot children. On May 24, Young wrote to Imoda:

> The School Teachers report to me that three boys were absent from school this morning and were said to have accompanied you. I hope this is not true . . . Of course you are aware that I can neither permit School Children to be coaxed or abducted from the reservation.[24]

Imoda replied on May 27, explaining that, "Far from abducting or coaxing children from your school, to several that offered themselves to come with me, I invariably told that I would not take them unless they were brought to me by their parents or tutors."[25] Furthermore, he argued, since all three children had been assigned to him either by their parents or their tutors, his position was both morally and legally above reproach. Imoda then pointed out what was essentially true, that the reservation

23 *Ibid.* Emphasis in the original.
24 John Young to Father Imoda, May 24, 1880 (BAA).
25 Father Imoda to John Young, May 27, 1880 (BAA).

75

was very large and the government school was not reaching all of the children. Thus he saw no reason why St. Peter's and the agency could not strike up a productive relationship. "I hope," he said, "that we may continue to work in harmony for the same end, which is to help these poor Blackfeet to become civilized."[26]

Young persisted in his belief that Father Imoda had done something illegal, and on the twenty-second of the next month he wrote to Commissioner Trowbridge asking for a statement of policy which would illuminate the situation and give him guidance. The commissioner not only ordered Young to retrieve the boys but also stated his position concerning the agent's authority: "You as Agent for the Indians of the Blackfeet Agency have full supervision over them, subject to the orders of this office, and as such Agent you are the tutor and guardian of the Indian children, and no Indian or Indian child can legally leave or be taken from the reservation without your consent."[27] This single sentence embodied the central ideas of the policy of wardship over Indian life and property. Imoda was arguing on the basis of the consent of the parents which, for the commissioner, had no validity. Evidently, Young had echoed the commissioner's language in a communication written to Imoda a few weeks before the official statement. Imoda's response was testy: "I find your claim of being the tutor and guardian of Indian children *against the will of their parents* quite a novelty, to say the least."[28]

Meanwhile, Young had informed the commissioner that Imoda's action was a threat to the education of the Blackfeet. "If this thing is allowed," he argued, "my school efforts are futile, as the most advanced boys or girls may be spirited away at any time."[29] In order to clinch his argument, Young reported that all the Indians were very concerned and were watching to see what the government would do. Furthermore, he said that the Blackfeet "altogether disapprove" of Imoda's actions.

At this point the director of Catholic Indian Missions, Father Brouillet, wrote to the commissioner of Indian affairs asking permission to educate Indian children at St. Peter's. In his letter

26 *Ibid.*
27 Commissioner Trowbridge to John Young, July 15, 1880 (BAA).
28 Father Imoda to John Young, June 16, 1880 (BAA). My emphasis.
29 John Young to Commissioner Trowbridge, August 11, 1880 (BAA).

Brouillet pointed out the inadequacies of the school at the agency and emphasized that means for training the boys in agriculture were limited. Indeed, the director went so far as to say that St. Peter's was large enough to accommodate the entire Blackfoot population—if they would take up residence about the school.[30] Evidently Brouillet had been informed of Imoda's difficulties and was seeking to establish a legal relationship between St. Peter's and the Blackfeet. His language clearly betrayed his active interest in maintaining a strong missionary connection with the entire tribe.

Young recommended that the Catholic request be denied on the grounds that St. Peter's was more than one hundred miles from the reservation and that the Indians did not like to be separated from their children. Furthermore, he pointed out that since Imoda's action had remained unpunished, the Catholic request was simply a move to legitimate illegal acts.[31] However, decisions on Indian affairs in Washington had passed to Acting Commissioner Brooks who, in his initial correspondence with Young, could see real advantages to Brouillet's proposal: "In view of the limited school facilities at your agency his proposition seems to be an advantageous one, but before accepting it I desire to have your opinion as to its advisability and practicability."[32]

In the light of Young's reply citing all the reasons for not contracting with St. Peter's, and upon further review of the Imoda incident, the acting commissioner referred the whole matter to the Department of Justice and to the U.S. district attorney in Montana. The district attorney, J. L. Dryden, ran into difficulties in the courts when he unsuccessfully applied for a writ of habeas corpus. The judge of the First Judicial District of the Montana Territory held that Dryden was not legally entitled to the custody of the children. When Dryden then presented his case before the Supreme Court of the territory, "The Court held in substance, that this is an undertaking of the Indians themselves, and . . . does not warrant any interference by the govern-

---

[30] Rev. Brouillet to Commissioner Trowbridge, August 11, 1880 (BAA).
[31] John Young to Commissioner Trowbridge, August 31, 1880 (BAA).
[32] Acting Commissioner Brooks to John Young, August 14, 1880 (BAA).

ment." Furthermore, the court referred "the whole question back to the *authority of the parents* to apply for the return of the children . . . which in no way raises or determines the question of the rights of the United States in the premises."[33]

By 1881 the commissioner felt that since an appeal to the United States Supreme Court would be too time consuming and costly, Young should use the existing court opinion to try to get the boys back from St. Peter's. The commissioner instructed Young to assert the parents' rights and thus avoid the whole issue of the agent's authority and jurisdiction.[34] And, although Dryden did not agree, this was where the matter stood.[35] The issue of who had the right to decide where and how Indian children would be educated was still not clearly settled, and the shifting personnel at the federal level produced differing judgments in the matter. There is no evidence to indicate what the final outcome of the controversy was, but its consequences for Protestant-Catholic relations at the reservation level were clear. Young's attitude toward the priests had soured, and in turn, they came more and more to see Young as their archenemy. They were partly responsible for attributing to Young the guilt for the tribe's disastrous starvation winter.

Between 1881 and 1883, Young also came into conflict with another priest, the vital Father Peter Prando. The substance of the conflict between these two strong-willed men cannot be reconstructed in its entirety, but it is possible to recover some of its motifs. Young stated at least two explanations for his attitudes toward Prando. First, he said that Prando was of the same general type as Imoda, who had abducted Indian boys and disregarded his authority as agent.[36] Furthermore, Young claimed that Prando undermined his authority even more by spreading "false statements to the Indians, tending to make them dissatisfied with the management here."[37] A second reason for Young's opposition to Prando was his conviction that Roman Catholic missionaries had done little toward Christianizing and civilizing

33 J. L. Dryden to K. Raynor, January 12, 1881 (BAA). My emphasis.
34 Commissioner to John Young, January 29, 1881 (BAA).
35 Dryden to Young, March 3, 1881 (BAA).
36 John Young to (name illegible), July 2, 1882 (BAA).
37 John Young to Commissioner Price, January 2, 1882 (BAA).

the Blackfeet. Writing to Commissioner Price concerning another request by Brouillet for permission to educate children at St. Peter's, Young said sharply:

> I have no confidence in these missionaries, nor have I seen any good resulting from their many years occasional visits to these tribes. None of the heathenish practices abated, no civilization in any shape taught, and the Indians were never shown how to build a house, plant a potato, or raise any kind of crop.[38]

A third reason also appeared in Young's correspondence, although he did not state his views explicitly in relation to Prando. Young had strong hopes that the Methodist would soon establish themselves on the reservation—a hope that was to remain unfulfilled. To a request by Rev. E. J. Clemens concerning the possibility of becoming a missionary, Young indicated that he had no power to appoint missionaries—despite the fact that Clemens had offered to provide for his own support. Young referred the minister to appropriate officials in the Methodist church and closed his letter with a warmth he never showed for the Catholics: "The field is white unto the harvest and should you come you may be assured of a hearty welcome."[39] And he expressed real elation to Commissioner Hoyt at the prospect of Methodist participation in civilizing the Blackfeet: "With the proper men (and without doubt such would be selected by the Missionary Committee), no more efficient plan for the benefit and civilization of these tribes could be devised."[40] Whatever motivated Young, the final consequence for Prando was his exclusion from the reservation, although there is no evidence that Young ever received instructions from Washington to banish the Catholics.[41]

From Prando's point of view, Young's actions were motivated by anti-Catholic passions and greed: "Our agent is a Protestant, and an open enemy of Catholicism. His only aim is to get rich

[38] *Ibid.*
[39] John Young to Rev. E. J. Clemens, October 23, 1879 (BAA).
[40] John Young to Commissioner Hoyt, October 21, 1879 (BAA).
[41] Whenever this happened, it tended to drive Roman Catholic missions underground. See Peter J. Rahill, *The Catholic Indian Missions and Grant's Peace Policy*, 42ff.

and, meantime, live as comfortably as possible."[42] While there is evidence that Young favored Methodist missions because he was himself a Methodist minister, there is little support for Prando's charge of official corruption. Conditions on the reservation at this time were really beyond the agent's control—the buffalo had disappeared, he could get only minimal response from Washington, and starvation was beginning to threaten the Blackfeet. However, the situation was not helped by the circulation of rumors and charges followed by more rumors and counter-charges.[43]

At the end of May, 1882, Prando was finally banished from the reservation. But by the twelfth of June he was celebrating the first mass in his new chapel located just across Birch Creek.[44] From this base, only a few yards outside Young's jurisdiction, Prando continued his work unabated:

> As soon as my Indians learned of my expulsion, they became convinced that the agent was doing all in his power to ill-treat me, and as I could not enter the reservation, it remained for the Indians to cross the creek and visit me at my residence, and they did this every Sunday, in order to be present at Mass.[45]

In his tiny chapel, twenty feet wide and forty-eight feet long, Prando baptized almost seven hundred Blackfeet and performed fifty-five marriages.[46] Thus, he extended Roman Catholic power on the reservation despite the action of Young and the Peace Policy.

It is clear that while Young laid the foundation for future Methodist activity among the Blackfeet, he was unable to gain control of other powerful historical factors. He could not undo the damage done by the Baker massacre; he could not bring back the buffalo; he could not force Congress to appropriate more money for provisions and therefore was unable to avoid the star-

---

42 *W.L.*, Vol. XII, No. 3 (1883), 315.
43 *Ibid.*
44 *Ibid.*, 319.
45 *Ibid.*, 316.
46 Bischoff, *Old Oregon*, 91. The record of these "bootleg baptisms" is preserved, along with Prando's fascinating marginal notes, in the files of Little Flower Church, Browning, Montana.

vation winter. And because he was a principled, stubborn man, he could not avoid conflicts with other principled, stubborn men—the Jesuits. To the Blackfeet, beaten to their knees by the army and coming closer to starvation each year, the conflicts between Young and the Black Robes must have seemed as confusing as were the priest's attacks upon their culture. In a strange, ambiguous way Young joined the Jesuits for he shared their lofty motivations, but, like the priests, he finally bowed to the darker powers of the historical situation.

CHAPTER

VI

Civilizing and Christianizing

During the last decades of the nineteenth century the United States government developed a policy designed to transform Indians into fully assimilated American citizens. In order to accomplish this goal, Indians were to be stripped of their culture and clothed with the life style of the white majority. As well as making systematic attempts to break up tribalism and to undermine the influence of the Indian family, efforts were made to suppress the language, religion, and values of traditional Indian cultures. The General Allotment Act of 1887, the Dawes Act, was a symbol of this policy of forced acculturation because it was designed to break up tribal lands and to make each Indian an independent property owner.[1]

Legislation and federal action during this period were motivated by great hostility toward Indian culture, and very few people questioned the inherent superiority of the white culture offered to the Indians. For example, in the 1880's Senator Pendleton of Ohio, moved by idealism and the tenets of Social Darwinism, argued that Indians:

. . . must either change their mode of life or they must die . . .

1 Allotment of 320 acres to each Indian on the Blackfeet Reservation was not completed until 1912. Ewers, *Blackfeet*, 318.

We must stimulate within them to the very largest degree, the idea of home, of family, and of property. These are the very anchorages of civilization; the commencement of the dawning of these ideas in the mind is the commencement of the civilization of any race, and these Indians are no exception.[2]

No one doubted that civilization would come to the Blackfeet through a process of education supplemented by the beneficial effects of Christianization at the hands of Protestant and Catholic missionaries. In the opinion of most policy makers, the task could be accomplished in little more than a generation.

To officials the boarding school seemed to be the logical institution in which to educate the Indian, for there he could be isolated from pernicious tribal and family influences. The growth of the Roman Catholic mission on the Blackfeet Reservation coincided favorably with the government's purposes, for in the last decade of the nineteenth century the Catholic missionaries founded a school designed to fulfill many of the ideas of the commissioner of Indian affairs. The commissioner believed that:

> To civilize . . . is to educate, and to educate means breaking up of tribal customs, manners, and barbarous usages, and the assumption of the manners, usages, and customs of the superior race with whom they are thereafter to be thrown into contact.[3]

This task inevitably involved coercion and, despite the loss of Blackfoot political and economic autonomy, provoked a surprising cultural resistance which frustrated many plans of both church and state.

Before the starvation winter, the establishment of permanent educational facilities on the reservation was prevented by the

---

[2] U.S., *Congressional Record*, 46 Cong., 3 sess., 1881, Vol. XI. Cited by D'Arcy McNickle, "Indian and European: Indian-White Relations from Discovery to 1887," in George E. Simpson and J. Milton Yinger (eds.), "American Indians and American Life," *The Annals of the American Academy of Political and Social Science*, Vol. CCCXI (May, 1957), 11. Concerning Theodore Roosevelt's hard realism, see also Wilcomb E. Washburn (ed.), *The Indian and the White Man*, 132–33.

[3] U.S., *Report*, 1901, 15.

limited resources of the churches, the exclusion of the Jesuits from the reservation, and the unsettled context surrounding the Blackfeet. The nearest Roman Catholic school was St. Peter's, a hundred miles away. As early as 1881 Father Prando had pointed out that the condition of the Blackfeet was desperate and that it was imperative to move beyond mere spiritual and sacramental ministries. The Blackfeet, he said, "need beyond all to be trained and encouraged to agricultural labors: they themselves now admit the necessity of this, and are anxious to receive instruction."[4] (This report actually tells more about Prando's ideas than it does about the true desire of the Blackfeet—who consistently resisted attempts to make them farmers.) Such missionary desires remained unrealized even four years after the winter of 1883 when Agent Baldwin reported to the commissioner:

> . . . that there is no church, missionary, educational or religious societies located within the limits of this agency. The National Women's Indian Association obtained permission in July 1886, to establish a mission at this agency, also I am advised that in 1885 like permission was granted the Catholic Church. As yet neither have selected sites.[5]

At about the time this letter was written, Father Damiani, who continued the work of Father Prando on Birch Creek, was completing a residence and a small log chapel on Two Medicine River. Then, in 1887 Chief White Calf contributed land for the building of a school which was completed and formally opened in September, 1890.[6] The mission was named Holy Family. It was located on a site that recalled better days among the Blackfeet. Built on the banks of the Two Medicine River in a narrow valley at the edge of a cottonwood grove, the mission buildings were surrounded on the north and west by stark cliffs over which the Blackfeet had driven buffalo in earlier times. In this setting, Father Damiani, along with three Ursuline sisters, mounted the Catholic church's most impressive experiment designed to civilize and Christianize Blackfoot children. By 1892 there were one hundred Blackfoot children enrolled in the agency school west

4 *W.L.*, Vol. XII, No. 1 (1883), 37.
5 Agent Baldwin to Commissioner, August 30, 1887 (BAA).
6 U.S., *Report*, 1890, 115.

of Browning on Willow Creek and one hundred in Holy Family Mission school. The agent commented that under the priest's care, "The children . . . have at all times shown that they were well cared for, and their advancement has been good."[7] By the turn of the century, Holy Family Mission was well established. It was an ordered world which, over a long period of time, made some impact upon the Blackfeet—even though the goals of civilization and Christianization were never fully accomplished. The mission diaries for the years 1908 through 1938 reveal a number of themes which together made up the daily rhythm of life at the mission.

In order to keep more than one hundred people alive the year round, sufficient food, clothing, and shelter had to be provided and maintained. These tasks were central in a number of daily routines which commanded much attention from the mission superiors. The farm had to be cared for, not only for food but also for training the children in the pursuit of agriculture. Baking and cooking had to be done, again not only out of necessity but also because the girls had to learn the skills which would make them good wives and mothers. And there was the daily routine of educating over one hundred restless Indian children, a chore which consumed much of the entire staff's time and energy.

Efforts to civilize the Blackfeet did produce some visible results as the children adjusted to life at Holy Family. Despite the occasional harshness of discipline, the priest and sisters were usually extremely kind, treating the children with warmth and affection.[8] No doubt they felt rewarded in their efforts when the Holy Family Mission Band received ovations in the surrounding communities. And they may have been even more impressed in 1939 when one of the children achieved fame in the mecca of American competition and adulation—Hollywood. Martin Pepion, a thirteen-year-old full blood, played opposite Shirley Temple in *Susannah of the Mounties*. Martin, who took the name Goodrider for the film, was apparently quite a success

7 U.S., *Report*, 1892, 281.
8 See Sister M. Irene to Dr. Martin, November 27, 1893; Sister M. Irene to Agent Cooke, November 14, 1893; Sister M. Irene to Agent Cooke, November 24, 1893; and Dr. Martin to Agent Cooke, November 10, 1893 (BAA).

in his role. When Twentieth Century Fox hired Blackfeet Indians for mass parts in the movie, the raiders of the plains had a brief moment in the sun.[9]

Of course, the boarding school required long-term commitments of time and energy by the staff. The Jesuit priests, the Ursuline sisters, and the Lamennais Brothers of Christian Instruction—a French teaching order—provided just such committed personnel. And although there were normal changes among the mission's workers, some gave their most productive years to the Blackfeet.[10]

The priests, possessing powerful personal traits and a variety of competences, dedicated their best energies to civilizing and Christianizing the Blackfeet. They worked especially hard with their considerable linguistic talents in order to improve communications with the Indians. For instance, Father Bougis, in addition to his heavy administrative duties, composed a grammar of the Blackfoot language, wrote numerous questions for confession, and authored an introduction to Blackfoot grammar for missionaries and teachers. Father Soer was also busy translating liturgical and Biblical texts into the Blackfoot tongue. And among the anonymous manuscripts produced at Holy Family were miscellaneous prayers, songs, vocabularies, and instructions for catechumens.[11]

Despite the priests' skills and occasionally dramatic successes, their efforts met with considerable Blackfoot resistance. To accomplish its aims, the church had to come into direct conflict with the whole range of traditional values which remained after the demise of Blackfoot economic and political institutions. The institution which continued to embody these values and to pass them on to succeeding generations was the Blackfoot family; here children still acquired their sense of identity, their sexual and work roles, their values, and their feeling for the religious life.

Holy Family Mission was designed to displace and replace the functions performed by the traditional home. The children

9 *Newspaper Files*, Vol. XLVIII, 129; Vol. L, 63 (CA).

10 Sister Thomas, for instance, was among the Blackfeet for almost fifty years. *The Indian Sentinel*, Second Series, Vol. XII, No. 3 (Summer, 1933).

11 Landar, *Bibliography* (JA).

were taken from their families and lived at the mission most of the year, except for a brief vacation. Parents were allowed to visit their children, but the mission took over the parents' role in teaching the children. Thus, the priests faced the twin difficulties of obtaining children for the school and keeping them in school once they were there. At this juncture the purposes of the federal government and those of the mission were in harmony; therefore, the power of the government was used to coerce recalcitrant Blackfoot parents and children.

It is doubtful that the federal Indian School superintendent realized the crushing effect his policy would have on the Indian family when he said, in 1886, "Only by complete isolation of the Indian child from his savage antecedents can he satisfactorily be educated."[12] But the agents certainly were aware of the parents' resistance to the isolation of their children from the family. In 1885, after the departure of Agent Young, the Peace Policy waned and priests were again on the reservation recruiting children for St. Peter's and for St. Ignatius Mission, located west of the Rocky Mountains in the Bitterroot Valley. In March of that year Agent Allen reported:

> Father Imoda is here trying to secure pupils for the school at St. Peter's Mission, with fair prospects of success. The Indians dislike very much to see their children taken away, but, as St. Peter's Mission is not a great way from the Agency, they do not object to sending them there as to more distant points.[13]

No doubt the priests at Holy Family Mission were aware that they would meet parental opposition when they actively began to fill the school. But they could call on the strong coercive powers of the government for assistance. By 1892, the co-operation between the agent and the priests at Holy Family had developed to such a degree that parents who resisted often had to tighten their belts. Father Bougis, an assistant to the superior, Father Damiani, described the tactics with striking clarity.

> New Years day (1892), several of our pupils were taken

12 U.S., *Report*, 1886, LXI.
13 Agent Allen to Commissioner, March 1, 1885 (BAA).

from school by their parents. I complained to the agent . . .
*Not only did he send his police to apprehend the deserters,
but he also held back the parents' requisitions for provisions
from the Government.*[14]

The practical consequences of Agent Young's earlier claims to
authority over the life and person of Indians could be devas-
tatingly effective.

The agent who withheld Indian rations to force compliance
with the government's educational policy was George Steell, a
man who gave no quarter when his principles were at stake. There
is little evidence to indicate that Steell was either a cruel or a
stupid man. He was aware that Indians could be pushed only
so far before policies began to produce fewer results. These feelings were uppermost in his mind when he wrote in December,
1892:

I feel now that we are crowding these people a little too
fast, they having been so opposed to sending their children
to school, and having already nearly doubled the number
over former years. We ought to take a rest, and so maybe
in the end make greater progress. Although I believe every-
one of school age ought to be in school as early as it can be
accomplished without setting the Indians against our work,
*a good deal of coaxing and a little driving will give better
results than all driving.*[15]

Under pressure, however, Steell was true to his principles and
used as much force as was necessary. The very next year, when
he was trying to get sufficient numbers of students for St. Peter's
and Holy Family, he wrote to Father Damiani: "I have the police
now out, telling them that they must get more boys for St. Peter's,
and they must be got before tomorrow."[16]

Under these conditions, it is little wonder that parents often
felt that the government and the church were robbing them of
their children, who were loved and well cared for in Blackfoot
families. In contrast to the agents, parents especially disliked the
use of coercion and would go to any means to prevent this ex-

[14] Cited by Bischoff, *Old Oregon*, 102–103. My emphasis.
[15] Agent Steell to Dr. Daniel Dorchester, December 19, 1892 (BAA). My emphasis.
[16] Agent Steell to Father Damiani, January 4, 1893 (BAA).

pedient from being applied to their children. A writer in *The Indian Sentinel* reported in 1912 that Indian parents would say to the missionaries: "If my child does wrong, tell him how he must behave; but do not strike or punish him . . . Physical pain . . . makes our children timid, and cowards, like pale-faced men; but let them be kept in ignorance of pain, and when the young brave will take the war path, there will be nothing to daunt his courage and he will fight like a mountain lion."[17] With the agents' and the missionaries' propensity to use force, it is little wonder that parents should have communicated their negative attitudes toward the mission school to their children. That the children learned some of these attitudes is apparent in the difficulty missionaries had with runaways during the early years of Holy Family Mission.

In December, 1891, the priests, sisters, and other employees —a total of fourteen adults—had charge of one hundred and seven Piegan children, ranging in age from fifteen to six.[18] Both the size of the school and the character of the student population remained the same between 1891 and 1896, and during these years the mission was plagued by a number of runaway children. In October, 1893, Father Bougis complained to Agent Cooke about one runaway boy and suggested that the boy be disciplined.[19] In January of the following year, Bougis again contacted the agent concerning boys who had left the mission.[20] And in January, 1895, two boys ran away from the mission during bitter weather. One boy froze to death, and the other had his feet badly frostbitten.[21] In February of the next year Father Damiani reported to Agent Steell that four boys had run away from the mission.[22]

While the number of *reported* runaways is not a significant percentage of the total student population, it is probably true that not all of the cases, and certainly not all attempts, were re-

[17] *The Indian Sentinel*, 1912, First Series, 36. Cf. Wissler, "Social Life," *Anthropological Papers, Am. Mus. Nat. Hist.*, Vol. VII, Part 1 (1911), 29–30.
[18] "Quarterly Report of Indian Schools," December 31, 1891 (BAA).
[19] Bougis to Cooke, October 20, 1893 (BAA).
[20] Bougis to Cooke, January 31, 1894 (BAA).
[21] Father Damiani to Agent Cooke, January 29, 1895 (BAA).
[22] Damiani to Steell, February 12, 1896 (BAA).

ported. Furthermore, the fact that the children would run away during the winter, often in the midst of the coldest weather, is significant. Finally, the daily records kept at the mission reveal that the problem of keeping the children on the grounds was one which received considerable comment. Occasionally, as in 1918, harsh measures were taken to curb the children. When three girls ran away in January of that year, the Indian police were immediately dispatched.

> Two of the runaways were brought back by the police & given a public flogging by him with a promise of more next time—The oldest one, the leader of the bunch, was dismissed from the Mission School to be returned to the Gov't school from which she formerly came.[23]

Both the persistence of runaways at the mission and the negative attitudes of the parents toward the school offer evidence of continuing resistance to missionary attempts to civilize the Blackfeet.

Unco-operative parents and runaway children were also signs that during the 1880's and 1890's, despite the cultural traumas which the Blackfeet were undergoing, there was more than a vestige of traditional culture left. For instance, in 1889, despite attempts to end polygamy, the agent complained that the "one relic of barbarism which the older Indians do not relish abandoning is the system of polygamous marriages."[24] And as early as 1881 Commissioner Price said to John Young:

> ... it is the policy of this Department ... to discourage by every judicious means, all barbarous Indian dances, feasts, and savage customs, and to encourage the Indians to relinquish them as rapidly as possible.[25]

Yet over a decade later, in 1892, a realistic appraisal by the agency physician indicated that the power of traditional ideas and practices was still very much in evidence.[26] Agent Steell found it necessary to refuse permission for such time-consuming activities as the medicine lodge, bundle openings, and dancing in order to

---

23 Holy Family Mission Diary, January 1918–December 1931 (JA).
24 U.S., *Report*, 1889, 222.
25 Commissioner Price to John Young, November 3, 1881 (BAA).
26 U.S., *Report*, 1892, 282.

A signal that buffalo are near the camp, as drawn by Father Point.
Oregon Province Archives of the Society of Jesus.

A chief telling the camp that buffalo are near, in a drawing by Father Point. Oregon Province Archives of the Society of Jesus.

Pierre-Jean De Smet, S.J. Oregon Province Archives of the Society of Jesus.

Father Point's likeness of Wolf's Son, perhaps the first Blackfoot to receive baptism. Oregon Province Archives of the Society of Jesus.

Peter Prando, S.J. Oregon Province Archives of the Society of Jesus.

Chief White Calf (third from left), who had been baptized at Father Prando's Birch Creek Chapel, and members of his band (1888). Oregon Province Archives of the Society of Jesus.

Ursuline Sisters and Indian girls at St. Peter's Mission. Oregon Province Archives of the Society of Jesus.

Holy Family Mission. Oregon Province Archives of the Society of Jesus.

get the Indians to work.[27] Although it was perfectly possible for government employees to make glowing reports of changes in such crude measures of civilization as the adoption of Western clothing ("citizen's dress"), these changes did not alter the value-laden cultural tradition which persisted.[28]

As the priests pursued their goal of Christianization outside the school, they encountered cultural resistance there, too. For instance, in 1909 Father Bruckert came into conflict with a man and woman living together without benefit of Catholic marriage. The man, extremely ill, had asked to be buried in the cemetery at Holy Family. His request was refused, and according to the diarist recording the event, this show of authority made a deep impression upon the other Indians who were living in sin.[29] Often, however, the priests either had to compromise with the devil or to make other distasteful concessions made necessary by the circumstances. These compromises often revolved about marriage. In reporting one such incident in 1918, Father Grant detailed the problem very clearly. He had performed a marriage, but he was not exceedingly happy with the results as is evident from his description of the couple:

> Both had been to Gov't schools and neither knew anything about their religion—they had been baptized Catholics & that was the only Sac. they had ever received—It was quite a task to instruct them enough for confession & marriage. The danger of putting them off is that they would live together without being married—So of two evils, chose the less.[30]

As late as 1934 the priests were still having altercations with full bloods concerning medicine ceremonies and the sun dance. The Jesuits took every opportunity to suppress the last vestiges of these devilish ceremonies, which nonetheless seemed to continue year after year. They did have a source of power, however, in extreme unction, for dying Blackfeet who had been baptized

---

27 Agent Steell to Indian Commissioner, Regina, NWT, August 4, 1892 (BAA).
28 It was reported in 1903, for instance, that the number of Indians wearing citizen's dress rose from 1,200 in 1890 to 2,401 in 1903. Estelle Reel, Supt. of Indian Schools to Supt. of the Blackfeet Boarding School, July 31, 1903 (BAA).
29 Diary, September 1908–December 1917 (JA).
30 Diary, 1918–1931 (JA).

were extremely anxious to receive this sacrament. In one such situation the person involved had been the medicine woman at a sun dance. Father Kane refused to administer the last rites of the church to this woman without a public confession. After three days of discussion and conflict with the woman and her relatives, the priest finally won the battle.

> The Old Lady was willing to make her promise not to have anything to do with Sun Worship or Indian Medicine. Father Kane gave a short talk on obedience to the voice of the Church and the privilege of dying with the Sacraments of the Church.[31]

The diarist's comment upon this incident probably contains a great deal of truth: "The Father argued a whole hour with the Indians about the evil of Sun Worship but whether any impression was made is doubtful."[32]

In addition to the stubborn persistence of Blackfoot culture, Holy Family Mission also faced a number of purely physical threats. Central among these hazards was the weather. Even though Holy Family was located in an aesthetically pleasing spot, winters could be extremely bitter, the temperature frequently plunging to forty degrees below zero. In addition to the blowing and drifting snow in winter, violent climactic disturbances accompanied the changes in season. In June of 1934, for example, hail devastated the mission:

> The hail was as large as hen's eggs and broke over 300 panes of glass, tore off many shingles so that the rain came through. It tore the leaves off the trees around the Mission so much so that it looked as if it were in the fall of the year. Very many of the cattle were bruised by the falling hail. The crop to a very large extent has been destroyed.[33]

Floods were also a continual threat, for during the spring the Two Medicine River could inundate the entire area where the mission was situated. Furthermore, the river had a life of its own which did not always take into account the plans of the mis-

31 Diary, January 1932–1937 (JA).
32 *Ibid.*
33 Diary, January 1932–September 1937 (JA).

sionaries. In 1927 it began to change its course, stripping away about two thousand feet of the mission land. A hasty appeal for money to finance a project for containing the river and diverting it back to its old course was successful, and fortunately the mission buildings were saved.[34]

Miserable weather, floods, and resistance by the Blackfeet all failed to undermine the will of the priests at Holy Family Mission. Their vision of the world and their view of the importance of their sacramental activity gave their efforts meaning when, to the outside observer, the mission was in shambles. Year after year they continued baptizing children, teaching catechism, performing marriages, saying masses, and burying the dead. During part of this period, between 1902 and 1939, they recorded 2,090 baptisms of children, 78 adult baptisms, 848 burials, 837 confirmations, and 339 marriages.[35] To the Catholic missionaries, the religious statistics they compiled were evidence of the extent to which the Blackfeet were responding to the Christianization program. However, because traditional culture and its values continued to manifest themselves in the conflicts which the priests reported, it is obvious that the goal of full Christianization remained unrealized. On the other hand, a more significant attempt to Christianize the Blackfeet had not yet been made.

Ironically, despite the motivations, skill, and dedication of the Jesuits, their attempt to Christianize the Blackfeet was destructive as well as constructive. Their efforts were destructive because they further undermined social order without fully convincing the Indians to adopt Western culture and constructive because Holy Family Mission became a center of order and meaningful activity for Indians who came deeply under its influence. Unfortunately, the number of Indians thus affected by the mission seems to have been very small; the majority, while they may have been baptized, often had little relation to the church until they required the last rites and Christian burial.

[34] *The Indian Sentinel*, Second Series, Vol. IX, No. 2 (Spring, 1929), 66; Vol. IX, No. 4 (Fall, 1929), 161.

[35] Holy Family Mission *Annual Reports*, 1902–1939 (CA). Reports for the years 1903, 1904, 1912, 1930, 1931, 1932, and 1934 are missing. Also, the records make a distinction between marriages performed by a priest and common law, civil, or Protestant marriages which were legitimated later by a priest.

The problem which finally took the life of Holy Family Mission was neither Blackfoot resistance nor floods, neither lack of success nor flagging commitment. It was money. The initial funds for the mission had come from the Drexel family of Philadelphia. Drexel, a banker, left a large fortune to his two daughters, Katherine and Elizabeth. Katherine became a nun and eventually founded the Sisters of the Blessed Sacrament. Through the coffers of the Bureau of Catholic Indian Missions, the two Drexel sisters funneled a great deal of money for supporting and extending Indian missions. Of this money, $14,000 went to build the first Holy Family Mission school.[36] Continuing support by the Drexels and the Bureau of Catholic Indian Missions plus the contract relationship maintained with the federal government[37] kept the mission solvent during the first decade of its existence.

But by 1899 the withdrawal of federal funds began to have an effect on the mission. Therefore, the archbishops of the United States, at their annual meeting in 1899, granted permission to the bishops of dioceses containing Indian missions to make collections of money from Catholic congregations in other parts of the country. The Right Reverend John B. Brondel of the Diocese of Helena collected over $10,000 for Indian missions, including Holy Family, when he visited the provinces of Philadelphia, New York, Baltimore, and Boston.[38]

Despite the initiative taken by the bishop and the continuing support by Catholic agencies including the Marquette League and the Bureau of Catholic Indian Missions, Holy Family was in a state of continual financial crisis. Regular appeals for aid appeared in such publications as *The Indian Sentinel*. For example, in the winter of 1929–30, Father Dumbeck appealed for a gift to aid in the purchase of a Diesel engine to run a generator he had recently acquired. In describing the needs of the mission, Dumbeck added:

[36] Mother Katherine Drexel continued to provide support for many other Indian schools. In 1907, for example, she gave more than $125,000 for this purpose. *Report of the Director of the Bureau of Catholic Indian Missions for 1907*, 33 (JA).

[37] For a time the government provided funds for children educated in church-related reservation schools. The total amount appropriated for the years from 1886 through 1893 for this purpose was $3,767,951. U.S., *Report*, 1892, 285.

[38] "Indian File" (CA).

The generator is in perfect condition and will handle all the machinery we need, for instance, a dishwashing machine to take the place of all the drudgery of dishes for one hundred and six children.[39]

Continuing financial difficulties finally forced the closing of Holy Family in 1940. On January 1, the total indebtedness of the mission was $74,117.02 and the cash on hand a mere $21.71.[40] At this point a conflict ensued over who was responsible for the debt. The parties to the conflict were the Diocese of Helena, the Oregon Province of the Society of Jesus, the Bureau of Catholic Indian Missions, and the local staff of the mission. Each group, of course, had a slightly different view of the situation. A central question concerned the ownership of the land, for it was felt that if ownership could be firmly established, then responsibility for the indebtedness could legally be assigned. From the Jesuits' point of view, it was absurd to assume responsibility for a debt upon property for which they had no title—even though they had been working at the mission for fifty years. Upon investigation, it was discovered that the Bureau of Catholic Indian Missions held the title to the property and had refused to assign it to the Jesuits. As the conflict matured, the entire matter became entangled in the courts and finally in the labyrinth of canon law. The final judgment of superior ecclesiastical authorities was that the Bureau of Catholic Indian Missions and the Oregon Province of the Society of Jesus should each assume half of the debt. At this point the Jesuits withdrew, and after a half century of missionary labors among the Blackfeet, Holy Family Mission closed its doors.[41]

Days are bright and gusty now at Holy Family, especially in the month of July. Sunshine spatters over the entire area, playfully drenching the deserted buildings. And inside the buildings wind blows through the collected rubble, occasionally making a loose shutter rattle. In the dirt the careful eye can see here the remains of an altar, there the broken form of one of the saints.

[39] *The Indian Sentinel,* Second Series, Vol. X, No. 1 (Winter, 1929–30), 23.
[40] "Financial Status of Holy Family Mission," January 1, 1940 (JA).
[41] Full coverage of all aspects of this complicated case can be found in the files of the Jesuit Archives.

But the sound of children's voices, the smells of freshly baked bread or newly killed hogs, and the busy routine of mission life —all are gone. Broken windows sightlessly stare toward the rimrock where Blackfeet once drove buffalo to their death. The rimrock remains, as do the buffalo bones imbedded at the base of the cliffs; the Two Medicine River still flows quietly through the cottonwood grove. But like the buffalo, all that was living and vital at the mission is forever lost except to memory and occasionally to imagination. Only the bones remain.

CHAPTER

VII

The Resistance of Satan

During its fifty years of existence, Holy Family Mission was the center from which the priests spread over the reservation, seeking to extend the power of the church against the Hosts of Darkness. Two of these outposts grew into mission churches. One church, St. Peter Claver, was dedicated by Father Soer on August 13, 1911, in the community of Heart Butte, a traditional full blood stronghold.[1] For almost a quarter of a century the church at Heart Butte remained dependent upon Holy Family Mission and was without a resident priest. Then, in 1931 the Diocese of Helena assigned to the mission a secular priest, Father Joseph Hannon.[2] He remained only three years, and in 1935 the Jesuits resumed control when Father Egon Mallman became the resident priest at Heart Butte.[3] He has remained at this outpost for a total of thirty-five years, and now only his work continues the Jesuit heritage among the Blackfeet.[4]

Another center finally developed into a church in the town of Browning. Beginning as a mission station on Willow Creek, St. Michael's Church was built in 1904. Father John B. Carroll,

---

[1] Wilfred P. Schoenberg, S.J., *Jesuits in Montana, 1840–1960,* 51.
[2] A secular priest is one who belongs to a diocese rather than a religious order.
[3] Schoenberg, *Jesuits,* 52.
[4] Father Mallman's activity will be treated more substantially in Ch. XII.

S. J., who was responsible for its construction, remained as priest from 1904 until 1916.[5] Because Browning evolved into a center of population and social activity, in 1910 Carroll decided to move the church into the village. St. Michael's was an all-Indian church, except for the priest and an occasional white Catholic who came to the village. By contrast, virtually all the whites in Browning were nominally Protestant, and thus those who went to church attended either the Methodist or the Presbyterian church.[6]

After the location of St. Michael's was settled, Father Carroll turned his attention to driving out the demons of Indian superstition and confronting the evils of Indian culture. This priest was perhaps the clearest example of a man righteously identified with his religious culture and determined to displace Indian culture with his own. Furthermore, Carroll was one of the priests who made the harshest recommendations for coercion by the government. Had he possessed the authority, he would have marched at the head of an army to engage in holy war on the reservation.

Carroll's attitudes and the cultural values which motivated him can be seen in his reactions to the Blackfoot celebration of Fourth of July. After the turn of the century, the Blackfeet increasingly used this holiday as an occasion for traditional celebrations, often including a sun dance. Besides its tribal significance, the event was economically profitable because white tourists were lured into Browning.[7]

Carroll hated the way in which the Blackfeet celebrated the Fourth of July. It was, he said, "a disgrace to our country and a stain upon our flag."[8] He was less concerned with the country's honor than he was with the threat which the celebrations posed to programs for civilizing and Christianizing the tribe. For Car-

---

[5] For four years between 1904 and 1908 the mission was tended by Father Soer (in addition to his duties at Heart Butte) while Carroll was in Alaska. In May, 1916, the Jesuits were replaced in Browning by regular diocesan clergy. Wilfred P. Schoenberg, S.J., *A Chronicle of the Catholic History of the Pacific Northwest: 1743-1960*, 225.

[6] See Ch. VIII.

[7] This celebration has developed into what is now called North American Indian Days, a largely commercial event.

[8] J. B. Carroll, "The Fourth of July Dishonored," *The Indian Sentinel*, 1910, First Series, 28.

roll, the sun dance symbolized one of the most dangerous and subtle weapons in Satan's arsenal. It strengthened the forces which held the Blackfeet captive.

> It animates the Indians with the spirit of dancing, belief in Indian medicine, a passion for painting and dressing in heathen fashion, and strengthens their inborn disposition to be superstitious . . . It certainly does retard advancement in Christianity and true civilization. It converts the blessings of civilization into moral evils to hedge in and make more desperate their situation in the realm of darkness, to make them more blind and obdurate, so as not to perceive the light of true civilization.[9]

Against such an enemy there could be no compromise. Carroll's perspective did not allow him to find values in Indian religion upon which to erect a program of Christianization. Instead, the cultural ground had to be cleared and purified before true Christianity could take root. In the face of cultural compromise, Carroll found the Blackfeet stubbornly claimed "that their old heathen customs are just as good as civilized customs, and even more venerable."[10]

As well as showing the emotionality of his own perspective, the pyrotechnics of Carroll's reaction are indirect evidence that traditional Blackfoot values survived and remained resistant to acculturation. His evaluation of the religious behavior of baptized Catholic Indians strengthens the view that Jesuit sacramentalism had little power to transform entirely Blackfoot religious culture. Rather than transformation, there was a blending of the two cultures, and at this time religious behavior was often only minimally Christian. Except for their performance of Easter duties, argued Carroll:

> They have very little Christian sincerity. Seldom will they go to church on Sunday. Very commonly they seem to be persuaded that once or twice a year is enough to go to church, and seem to think themselves very good and strong Christians if they condescend to that much. Even on Sunday will some of them, baptized Christians, who are near the church,

9 *Ibid.*
10 *Ibid.*, 29.

leave without hearing Mass and go far away to a medicine dance, or go fishing, or hunting, or to do anything that best pleases them.[11]

When this behavior is placed against the backdrop of Blackfoot culture, it is easy to see that the Indians were treating Christianity in conformity with their ancient ways. After all, the sun dance was not, like the mass, held every week; there was no one sacred day in each week, and thus the idea of the Sabbath was foreign. Similarly, they felt no radical separation between religion and everyday activities such as hunting, fishing, making love, or making war.

To the Jesuits, of course, the Kingdom of Darkness stood in opposition to the Kingdom of Heaven. Behind this view lay a distinction between the eternal realm and the realm of earth and time. Man's true home, according to the priests, was in the eternal realm, and his entire life was a continuous movement toward this great end. By contrast, the Blackfeet were radically this-worldly in their orientation. Carroll's reaction to this fact was negative: "They are worldly, grossly so."[12] But from the perspective of the Blackfeet, the world was the arena within which life was lived; there was no other world. They believed that after death spirits ultimately took up residence in the Sand Hills, a lonely and empty region south of the Saskatchewan River. There, people pursued life in much the same fashion as they did before death. Of the dead, Blackfeet believed that "Their ghosts sometimes visit the living and talk to them in a whistling sound which they hear in the sighing of the wind, the creaking of lodgepoles, and the rustling of the leaves."[13]

In 1910 Father Carroll was confronting a rather powerful expression of Indian culture which Father Point had analyzed perceptively more than sixty years before. Point exhibited great

---

[11] *Ibid.*, 32.

[12] *Ibid.* Not all Jesuits were as dualistic in their understanding of the world as was Carroll, of course. Certainly Point and later Prando were more sympathetic toward Blackfoot culture. And historically tendencies toward dualism would have been softened by the Catholic understanding of natural law.

[13] "Bradley Manuscript," Book 2, 197 (MHS). Cf. Wissler and Duvall, "Mythology," *Anthropological Papers Am. Mus. Nat. Hist.*, Vol. II, Part 1 (1908), 163, and Wissler, "Social Life," *Anthropological Papers Am. Mus. Nat. Hist.*, Vol. VII, Part 1 (1911), 30–32.

sensitivity to cultural meanings and understood that when he spoke of heaven, the Blackfeet would immediately think of the sky rather than Catholic theology's eternal realm. Furthermore, even though they were interested in Point's religion, they could not understand how there could be a heaven so radically different from earth. Writing in 1846, Point indicated that while the Blackfeet had some notion of an afterlife:

> These notions were still so obscure that, when one spoke to them of the happiness of Heaven, they asked very seriously whether there were many buffalo in our heaven, since they thought they were unable to do any kind of good without this.[14]

Even though the buffalo were gone in 1910, Blackfeet were still not able to see the superiority of the Christian heaven.

The Blackfoot outlook on life continually undermined Carroll's authority. He could threaten the Indians with the fires of hell; he could refuse them the sacraments. But all his efforts did very little to alter their conception of the good life on earth: "Their desires, their passions must rule. About the salvation of their souls and the life to come they seem to take scarcely any thought."[15] Apparently Carroll thought the Blackfoot desires and passions evil, but he made little progress in convincing them to mortify the flesh. Even in 1910 they were still close to their traditional view of the good life and its rewards which Father Point described so graphically:

> According to them, what are the goods enjoyed by those who have lived a good life? The pleasures of good meat, of the calumet, of good conversation. And where is the place of these pleasures? In the sand hills that rise up in their country.[16]

And to Carroll's consternation, the Blackfeet continued to pray for "worldly blessings, such as good health, a long life, healthy children, large numbers of horses and cattle, abundant grass and plenty to eat; *so in their meager practice of Christianity, their*

14 Point, *Wilderness Kingdom*, 202.
15 *The Indian Sentinel*, 1910, First Series, 32.
16 Point, *Wilderness Kingdom*, 202.

prayers and promises to God seem to chiefly concern these earthly favors."[17]

The priest was especially offended by the way the display of Indian religion on the Fourth of July reversed his labors with children. "Little baptized children, upon whom much care and labor have been lavished in the different schools, you can see decked out in paints and feathers, looking like young demons that have just emerged from the lower regions."[18] In all of this display, Carroll could see only evil. And he was convinced that the darkness had manifested itself most clearly in the continuation of the sun dance. Believing this, he could argue that Blackfoot religious expressions required no protection by the Constitution for, to his mind, the Constitution's protection of conscience applied only to *true* worship of God. Therefore, the Constitution should not protect any religion based upon "the direct worship of the devil, the arch-enemy of the Creator and Great Father, from whom every good comes. *Now, the religion of the Piegan Indians is devil-worship, clearly so.*"[19]

Because Carroll felt the religion of the Blackfeet was devil worship, he believed it was to be given no quarter and indeed should be dealt with harshly. Carroll recommended that government and church work together to wipe out the medicine lodge and all that it stood for. This would be a righteous act, for God was clearly on the side of government and church. Carroll claimed that just as the Christian God had been opposed to the idolatry of the Israelites in their worship of the Golden Calf, He was opposed to the idolatry of the medicine lodge. He even went so far as to hint that violence might be justified, illustrating his point by reference to the destruction of twenty-three thousand Israelites for their crime of idolatry.[20] Not even destroying the body was too harsh a measure when compared to the suffering after death which awaited the Blackfoot who persisted in idolatry. Thus, Carroll could in perfect sincerity give a benediction which might sound demonic to ears conditioned by a different culture:

[17] *The Indian Sentinel,* 1910, First Series, 32. My emphasis.
[18] *Ibid.,* 30.
[19] *Ibid.,* 33. My emphasis.
[20] *Ibid.*

And may the good God send His divine light and grace into the minds and hearts of the poor benighted Indians to accomplish the salvation of their souls, that, being miserable in this poor world, they may not be infinitely more miserable in the endless ages of the world to come![21]

Since Father Carroll expressed these ideas in 1910, exactly half-way through his ministry among the Blackfeet, it is likely that they represent a seasoned perspective. However, after the Jesuits were replaced by diocesan clergy in 1916, the war against Satan, so implacably pursued by many Jesuits, began to slacken. Cultural resistance to Roman Catholic religious forms persisted, but the demonic was in a sense relocated. More and more the devil made himself felt in the depressing conditions in Browning which surrounded the priests. For instance, in commenting upon the arrival of Father T. J. McCormack in April, 1918, the diarist at Holy Family Mission said: "The poor man was already disheartened before taking up the burden and remarked that the Bp. [bishop] had no heart when he would send a priest to a place like Browning."[22]

When Father M. J. Halligan arrived in 1920, both physical and spiritual conditions had improved very little. But Halligan reacted differently to expressions of traditional Blackfoot culture and was able to make an impact upon the personal lives of many Blackfeet. When he arrived on the reservation, he found that some of the older Indians were still living in polygamy. In discussing this situation with one husband, Halligan insisted that the man could not be baptized until he gave up two of his three wives. But there was no rejection of the individual, no identification of his culture with the demonic, and certainly no analysis of his religion as devil worship or idolatry. While Halligan shared the Jesuits' view of the steps by which Blackfeet could become Christians, he was at the same time appreciative and tolerant of their culture.[23]

Halligan faced an enormously difficult situation. The consequences of decades of Blackfoot resistance combined with the

21 *Ibid.*
22 Diary, 1918–1931 (JA).
23 This judgment is based partially upon an interview with M. J. Halligan, July, 1969.

Indians' erratic participation in the sacraments, often limited to baptism, had issued in a superficial assimilation of Christianity. Furthermore, far too many Indians were scattered over too extensive an area for the priest to be able to make a deep impression. At places like Cut Bank School the level of the Christian instruction received by the children was minimal. Carroll, who had become the bishop, wrote to Father McCormack in 1919 concerning this problem: "On the occasion of my last visit," he said, "very few of the boys knew how to make the sign of the Cross, and, of course, they knew absolutely nothing about the principal mysteries of religion."[24]

The decade between 1920 and 1930 found Halligan engaged in the routine of ministering to Blackfeet who were also the subjects of several idealistic government ventures designed to contribute to their civilization. During the first decade of the twentieth century, irrigation was supposed to be the final solution to Blackfoot poverty. But when a member of the Board of Indian Commissioners visited the reservation in 1926, the Blackfeet were farming only a little over 1 per cent of the land which had been irrigated. His analysis of the project was devastating. It was, he said, "a monument to the unthinking enthusiasm with which this country 20 years ago embarked upon its reclamation projects."[25]

This government experiment to transform the Blackfeet into farmers had failed—as had all the others before. But government experiments with cattle were more congenial to traditional Blackfoot values. These ventures succeeded among many of the mixed bloods on the reservation, and they became affluent. When cattle prices soared during World War I, Blackfoot ranchers profited in the war economy. But in 1919 a summer drought destroyed crops, and in the severe winter which followed most of the cattle froze to death.[26] It is little wonder that Father McCormack was depressed with Browning. And Halligan's irenic perspective, especially since he arrived in 1920, is all the more interesting. To a mind such as Carroll's, events of this sort could

[24] Bishop Carroll to T. J. McCormack, April 25, 1919, "Little Flower Parish Correspondence, 1918–1940" (CA).
[25] Reports of the Board of Indian Commissioners, 1926, 30. Cited by Ewers, *Blackfeet*, 318. [26] Ewers, *Blackfeet*, 318–19.

be interpreted as the answer of divine wrath to Blackfoot per-versity—or as the wily attacks of Satan. Neither of these views appear to have been held by Halligan.

Much of Father Halligan's energy was consumed in the build-ing of the Little Flower Chapel which replaced old St. Michael's in 1932.[27] But his sacramental and pastoral duties were as criti-cal for furthering Roman Catholic institutional power as his church-building activities. By the time he finally left in 1946, he had baptized 1,796 children and 171 adults; he had buried 815, confirmed 2,205, and married 442.[28] Indian participation in the church was still minimal from one standpoint, but when compared with Protestant institutions, it was most impressive.[29]

When Little Flower Chapel was dedicated, participation by both the Indians and the Catholic church was significant. Four bishops joined in the dedication, an indication of the level of Roman Catholic commitment to Indian missions. And the fact that Indians had responsibility for arranging ceremonies at the dedication shows the indigenous nature of Little Flower Church. A partial list of Indians involved in the dedication included the names of Bird Rattler, White Calf, Heavy Breast, Cut Finger, Arrow Top Knot, Last Star, Wades in Water, Rides at the Door, Berry Child, Fish Wolf Robe, Black Weasel, Lazy Boy, Weasel Head, Night Gun, No Chief, Many Hides, Dusty Bull, and After Buffalo.[30]

Apparently there was very little conflict between Halligan and Protestants, although they evidently had little beyond a formal relationship. The kind of passionate anti-Protestantism en-gendered by Grant's Peace Policy was a part of the past Halligan did not fully reincarnate. He seemed mildly irritated that Prot-estants were engaged in widespread philanthropy, but he was secure in the belief that no harm would come to his flock. In 1936 he said:

Of late . . . others have entered the field, who, under the cloak of charity, are trying to rob them of that faith. Thank

27 See the story of the dedication of Little Flower Church in *The Calumet*, July, 1932. *The Calumet* is a Marquette League publication.
28 St. Michael/Little Flower Parish Statistical Reports, 1920–1946 (CA).
29 See Ch. VIII.
30 "Little Flower Parish Correspondence, 1918–1940" (CA).

God they are not making much headway, for while the Indians accept food and clothing, they remain faithful to the church.[31]

In the light of the past missionary efforts and the Blackfoot cultural perspective, Halligan was the sort of man who would make headway and be loved by the people. Firm, yet appreciative of their traditions, he quietly went about doing his work.

In the course of a century among the Blackfeet, the mission of the Roman Catholic church had passed through two distinct phases which corresponded to the two major dimensions of Blackfoot life. While the Blackfeet still roamed the plains, Black Robes were forced to do the same, and their religion was accepted largely on Indian terms. When the Blackfeet lost their autonomy, the missionary movement became one among several forces which functioned to destroy Indian life. With the turn of the century, and certainly by the time of World War II, the outlines of a new phase in Indian life were emerging. The memories of buffalo days were dying, and those who did remember were such a tiny minority that their influence was waning. Although the tribe certainly had not completely conformed to white society and still preserved a distinctly Indian flavor, acculturation had done its work.

The participation of many Indians in the mission churches was symbolic of a Blackfoot movement toward new identity and illustrated the stages in that process. A few still rejected the church; for some the importance of the church remained marginal, their participation being confined to baptism; but for others the church had replaced the religion of their fathers. Between the extremes of loyalty to traditional religion and full assimilation of Roman Catholic Christianity were many variations in behavior. But at least one thing was clear. In the end the priests' sacrifices and commitment, combined with their competence and persistence, had produced an indigenous religious institution which had some positive influence upon the quality of Indian life. In this limited sense, the goal of Christianization, ambiguous though it was, had partially been realized.

[31] Father Halligan to Bishop O'Brien, December 15, 1936, "Correspondence" (CA).

PART III

Protestant Missions
Struggle for Identity

VIII

Short Coats and Civilization

Protestant missionary institutions developed among the Blackfeet after the tribe lost its autonomy and long after Roman Catholic missions were well-established. Planted during the heyday of forced acculturation, Protestant missions naturally reflected the ideology of the times in their programs. In this sense, they also contributed to some of the social forces which continued to undermine the Blackfoot way of life. In contrast to Roman Catholic missions, however, Protestant institutions faced a serious problem of identity—a problem which has deeply conditioned Protestant missions from the beginning of the twentieth century until the present.

Simply stated, the issue was this: Was the Protestant church to be an Indian mission, a white congregation, or a mixture of both? And if it was to be a mixed institution, upon what principles were white and Indian participation to be organized? Roman Catholics had never had real difficulty with this question. For them, there was no option; they were missionaries to the Blackfeet. By contrast, Protestant ministers were not always clear about their role—especially as the century matured. Similarly, the institutions they created reflected and often fostered the minister's role conflicts. An examination of the evolution of Protestant institutions, focusing upon their identity problem, not only provides important clues for understanding their historic role among the Blackfeet but also insight into their present shape.

After the harrowing winter of 1883, Agent Young left the reservation a broken, embittered man. It was fully a decade later before the Methodist church had sufficient personnel to establish any permanent missionary activity among the Blackfeet. But as transportation and communication improved in Montana and as the rudiments of civilization began to appear, church officials found it increasingly easy to recruit ministers to serve the state's white population. The decade of the 1880's brought an influx of thirty-seven ministers, twelve of whom remained in Montana for the remainder of their lives. In the decade and a half following 1890, one hundred and forty Methodist ministers were appointed to churches in Montana.[1] Then, more than a half-century after Father De Smet baptized the first Blackfeet, Protestant missionary institutions were established on the reservation.

In 1891, one hundred and sixty acres of reservation land were granted to the Brooklyn and Bay Ridge branches of the Woman's National Indian Association.[2] Rev. and Mrs. E. S. Dutcher went to the reservation in 1893 as employees of the association. Dutcher was a member of the West Nebraska Methodist Conference but was transferred to the North Montana Mission upon his arrival at the reservation. In July, 1894, the mission was transferred from the Woman's National Indian Association to the Methodist church and was placed under the administration of the Missionary Society.

The new Epworth Piegan Mission was located on land adjoining the agency boarding school on Willow Creek. Agent Steell reported in 1893 that Dutcher was busily "engaged in completing a residence for himself and family. A chapel is to be erected soon."[3] The chapel, about twenty-six by forty-five feet in size, was built with the assistance of interested Indians. When

1 Mills, *Plains, Peaks and Pioneers*, 56–57.
2 Barclay, *Methodist Missions*, Vol. III, 350–51. Apparently the Woman's National Indian Association was an organization distinct from the Methodist church.
3 U.S., *Report*, 1893, 174.

the lumber for the Methodist venture arrived at Durham Station, some three and one-half miles from the church site, Indians came with twenty-two teams and hauled the lumber to the location.[4]

Dutcher proved to be an extremely vigorous man, well-equipped to survive the frustrations of life on the reservation. He also brought to his work previous experience as a missionary among the Navahos. Before long the Blackfeet dubbed him the "priest with a coat."[5] His conception of the mission's goals very closely followed the ideology of his time. Thus, the twin themes of civilization and Christianization, enunciated by the government and pursued by the Roman Catholic missionaries, became the organizing principles for Dutcher's work as well.

To Dutcher, civilization primarily meant education and the acquisition of the Protestant work ethic expressed in an agricultural setting. Dutcher tried to teach the Blackfeet agricultural responsibility through the familiar device of the demonstration farm. This enterprise was based on the assumption that if the value of farming could be successfully demonstrated to the Indians, they would freely adopt the better way for themselves. Dutcher felt that the mission farm was designed to be "an industrial object lesson to the Indian and a place where the pure and simple truth of the gospel are taught."[6] In translating these agricultural aspirations into reality, he raised in the mission garden twelve thousand pounds of potatoes, three thousand pounds of rutabagas, one thousand pounds of turnips, one hundred and fifty heads of cabbage, and fifty pounds of beets.[7]

Although there is little evidence that Dutcher made a large number of converts to farming, he did continue his activity undaunted. In 1895 he proceeded to fence the land and build a house for his family. Since cash was in short supply at the mission, he also marketed his other skills in the nearby village of

[4] *Montana Christian Advocate* (hereafter cited as *MCA*), First Series, Vol. 9, No. 16 (October, 1894).

[5] George Logan, *Histories of the North Montana Mission, Kalispell Mission and Montana Deaconess Hospital with some Biographical and Autobiographical Sketches*, 42.

[6] *MCA*, Vol. 9, No. 20 (December 20, 1894). Cf. also *Proceedings of the First Session North Montana Mission of the Methodist Episcopal Church* (hereafter cited as *Proceedings*, followed by appropriate year), 1893, 13 (CHC).

[7] *Ibid.*

Browning. "The missionary," it was reported, "who is a practical mechanic, has earned from doing carpenter work at $4 per day more than $40."[8]

Dutcher also had educational goals for the Indians which he was never able to realize. He wanted to begin a day school, which he believed was greatly desired by the Blackfeet.[9] One significant difference between Protestant and Catholic institutions was the absence of a Protestant mission school. However, the government boarding school on Willow Creek functioned essentially as a Protestant school because it was run by a Methodist minister. At the time of Dutcher's appointment in 1893, Rev. W. H. Matson was named superintendent of the Blackfeet Boarding School, a position he held for more than a decade. And even though he was not considered part of the active ministry in Montana—that is, he was not the pastor of a church—he did initiate and support numerous religious activities such as Sunday schools and other programs of religious instruction.[10] Despite the fact that with Dutcher at the mission and Matson at the school there was a kind of Protestant establishment on Willow Creek, nothing like the school at Holy Family developed out of these beginnings.

Although the Methodists shared the priests' goals of civilizing and Christianizing the tribe, important differences resulting from their contrasting theological perspectives were also evident. The sacramental world of the Roman Catholic missionary was not that of the Methodist minister. The Methodists did baptize, of course, but to them baptism was not a sacrament which regenerated the soul by its own power; rather, baptism symbolized but did not cause regeneration.[11] For this reason, the ministers did not have the intense motivation, as did their Roman Catholic counterparts, to harvest souls by this method. Likewise, while the Methodists celebrated the Lord's Supper, it was conceived of

---

8 *MCA*, Vol. 9, No. 32 (August, 1895).

9 *MCA*, Vol. 10, No. 10 (December, 1896).

10 Logan, *North Montana Mission*, 61.

11 The theological distinction here is between a view that connects baptism causally with regeneration and a view that makes baptism a sign rather than a cause of regeneration. The Roman Catholics tended to hold the former view and the Methodists the latter.

more as a memorial meal than as a re-enactment of Christ's actual sacrifice—the Roman Catholic view. Therefore, they gave less attention to the supper than the priests did to the mass.

For the Methodists, preaching and personal relationships, rather than sacramental activity, primarily defined their role. It was through preaching that they would harvest souls. Preaching taught people the gospel, brought them to repentance, and then pushed them into the maelstrom of conversion. Out of this emotional turmoil emerged newborn Christians. Furthermore, it was through personal relationships, with all their idiosyncrasies, and not through a sacramental system, that Protestant grace was imparted. In the final analysis, the personality of the minister was the instrument of evangelism. Through his formal preaching, as well as his visits to the homes, the minister believed that he was revealing the gospel to the Blackfeet.

A typical instance of Protestant religious activity appears in a report describing Easter Sunday worship services in 1894. Rev. Van Orsdel and Rev. Dutcher addressed over one hundred Blackfeet through interpreters. Van Orsdel was optimistic in his analysis of the response by the Blackfeet to his presentation of the gospel: "I never saw a congregation more interested in the story of Jesus and his love."[12] After the sermon, fourteen Indian children were baptized. A number of whites and one Indian then participated in the Lord's Supper. To close the service, the missionaries took up a collection "which amounted to $36.75, a number of the Indian girls and boys giving from 5 to 50 cents each."[13] Although Van Orsdel's enthusiastic views have to be tempered, at least some Blackfeet expressed positive dispositions toward the first Protestant missionaries.

For Dutcher, giving religious instruction to children was also a task of great importance on the missionary agenda. Even though he was busy with his many agricultural projects, he still had time and energy left to pursue programs he considered edifying for the Blackfoot child. After describing a number of his other duties, he was quick to add:

While all this work has been done, do not think we have

[12] *MCA*, Vol. 9, No. 5 (April, 1894).
[13] *Ibid.*

neglected the spiritual interest of the people, for we have maintained a Sunday-school since the last Sunday in March last, the average attendance of which has been 130.[14]

Furthermore, Dutcher did not have a monopoly on Protestant Sunday schools for they sprang up at other places on the reservation, usually in response to the interest of a white official. For instance, in 1898, Dr. Z. T. Daniel, a physician at the agency hospital, set up his own Sunday school. "When I came I instituted a Sunday school in the hospital, and every Sabbath during the school months we had Sunday school, with myself as superintendent."[15] An interested woman in New York, Mrs. A. T. Wheelock, provided "Bible lesson pictures, cards, and a little newspaper, the Sunbeam, one of which each pupil and inmate receives each Sabbath."[16] The doctor felt, "The Sunday school helps to prevent the hospital children from idling about the agency on the Sabbath day."[17]

Dutcher continued his program of civilizing through agriculture, preaching, and instructing children in religion. However, beyond the record of fourteen children baptized in 1894, there is no evidence indicating how many Indians responded seriously enough to join the Methodist church. Apparently not many adults actually joined, although church gatherings usually had considerable Indian attendance. At this point, while it is possible to tell what Protestants and Catholics believed about their work, it is as difficult to determine the impact of the Protestant church on the Blackfeet as it is to determine the actual impact which Roman Catholic baptism had. Certainly, the glowing statement appearing in the *Montana Christian Advocate* in 1895 was hardly an accurate prediction of the Protestant future: "Bro. and Sister Dutcher are abundant in labors among these Indians. *They are doing a work that will live forever.*"[18]

In 1899, after his exhausting work among the Blackfeet, Dutcher left the mission buildings and the farm to his successor, Rev. Francis Asbury Riggin. Riggin had come to Montana as

14 *MCA*, Vol. 9, No. 32 (August, 1895).
15 U.S., *Report*, 1898, 185.
16 *Ibid.*
17 *Ibid.*
18 *MCA*, Vol. 9, No. 28 (May, 1895). My emphasis.

a Methodist minister more than twenty-five years earlier, in 1872. In his long ministry he had assumed both administrative and pastoral responsibilities and had served as superintendent of the North Montana Mission in 1880. Because the area of his superintendency had included the church among the Blackfeet, Riggin had considerable knowledge and certainly great interest in the Blackfeet before he actually moved onto the reservation.[19]

From 1899 until 1913, Riggin remained in charge of the Epworth Piegan Mission. During this significant period certain social forces exerted tremendous influence upon the development of Methodist missionary institutions. The most important of these forces was the emergence of the village of Browning as a white-dominated settlement on the reservation. Eventually, the Methodist church moved its activities from Willow Creek into Browning, a change which finally separated the mission from the Blackfeet. It also set in motion processes which, later in the twentieth century, involved the Methodist mission in the intolerable contradiction of segregation.

Despite Riggin's good will, dedication, and sincerity, his perspective on the work of the mission nurtured the processes which ultimately were so destructive. In this respect, Riggin was simply a man of his time, sharing the assumptions of his time about the place and future of Indians in American society. Other men who shared these views often used them as tools for exploitation. Riggin was not one of these men. Instead, Riggin illustrates nicely the flowering of that benign evolutionary optimism concerning social forces which was the heritage of the nineteenth century. For him, it seemed that history itself, in a steady upward progression, would solve all the problems connected with the conquest of Indians. One of the signs of history's beneficence was the process of assimilation. Riggin believed that assimilation was both the goal toward which church and state should work and an inevitable consequence operative within history itself. Of the Blackfeet, he could say confidently, "It is only a matter of time when they will become absorbed by our commonwealth."[20]

[19] For a description of his early ministry, see F. A. Riggin, "Recollections of Methodism in Montana From the Early Seventies," *The Messenger*, Vol. VII, No. 2 (February 1, 1911).
[20] *Proceedings*, 1900, 28–29 (CHC).

Furthermore, Riggin firmly believed that he was presenting to the Blackfeet the best of Christian civilization and that the Indians were eager for these benefits: "They are now reaching out with both hands for the benefits and helpfulness of our Christian civilization."[21]

Undoubtedly, Riggin felt that divine intentions worked through the programs of civilization and Christianization. Riggin was certain that he could see signs of progress toward civilization on every side, and he naturally believed that the church should co-operate with the government throughout this process.[22] For this reason he could make an unqualified affirmation of what he saw as a sign of divine providence, namely the government's beneficent control over the Indian family. He thoroughly approved of the fact that "Children of all ages are taken from the tepees and as much as possible of the Indian life is trained out of them and as much as possible of our life is developed within them."[23]

In support of this government policy, the missionary continued the operation of Dutcher's farm. In addition, he was convinced that a demonstration of the best qualities of the Protestant home would make a favorable impression upon the Blackfeet. His optimism overreached itself in 1906 when he reported that one of the agency employees had assured him that if the government could duplicate his example among the Indians, they "could practically settle the Indian question from the standpoint of home life."[24]

Riggin passionately believed that through co-operation between government and churches, a generation of Blackfeet would emerge who could take their place as full participants in American life. Consequently, he had extremely high expectations of the impact upon the tribe which returning Blackfoot children would have after they had received the benefits of education. "As they come back to the reservation," he said, "they have re-

---

[21] *Ibid.*

[22] *Proceedings*, 1907, 62 (CHC).

[23] F. A. Riggin, "Piegan Indian Mission," *Methodism and the Republic* (ed. by Ward Platt), 303.

[24] *Proceedings*, 1906, 26 (CHC).

ceived impulses to a nobler life not easily effaced."[25] With the passage of time and the continuing work of government and churches, the wounds of the past would be healed, and the Blackfeet could move into a new day.

> Thank God, the days of butchery on their part and on our part are over ... Today they are pursuing the arts of peace, each year steadily advancing toward that high attainment so richly prized by us, viz: *citizenship of the greatest nation on earth.*[26]

Riggin's estimation of the progress of civilization among the Blackfeet was not matched by reservation realities, and he continued to fail in making any significant impact upon adults. *"My spiritual work in the Mission,"* he reported, *"has been chiefly among the children."*[27] The Sunday school and the children who participated in it were the most impressive fruits which the missionary could show for his efforts. With his confidence in the younger generation, however, he felt that his work was a great success.

> If there is no pentecost there [in the Sunday school] I am unable to discern the whisperings of the Spirit. No white Sunday School I have ever had has displayed more of the blessed Spirit. They sing beautifully. I can hardly contain myself when I hear them lisp forth His praises.[28]

As the first decade of the new century wore on, there were changes in Riggin's perspective, though not in his passion and dedication. The religious ideas which had motivated him throughout his life continued as he felt himself growing older. He could still cope with many of the external problems of the mission—the farm, the crops, the repairs on the building. Furthermore, he continued the missionary tradition of contributing money from his own budget for projects in which he believed.[29] But growing in his mind was a shadow which revealed itself in his more reflective moments. Characteristically, it was a mixture

25 *Proceedings*, 1905, 45–46 (CHC).
26 *Ibid.*, 45. My emphasis.
27 *Proceedings*, 1906, 26 (CHC). My emphasis.
28 *Ibid.*, 26–27.
29 *Ibid.*, 27.

of hope and optimism, but in contrast with some of his earlier views, he was no longer certain about the results of his work.

> I have felt, perhaps, I shall close my ministry with my work with these Indians. I have felt I was sitting by an iceberg at times, hard to melt. I do not know what you see. but I believe I see the glimmerings of the breaking day.[30]

Then he stated a belief which not only sustained him but which also explained what apparently had been slow and often discouraging progress.

> I have deemed it unwise to attempt any rapid or showy results. I would rather bide my time and wait in patience and silence if need be. But I have a blessed good conscience now that I have sown some gospel seed and done something to perpetuate Methodism. We had always fought shy of the work among Indians, because it don't [sic], perhaps, can't, claim glorious results . . . I hope we will never haul down the standard we have raised among the Blackfeet.[31]

During his last year at the mission, Riggin urged the Methodist church to exercise great care to send only the best of its ministers among the Blackfeet for he believed the religious purposes of the church could be fulfilled only by such men:

> We therefore recommend that those who labor among them be earnest and prayerful as to the best means of bringing them to our Christ mighty to save, our Christian education, to enlighten their minds, our Christian fellowship that teaches the brotherhood of races.[32]

Competent ministers, however, could not make up for the government failures which made reservation realities so destructive for the Blackfeet during this period. The school, of course, was the institution through which civilization was supposed to be implanted. But the Blackfeet Boarding School was in a deplorable state of decay. In 1901, after nine long years at the school, W. H. Matson described his frustration with the lack of funds for repairs, his continual overwork, the problems of shifting

---

30 *Ibid.*, 28.
31 *Ibid.*, 30.
32 *Proceedings*, 1912, 71 (CHC).

personnel, and the disease-ridden state of the children. His depressing portrayal of the building itself raises serious questions about Riggin's optimism:

> The school is sadly in need of improvements and repairs. An old wood shed, flooded with water when it rains . . . and filled with snow or dirt when it blows in winter, is still used for the boy's bathroom . . . The floors in the buildings are worn through in many places and patched with blocks of wood and pieces of tin. The plastering is falling in places by the foot and by the yard, while 25 windows are in need of glass, the size of which is not in stock.[33]

In the light of these conditions, it is not surprising that competent men would shun an appointment among the Blackfeet. Although he was depressed and frustrated, Matson's statement in 1902 was more realistic than were Riggin's rosy hopes: "Every employee worth retaining in the [Indian] service is casting about for some more desirable place."[34]

Despite the hard work of such men as Matson, the quality of education in the government school was not high. Experiences which Blackfoot children had there certainly did little to prepare them for life in the surrounding society. The poverty of the program of forced acculturation was evident in the subjection of children to the filth, disease, and general inefficiency characteristic of government institutions at this time. In striking contrast to the boarding school, the situation at Holy Family Mission was described as "modern, comfortable and substantial" by a Blackfoot agent in 1903.[35] Clearly, the institutional decay in the government school must have negated many positive values fostered by Holy Family. And above all, the government school was a symbol of the broader problems in which reservation institutions were sunk.

Nor did the situation improve during the ensuing decade. Just two years after Riggin left, a Joint Commission of the Congress investigated conditions on the reservation and found them most inadequate. Upon his return to Washington from a visit to

[33] U.S., *Report*, 1901, 258.
[34] U.S., *Report*, 1902, 229.
[35] U.S., *Report*, 1903, 189.

Browning, Senator Lane of Oregon recommended the removal of virtually the entire government staff, basing his judgment upon the following facts. There was almost no agricultural activity on the reservation, and the Blackfeet were virtually dependent upon government rations for subsistence. The condition of the old hunting bands which had settled around Heart Butte was especially wretched. There was very little food in the homes and almost no clothing for many of the children. Large families were living in one-room shacks. The rations consisted of ten pounds of flour a month, two and one-half pounds of beef for each person each week, three-fourths of a pound of beans a month, and two and one-half pounds of sugar—hardly sufficient for human nutrition. The program of education, for which government officials had expressed such high hopes, was still operating far below any reasonable expectations. Sixty years had elapsed since the United States had negotiated its first treaty with the Blackfeet, but in 1915, 631 out of the 950 children of school age were not in school.[36]

Even though Riggin's later perspective showed greater realism, he was never fully able to grasp the true situation on the reservation. Furthermore, there is a possibility that Riggin's view of matters masked more serious deficiencies which had developed at the mission. It would seem that divine providence had faltered during the last years of Riggin's tenure. His successor, Rev. A. W. Hammer, was brutal in his assessment of what he found when he arrived in January, 1913. The mission was:

> . . . in a deplorable condition; the property was in a most run down shape; the church had 48 window lights broken out and the snow was from two to three feet deep over the entire floor. There had not been a service held in the church for several years, and all the other property was in like neglected condition. There were no records to show who had been members or who had been baptized or married.[37]

While the full account of what had happened is lost in the

---

[36] U.S. Congress, "Blackfeet Indian Reservation," Serial 2, *Hearings Before the Joint Commission of the Congress of the United States,* 1915.
[37] *Proceedings,* 1917, 67 (CHC).

biases of Riggin and Hammer, it is obvious that activities at the mission had diminished. However, Hammer's report detailed some circumstances which were not uncharacteristic of Methodist churches, either past or present. For instance, records, especially in small churches, were very seldom complete, and sometimes none were extant. Furthermore, there were records of marriages performed by both Dutcher and Riggin in the Blackfeet Agency Archives, since the ministers were required to report marriages to the agent. As to the condition of the property, it is probably true that a decline had begun.

Hammer's negative analysis of the mission was partly realistic and partly the result of his own conception of what the mission should be and do. Fundamental to his perspective was his belief that new realities were emerging on the reservation, of which the most visible and impressive was the population growth in the village of Browning. Since the establishment of the Blackfeet Agency at Browning in 1895, white social and economic activities had steadily increased. And it seemed natural to Hammer that Methodists ought to be at the center of these new institutional developments.

In order to be nearer the center of reservation life and in an environment favorable to institutional health and growth, Hammer recommended strongly that the mission be relocated in Browning. In support of this change, he pointed to the power of the Roman Catholic church and the corresponding weakness of the Methodist mission. He estimated that of the some 2,700 mixed and full bloods on the reservation:

> About two-thirds of these are affiliated with the Roman Catholic Church. Probably two hundred claim affiliation with the protestant churches. *Of this number, thirty-five are Methodists.*[38]

If his figures were correct, the church could not possibly have survived with Indian members alone, and in order to get more white members it seemed necessary to move into town.

A nucleus of white Protestants probably had been meeting

[38] *Proceedings*, 1913, 73 (CHC). My emphasis. Hammer's estimate of the total Protestant strength among the Indians may well have been inflated, although his estimate of Methodist members seems reasonably correct.

in town for some time, since as early as 1905, at the request of the "ladies of Browning," Riggin had asked for and received permission to hold religious services in one of the agency buildings.[39] Hammer also claimed that white members increasingly resisted driving outside Browning to attend church.[40] Whatever the situation was, the mission was moved from its location on Willow Creek into Browning during the first year of Hammer's ministry. When this action was ratified by the Methodist Conference, Hammer looked forward to better days.[41]

After moving the church into the village, the minister was able to report a membership of seventy-one persons. If his former estimate of Methodist converts was correct and if all the Indian members survived the move, then exactly half of the reported membership was Indian. And among the Indians, in the church and out, Hammer fully believed that processes of civilization had been so extensive that "old things are passing away, soon there will be no Wards of the government."[42] Furthermore, he felt that this great change had produced a new set of conditions for the Methodist church. "The day we have been looking for so long has come," he said, "and a new plan must be worked out and the Methodist Church will have a great field *not only among the Indians but also among the whites.*"[43] The incorporation of the town of Browning in 1919,[44] the year in which Hammer's prediction was written, lent support to his vision of the Methodist future.

Neither Hammer nor Riggin dealt with the problem of how the white membership would relate to the Indians. When Hammer left the reservation in 1921 and Rev. Henry Mecklenburg arrived, the relationship between the two groups was characterized by a kind of parallelism. Both the re-establishment of the Presbyterian church on the reservation and the policies of the new minister strengthened the parallelism which had developed.

In 1912, fifty-six years after Elkanah Mackey and his wife left

39 Agent Dare to F. A. Riggin, November 7, 1905 (BAA).
40 *Proceedings*, 1917, 67 (CHC).
41 *Proceedings*, 1915, 87 (CHC).
42 *Proceedings*, 1919, 60 (CHC).
43 *Ibid.*, 60–61. My emphasis.
44 *Newspaper Files*, Vol. XX, 17 (CA).

the Blackfoot mission post at Fort Benton, the Presbyterian church sent Rev. James D. Gold to the reservation. Gold remained in Browning until 1926,[45] and it was under his leadership that the church developed functions which ultimately made it a predominantly white church. When the church was established, the government set aside reservation lands roughly equal to the holdings of the Methodist and Roman Catholic churches. The Presbyterians' land was some distance from Browning on Cut Bank Creek, but they decided to locate their church in the village.[46] Gold requested in March, 1916, that in addition to the two hundred and eighty acres set aside for his church, forty acres more be granted.[47] The commissioner of Indian affairs asked for information about how the two hundred and eighty acres were being used. Upon investigation, Agent Ellis learned that the land had been leased to a member of the Presbyterian church, Mr. James A. Perrine.[48] The commissioner's reply is instructive, especially in the light of what happened to the Methodist property a few years later.

> When lands are set apart for mission purposes it is with the understanding that they are needed for immediate use and not that they are to be held merely for future use. The leasing of such lands is not held to be used for mission purposes, and in several instances the right to retain lands so leased has been forfeited. Please notify Mr. Gold accordingly.[49]

Gold withdrew his request.

Even though the Presbyterians claimed to have a predominantly Indian membership, the evidence seems to point in the opposite direction. Since their estimate of Blackfeet membership appeared within the context of Gold's request, it could have

---

[45] Douglas Gold, *A Schoolmaster Among the Blackfeet Indians*, 1. Douglas Gold's father, Rev. James D. Gold, went to Browning as a Presbyterian minister in 1912. According to official sources, he remained until 1926, when he retired and moved to Belton, Montana. *Minutes of the General Assembly of the Presbyterian Church in the U.S.A.* (hereafter cited as *Minutes*) Part I (1926), 451.

[46] C. L. Ellis to Commissioner, June 16, 1916 (BAA).

[47] C. T. Hawke to C. L. Ellis, May 17, 1916 (BAA).

[48] C. L. Ellis to Commissioner, June 13, 1916 (BAA).

[49] Cited by Agent Ellis in correspondence with Rev. J. D. Gold, June 29, 1916 (BAA).

been propaganda designed to acquire the extra forty acres of land.[50] Mecklenburg's analysis was that the membership of the Presbyterian church primarily was formed of agency employees, teachers, white businessmen, and cattlemen. By the 1920's the church included all the "prominent" people in Browning. It featured such attractions as intellectually oriented sermons, which were not designed to appeal to Blackfeet with little formal education.[51] Furthermore, there is no evidence that the Browning Presbyterian Church was ever defined by the denomination as an Indian mission, although the local church did receive some mission funds from the national organization.[52]

If this analysis is correct, then Browning had at this time two Protestant churches, one largely white, the other both white and Indian. As late as 1924, there were a number of full-blood Blackfoot members in the Methodist church. According to a deaconess who worked at the mission during this period, "The Indians that came to the Methodist Church were, primarily, the full-blood Indians."[53] Henry Mecklenburg, the Methodist missionary, developed a system of parallel institutions which distinguished the two memberships in the church and prevented any serious tensions from arising. The division of labor between the Presbyterian and Methodist churches, supplemented by institutional parallelism within the Methodist church, remained the *status quo* until 1930, temporarily solving the identity problem for both institutions.

During Mecklenburg's ministry, the morning worship service was attended by the white members while the evening worship service was reserved for the Indian members. Other church organizations, such as the women's groups, were also divided along racial lines. Beadwork made by the Indian women in their group found a ready market among tourists in Glacier Park. And although the minister's wife rather than an Indian woman was the

50 C. L. Ellis to Commissioner, June 13, 1916 (BAA).

51 Rev. Henry Mecklenburg, personal interview, October, 1963. Official sources indicate that Gold had both an honorary D.D. degree and an earned Ph.D. degree, which further supports Mecklenburg's interpretation. *Minutes*, Part I (1924), 1057.

52 Gerald W. Gillette, Research Historian, The Presbyterian Historical Society, personal correspondence, February 10, 1965.

53 Marian Lewis, personal interview, October, 1963.

leader of this group, there is evidence that the Indian women achieved some sense of meaning from participation in the group.[54] By maintaining separate groups within one institution, the dangers of friction between full-blood Blackfeet and white members were reduced, and at the same time the Blackfeet were kept within the institution. The Methodist missionary could not possibly foresee that twenty years later the principle of parallelism would develop into segregation.[55]

While the Methodists struggled to define their identity, it is apparent that their relationship with the Blackfeet was seriously deficient in the areas of language competence and knowledge of traditional culture. Despite the pastor's good will, there is painful evidence from the 1920's to indicate that his attempts to communicate with the full bloods were halting. For instance, Mecklenburg's wife described their visits to full-blood homes in language which leaves little to the imagination:

> We make a few casual remarks about the weather, the health of the children, or admire some new . . . blanket, or . . . piece of bead work that an old grandma is working on. Then on giving our invitation to them for a social at the church or urge their presence at the Sunday services, we bid them goodbye. We feel they have appreciated our call for they have asked us to come again.[56]

Obviously, without a significant sacramental role—which was absent from Protestantism—the missionary was reduced to attempting to form personal relationships. Unfortunately, these

---

54 Mecklenburg, interview.

55 Institutional parallelism was also a matter of conscious policy in the Baptist church on the Crow Reservation, and a comparison to the Methodist arrangement is illuminating. From early in its existence, the Baptist mission on the Crow Reservation was dominated by Indians and ultimately became an indigenous Indian church. As the white population increased on the reservation, the Crows invited white Baptists to participate in *their* church. The consequence was the development of two separate programs and organizational structures. Two sets of officers were elected each year, and two distinct worship services were conducted each Sunday. The white minister who was in charge of this church for more than thirty years thought that institutional parallelism was necessary to stabilize relationships between Indians and whites. Apparently, some of the same functions were performed by Mecklenburg's parallel programs. Rev. C. A. Bentley, personal interview, September, 1963.

56 Mrs. Henry Mecklenburg, "Work Among the Piegan Indians" (mimeographed), 2 (BMC).

relationships were often rendered superficial by his lack of training.

Mecklenburg's lack of linguistic competence and insufficient knowledge of Blackfoot culture increased the social distance separating him from the full bloods. He naturally found his ministry easier among the Indians who spoke English, some of whom had assimilated Western life styles. Describing the home of one of these Indians—a woman who had married a white cattleman—Mrs. Mecklenburg seemed to feel much more comfortable. Of the house, she said:

> At first sight you could not detect it from the average white home. There is a piano, perhaps a violin, there are books and magazines, good furniture tastefully arranged and the occupants are dressed as good as the average white person and often they are dressed better.[57]

The approval expressed by Mrs. Mecklenburg was apparently based upon a view stated by her husband in 1923: "We desire that the Indians may become self-supporting and progressive in both material and spiritual lines."[58] While this statement reveals her commitment to the value of assimilation, Mrs. Mecklenburg also evidenced a great sensitivity to the problem of displacing traditional Blackfoot values and religion.

> If we want to take away his rel[igion], we must give him something to take its place . . . We cannot condemn his rel[igion] if we can't replace it with something better. The thing to do is to draw out from his rel[igion] the good that there is in it and gradually get him to come into the Xn [Christian] realm. He worships a great Spirit and so do we.[59]

Such attitudes are in striking contrast with the traditional Jesuit fear of superstition. The Mecklenburgs were less concerned about doing battle with the Powers of Darkness than were the Roman Catholics. And their positive appreciation of Blackfoot religious life must have gone a long way toward overcoming the distance created by their lack of formal training in Blackfoot language and culture.

57 *Ibid.*
58 *Proceedings,* 1923, 46 (CHC).
59 Mecklenburg, "Work Among the Piegan Indians," 3 (BMC).

Another factor which increased the influence of Methodist missions during this period was Mecklenburg's practice of concentrating a considerable portion of his time on activities outside Browning. Meanwhile, the church in the village increasingly took on a traditional shape, conforming itself to the pattern of comparable white churches in other communities: "We had our Junior and Epworth League, Ladies' Aid, Brotherhood, C.F.G.'s [Camp Fire Girls] and Boy Scouts."[60] Mecklenburg also developed a Sunday school at East Glacier, as well as at four other points on the reservation. Furthermore, in a continuation of Riggin's earlier practice, Protestant and Catholic missionaries were allowed two hours a week for religious instruction at the Blackfoot Boarding School.[61] Such activity naturally extended the influence of Protestantism and made Indian participation in the Methodist church much easier.

At this point in the history of the Methodist church, the Blackfeet evidently did not perceive the church as exclusively white—as they did later. Baptisms of Indians proceeded to trickle in, and the Methodist church added to its rolls such colorful names as Split Ears, Eagle Child, White Dog, Little Dog, Torn Weasel Head, and Two Guns White Calf.[62] These Indians were not simply incorporated into the church on paper but were involved in the denomination's decision-making process.[63] This fact was a consequence of Mecklenburg's commitment to the development of indigenous Indian leadership.[64] And even though the social distance between the groups was great in the 1920's, there were many occasions for communication between the Indians and whites. Participation in the church—even through parallel programs—provided some Blackfeet who had lost their traditional autonomy a source for acquiring a new identity. Had this trend continued and been fully supported by the church, the impact of Methodist missions would have been vastly increased. Beginning in 1930, however, other institutional factors intervened to frustrate the development of strong Protestant missionary forms among the Blackfeet.

60 *Ibid.*, 1.
61 See Agent McFatridge to Commissioner, November 17, 1910 (BAA).
62 Mecklenburg, "Work Among the Piegan Indians," 1 (BMC).
63 *Proceedings*, 1923, 46–47 (CHC).
64 Mecklenburg, "Work Among the Piegan Indians," 1 (BMC).

The Church of the Little Sweet Pine

When Henry Mecklenburg left Browning in 1926, Methodist missions among the Blackfeet were firmly established. Despite formidable obstacles—the powerful Roman Catholic enclave, the Protestants' lack of formal training or linguistic competence, and the problems associated with moving the church into Browning—the Methodist church had begun a tradition on the reservation. The danger that separate institutional programs based on race would fall into patterns of segregation was implicit in the historical situation. But with the arrival of Rev. Allen C. Wilcox, the more ominous forces were curbed for a time. Unfortunately, the missionary's intentions were often frustrated by inefficiencies in church organization. Had his plans been fully realized, the development of Methodist missions probably would have been significantly different.

The first problem which confronted Wilcox was one all too common to both Protestants and Catholics—money. Especially serious was the lack of adequate housing for the minister. In March, 1929, Wilcox wrote to the Board of Home Missions and Church Extension in Philadelphia requesting financial aid.[1] This request produced a series of interchanges among the minister,

1 Allen C. Wilcox to F. W. Mueller, March 19, 1929 (PS).

church officials in Montana, and national church executives. These interchanges not only clarify the local situation but also bring into focus the institutional problems plaguing the Methodist church at this time.

Before requesting aid from Philadelphia, Wilcox and his wife had endured three rigorous years at the mission under difficult conditions. Facing Montana winters with small children in a parsonage in poor condition did not help the situation, although Wilcox did not complain at first. The house, which had been built by Hammer, was singularly unattractive according to Mrs. Wilcox's description:

> The parsonage was a 4-room house with a coal stove in the kitchen-dining room, and a coal heater in the living room. Out door plumbing, and all water carried in and out. Two bedrooms upstairs, and no electricity.[2]

At first, the unpleasant living conditions were offset by the press of work. In those first three years, said Mrs. Wilcox, "We had to work hard, and get up early because the Indians came to our house both early and late."[3] Wilcox evidently made an impression upon some of the Blackfeet. Even at this late date in their history, they saw him as possessing powers similar to their traditional doctors and medicine men: "They had great faith in Allen's prayers and he would be called any time in the night to pray for the sick."[4]

Wilcox's request for financial assistance from the Board of Home Missions initially was directed to the Department of Church Extension, which was responsible for building and the repair of churches. There was a long silence from the national officials. Between March, 1929, and February, 1930, Wilcox heard nothing from Philadelphia.[5] After spring and summer had passed and the missionary had tasted another winter in Browning under a leaking parsonage roof, he decided to direct his requests to a different agency within the Board of Home Missions—the Department of Evangelism. Wilcox communicated

---

2 Mrs. Allen C. Wilcox, personal correspondence, April 6, 1964.
3 *Ibid.*
4 *Ibid.*
5 Allen C. Wilcox to F. W. Mueller, February 14, 1930 (PS).

with this office in August, 1930, and was able to attract the attention and interest of George B. Dean, superintendent of the Department of Evangelism. The missionary explained to Dean that his letters and telegrams to the Board of Home Missions had gone unanswered.[6] In response, Dean made a personal visit to Browning and reported the seriousness of the situation to F. W. Mueller, the secretary of Church Extension, who had failed to respond to Wilcox's earlier correspondence.

"When I reached Browning," Dean reported, "I found a most discouraged missionary and his wife. They were planning on getting out of this work and were interviewing District Superintendents regarding work."[7] Then he went on to emphasize the necessity for immediate action to salvage a declining situation:

> Not for ten years have we had such good results from our work in Browning as we are having at this time. The whole field is ours because of the magnificent way in which this couple have handled themselves and the work. We must not let them go.[8]

Dean's specific recommendation was that Mueller expedite a grant of $750 for parsonage repairs. Furthermore, he strongly urged Mueller to answer the pastor's correspondence and to give Wilcox a definite date when he could expect the money. Concluding passionately, the superintendent pleaded, "If you knew the situation you would not hesitate for one moment. Please rush this matter through and wire Wilcox to go ahead."[9]

While Mueller and Dean were involved in correspondence, Wilcox was left without any assurance of support. In frustration, the missionary wrote another letter to Mueller expressing his disgust for the way in which he was being treated.

> Would you kindly explain the cause of the delay? Other applications from this district were acted upon favorably and there is no reason why you should discriminate against this one . . . I have tried to be patient with the conditions

[6] Allen C. Wilcox to George B. Dean, August 26, 1930 (PS).
[7] George B. Dean to F. W. Mueller, September 12, 1930 (PS).
[8] *Ibid.*
[9] *Ibid.*

under which we were working. I do feel that we are justified in urging this donation and we are fully expecting you to do your part. Will you kindly reply to this request?[10]

Finally, on September 17, 1930, Mueller sent a telegram to Wilcox assuring him that funds for repairing the parsonage would be made available.[11] On the same day Mueller composed a revealing letter in which he laid before the missionary some of the reasons for the delay.

> . . . we are painfully limited on account of funds, and hence are not always able to meet the situations that arise as promptly as we would like. I am confident, though, that you appreciate our difficulties . . . while at the same time we are endeavoring to visualize the needs of the field.[12]

In light of the facts, the benediction with which Mueller concluded his letter to Wilcox is especially ironic: "May God's choicest blessings ever be with you. However man may frequently forget, it is wonderfully comforting to know that God's watchful eye is ever over his faithful ones."[13]

At this time, the national boards of the Methodist church were in the throes of the national depression. Mueller was probably stating a fact when he wrote to Wilcox in October, "Our financial limitations are so severe that we hardly know which way to turn."[14] He did not say, however, that one of the major reasons for the long silences between Philadelphia and Browning was contained in his benediction to Wilcox. Man did indeed "forget." Dean and Mueller had made an oral agreement in June, 1930, concerning financial support for the Blackfoot mission.[15] Dean subsequently put this agreement in writing, but apparently Mueller's staff misplaced the memorandum. Mueller did not know how to respond to Wilcox's requests and showed evidence that he had completely forgotten his agreement with Dean. Finally, under pressure from the missionary, Mueller

10 Allen C. Wilcox to F. W. Mueller, September 13, 1930 (PS).

11 Telegram from F. W. Mueller to Allen C. Wilcox, September 17, 1930 (PS).

12 F. W. Mueller to Allen C. Wilcox, September 17, 1930 (PS).

13 *Ibid.*

14 F. W. Mueller to Allen C. Wilcox, October 27, 1930 (PS).

15 Interoffice Memorandum, George B. Dean to F. W. Mueller, June 23, 1930 (PS).

asked that Dean send another memorandum in order to refresh both their memories.[16]

The episode of the lost office memorandum symbolizes the communication difficulties which national officials were having with Browning. These institutional problems had the practical consequence of further deteriorating the local situation. Nor was this a simple obstacle. The problem which Protestant institutions faced involved at least four dimensions. First, there was real ambiguity at the national level concerning who had responsibility for the mission. Second, there were problems related to administrating a local situation through correspondence alone. Third, the administration of the mission by the Montana Conference of the Methodist church was ineffective. And fourth, there were conflicting conceptions of what the mission should be.

A typical example of confusion within the national board appeared when, as superintendent of the Department of Evangelism, Dean assumed responsibility for the mission which properly belonged to Mueller and the Department of Church Extension. In October, 1930, he wrote to Wilcox, "If any matter is not clear, please direct your letter to me so that I may be able to take it up with the department involved."[17] Dean's motives for assuming such a posture in relation to Browning are understandable, even though his action clearly exceeded his authority as defined by the *Discipline* of the Methodist church.[18] He had visited Wilcox and had been personally impressed by the needs of the mission. The formal church organization (represented by Mueller) did not have firsthand knowledge of the situation. By exceeding his formal authority, Dean hoped to avoid some of the problems which were frustrating action within the institution.

Dean's assumption of authority had unforeseen consequences which deeply affected the mission. Acting on the basis of assurances which he had received from Dean, the missionary embarked on an ambitious building program which obligated his

16 Margaret Krauss, Secretary to F. W. Mueller, to George B. Dean, September 11, 1930 (PS).

17 George B. Dean to Allen C. Wilcox, October 30, 1930 (PS).

18 See *Doctrines and Discipline of the Methodist Church*, 1916, para. 446. Cf. para. 438 on the Department of Church Extension.

church to considerable indebtedness. Unknown to the pastor, however, were difficulties which Dean had encountered. Dean had planned to fulfill his promises to Wilcox by transferring unused money, appropriated for a deaconess, from the Department of Evangelism to the Department of Church Extension. Another denominational executive, W. J. Elliott, refused to transfer the funds. First, he thought it was improper to use funds originally appropriated for evangelistic work for another purpose without the approval of the executive committee of the national board. Second, he seriously doubted if Dean could show evidence that the budget would justify such a transfer, even if it were approved.[19] As a result of these objections, funds were withheld. But the pastor was not informed and went ahead with his plans.

By August, 1932, the church in Browning was heavily in debt and in serious trouble. Wilcox wrote to his district superintendent that a lumber company had filed a lien against the church and had threatened to sue for foreclosure.[20] Although some of the money promised by Dean had by this time been sent to Wilcox, it was insufficient to cover the debt which he had incurred. Exasperated with this state of affairs, the national office in Philadelphia dispatched an official from San Francisco to survey the situation. After his trip to the mission, Walter Torbet reported to Mueller that the local church was $1,510.95 in debt.[21] Torbet thought Wilcox had managed the job very poorly and was not adapted to mission work at all. His solution was devastatingly simple: *"A new preacher, carefully selected, is needed."*[22] Torbet was unaware of the factors which had contributed to the situation he was analyzing. Certainly, if there was failure, the blame had to be shared by the national board. At this point a change in local leadership was hardly an adequate solution to the difficulties.

The second dimension of the institutional problem here became clear; it was impossible to administer a local mission program by correspondence alone. For instance, if Wilcox had

[19] Interoffice Memorandum, W. J. Elliott to George B. Dean and F. W. Mueller, August 5, 1931 (PS).
[20] Allen C. Wilcox to Reuben Dutton, August 31, 1932 (PS).
[21] Walter Torbet to F. W. Mueller, October 27, 1932 (PS).
[22] *Ibid.* Emphasis in the original.

known the difficulties which plagued Dean, he probably would not have obligated the church to such a large debt. Furthermore, Philadelphia was too far from Montana to permit sufficient visits by national personnel. Mueller never did have adequate information to make an appropriate response, and Torbet was too unfamiliar with the context of the situation to make adequate judgments. Rather than seeking to assume control of Browning from Philadelphia, it would have been better if national officials had informed the Montana Conference and let officials there deal with the problem.

This issue suggests the third dimension of the problem, the ineffective administration of the Montana Conference. After the crisis of 1932, correspondence between the national and conference levels in the Methodist church became more frequent. The district superintendent obviously did not understand his relationship to the mission. Writing to Mueller, the superintendent said:

> District Superintendents as representatives of the Home Board will need to have a little more authority in the matter of building of churches, and remodeling, etc. I personally advised the pastor against proceeding with this project until some local money had been raised, but was told that Browning was a Home Missionary project, therefore I feel like assuming very little responsibility for the plight in which this church finds itself at the present time.[23]

Clearly the confusion concerning ecclesiastical responsibility for Browning was so great and communication so garbled that the district superintendent had almost completely withdrawn his leadership.

Mueller's reply to the district superintendent showed that the board had assumed that the Montana Conference approved Wilcox's building program. His answer also indicated what he felt was the normative relationship of national, conference, and local levels in the Methodist church.

The Board of Home Missions and Church Extension has no projects throughout the home mission field as in-

---

[23] Reuben Dutton to F. W. Mueller, July 20, 1933 (PS).

tegral units. All of the Methodist Church is related to the district and to the conference, and hence is under the leadership and jurisdiction of the sectional administrator . . . *Our activities . . . must channel through the district superintendent.*[24]

Even though such a relationship was typical, national officials had violated their own rules. Both Dean and Mueller had assumed direct relations to Browning and had actually by-passed the Montana Conference until after the 1932 crisis. Furthermore, the district superintendent's reaction to the pastor's statement that Browning was a "Home Missionary project" shows that he did not fully understand his role. Evidently neither Mueller nor Dean had bothered to write to the superintendent; and, from his point of view, it appeared that the mission was not really within his jurisdiction.

The difficulty was finally resolved when the national officials and the district superintendent came to the agreement that no further work would be done until the local debt was paid. The decision was then appropriately communicated to Wilcox by the district superintendent.[25] However, Wilcox was determined to finish the building he had begun despite the obstacles he had encountered; and in 1934, he again initiated correspondence with the national offices in Philadelphia. Mueller replied immediately, saying that he could not support any plan until it had the district superintendent's approval.[26] By May, 1935, Rev. Charles G. Cole, the district superintendent, had written to Mueller informing him that Wilcox's plans had been approved.[27] Funds were immediately forwarded from the national offices to complete the building program begun in 1930.[28] The normative relationship between the local church, its direct superior in the conference, and the national board had been re-established.

The fourth dimension of what was becoming a "Browning

---

24 F. W. Mueller to Reuben Dutton, July 28, 1933 (PS). My emphasis.

25 Reuben Dutton to Allen C. Wilcox, March 25, 1934; F. W. Mueller to Allen C. Wilcox, March 26, 1934 (PS).

26 F. W. Mueller to Allen C. Wilcox, October 25, 1934 (PS).

27 Charles G. Cole to F. W. Mueller, May 7, 1935 (PS).

28 Margaret Krauss, Secretary to F. W. Mueller, to Charles G. Cole, May 24, 1935 (PS).

syndrome" to the Philadelphia officials lay in the differing conceptions of what the mission was and what it should become. Two concepts were expressed by national officials, both of which were in basic conflict with Wilcox's understanding of the situation.

Dean was a passionate, sympathetic, and loyal administrator. But his comprehension of the mission was limited, even though his ideas had affinities with the Protestant tradition on the reservation as well as with the wider ethos of the Methodist church. Dean's was basically a philanthropic approach, as is revealed in his description of the shape which missions among the Blackfeet should take.

> Our thought is to make it [the Methodist mission] a kind of Goodwill Industry where many cast-off garments, etc., may be repaired by the Indians, thus giving them some training in this kind of work and also provide them with cheap garments, etc. "Not Charity but a Chance" will be our slogan and we hope thereby to give our Indian friend a new conception of life and service.[29]

Had this program actually been attempted, it might have further undermined the self-respect of the Blackfoot, rather than accomplishing the ends for which Dean hoped.

In contrast, Torbet felt that the church should realistically examine the consequences of its policy of philanthropy. Torbet believed that if the system were fairly scrutinized, its destructive consequences would become apparent. In his own analysis, he connected the traditional policies of the government with the policies developed by the church. For him, these policies were mutually reinforcing and destructive.

> The dole system that destroys the self-respect of the Indians has a like effect on the white people on the various reservations so that they expect the Board of Home Missions and Church Extension to do for them . . . what the government does for the Indians in the way of schools, rations, etc.[30]

[29] Interoffice Memorandum, George B. Dean to F. W. Mueller, June 23, 1930 (PS).
[30] Walter Torbet to F. W. Mueller, October 27, 1932 (PS).

In addition to suggesting that the missionary be disciplined, perhaps by removing him altogether or by cutting his salary, Torbet
expressed another idea which had been in Hammer's mind—
that the real future of the Methodist church in Browning lay in
its successful entrenchment in the white community. To this efficient San Francisco official it was obvious—and true—that the
white community was economically stable and could support an
institutional program much better than could the Indian membership. Torbet argued:

> With proper organization I am sure the people of the
> Agency and of the public schools and certain business ele-
> ments about the town can be brought into our church organ-
> ization *and make our Browning church program absolutely
> worth while.*[31]

Torbet's position illustrates a general tendency in the Methodist church, although it certainly was not limited to that body,
to assign great importance to institutional growth. If positive
social processes had been supported, the Methodist mission could
have become an indigenous Indian institution where Blackfeet
could seek a new cultural identity. Instead, processes were often
fostered which ultimately segregated the local church. The trends
which might have prevented such a separation were present in
Allen Wilcox's understanding of his task among the Blackfeet.
Despite his lack of either linguistic competence or formal training as an Indian missionary,[32] Wilcox was extremely sensitive.[33]
Whether by instinct, intuition, or shrewd intelligence, he formulated and worked for almost two decades out of a view of things
which was quite different from the views held by Dean and Torbet.

The most important aspect of Wilcox's self-understanding was
his image of what the ministry should be. Increasingly there was

---

[31] Walter Torbet to F. W. Mueller, December 28, 1932 (PS). My emphasis.

[32] Wilcox continually sought to train himself, and in 1940 he was elected president of the Northwest Region of the National Fellowship of Indian Workers.
Proceedings, 1940, 46 (CHC). There is little doubt that he understood himself to
be a missionary. Both Wilcox and his wife had been student volunteers for the
foreign mission field while they were in college. They understood Browning as
"a call to Home Missionary Service." *Proceedings*, 1944, 51 (CHC).

[33] See, for instance, *Proceedings*, 1928, 63, and *Proceedings*, 1930, 289 (CHC).

the possibility of developing a ministerial role in relation to two distinct groups. The minister could see himself as primarily oriented toward the church in Browning, focusing upon the membership who lived there; or the minister could see himself as oriented outside the community of Browning, focusing upon the local church as a base for ministries elsewhere on the reservation. After the church moved into Browning, these alternate conceptions of ministry increasingly held the potential for creating role conflict. For the choice between them was evolving into a choice between conforming to the expectations of a predominantly white membership or being an Indian missionary. The struggle for identity implicit in the Methodist heritage on the reservation now, in the ministry of Wilcox, became increasingly explicit.

After coping with the institutional difficulties confronting his building program, Wilcox continued to expand the style of ministry that he had assumed from the very beginning. He understood himself to be an Indian missionary, so he focused his energies upon projects outside Browning. He continued, as had Protestant missionaries before him, to have Sunday schools at various points on the reservation; he formulated a plan for the use of the land where the church once stood that would involve the establishment of a Folk School; he stimulated the development of Indian crafts and also placed high value on any evidence of Blackfoot artistic ability.[34] Even though many of his plans— such as the Folk School—never materialized, he clearly had a view of his role which oriented his work on the reservation primarily toward Indians.

Many of the elements of Wilcox's ministry were present either in the minds or the programs of other missionaries; thus, if he had not moved any further, his ministry would have been less significant than it was. But Wilcox did move further and addressed the problem which was perhaps the most difficult of all —the development of indigenous Indian missionary institutions. Unless such institutions could be developed, he reasoned, it was unlikely that an Indian clergy could be developed, and the church would remain essentially a missionary structure.[35] A part

34 Mrs. Allen C. Wilcox, personal correspondence.

of the indebtedness incurred in the 1930's resulted from money spent on a church that might have become an indigenous Indian institution.

In the summer of 1931, a movement arose among Indians living along the South Fork of Cut Bank Creek to build a church which would serve their needs. The Indians immediately began hauling logs from the surrounding mountains to the building site. During the winter of 1932 the building was erected. After the church was completed, Walter Torbet reported, "The little log church fourteen miles North of Browning in the woods, is a very comfortable building. The Indians like it. I think it cost entirely too much money—but that is neither here nor there—it has been done."[36] Although Torbet grudgingly accepted the idea of a church outside Browning, his real interest was riveted upon the institutional potential in the village. Of the Browning church he said, "The church when finally completed . . . will . . . be a credit to Methodism and will make an appeal to the people of the Agency."[37] Here, reflected in this national official's attitude, was the dilemma of the missionary—white pastor or Indian missionary? It was easy to see which side Torbet favored.

Though interesting but not very significant to national officials, the church in the woods had meaning to the Blackfeet involved. In choosing a name, they interpreted the site in terms of their own past, a different heritage from that embodied in the Browning church.

> Long before our grandmothers can remember, [a] Medicine Lodge . . . was held here. Instead of using the cottonwood and the quaking aspen trees as they did then and do now, on this particular Lodge they used the Sweet Pine branches. After that this creek was known to all as Sweet Pine Medicine Lodge Creek. We want to call our Church "The Church of the Little Sweet Pine."[38]

The church was constructed of materials from the surrounding mountains. The furniture and other appointments were left

---

35 The development of Blackfoot clergy—had this happened—would have been one significant measure of the impact of Protestant and Catholic missions.

36 Walter Torbet to F. W. Mueller, December 28, 1932 (PS).

37 *Ibid.*

38 Mrs. Allen C. Wilcox, personal correspondence.

unvarnished and unpainted. Soon the Church of the Little Sweet Pine became a social center as well as a place for the celebration of the significant events of life—birth, death, marriage, and baptism. It was distinctively an Indian church, built and dominated by Indians. By contrast, the Browning church increasingly exhibited the liturgical and theological traditions of a middle-class membership. The Church of the Little Sweet Pine was separated from the institutional tendencies of the Browning church and could have developed into a new center of order and identity for its members.

Such a future was altered both by a change in the course of the creek along which it was built and by disinterest in its support among ministers who succeeded Wilcox. The South Fork of Cut Bank Creek finally undermined the foundation, and the church fell into disuse. Not until after 1960 did the Methodist church attempt to establish comparable centers outside the community of Browning. Disinterest in the Church of the Little Sweet Pine as well as some active resistance were also present in the white membership. For example, a member of one of the most powerful white families in Browning, who belonged to the Methodist church during Wilcox's ministry, argued that the majority of the congregation did not approve of the building of the little church.[39] Although this opinion was not universal, it did represent a conception of the minister's role that conflicted with Wilcox's views and actually undermined the developing Indian institution which he had fostered.

The effects of the national depression upon church structures, the Board of Missions' organizational fumbling, and the inadequate supervision by the Montana Conference all created frustrations for Wilcox. More serious was the official confusion concerning the shape which a mission among the Blackfeet should take. Wilcox had a clear idea of what he wanted to do, and despite bureaucratic frustrations and insufficient support, he did what he could. Through sheer persistence and dedication—qualities which recall the Jesuits—he established a ministry on the reservation which was more significant than that of any Methodist missionary before him.

39 Mrs. Frank Sherburne, personal interview, September, 1963.

X

Short Coats and Segregation

The decades between 1940 and 1960 were years of tension and occasional conflict in the Methodist church for the church in Browning was struggling to resolve its identity problem. Was it to be a middle-class white church with a minority of largely assimilated middle-class Indian members? Or was it to be an institution which included a broad segment of the Indian population, not simply as objects of charity but as full participants? Related to these institutional questions was the continuing problem of the minister's role in Browning. Was he chiefly a minister to the town population, or was he primarily a missionary to the Blackfeet? The forces which had maintained an equilibrium between Indians and whites through parallel programs was upset when the Presbyterian church was closed. This event marked the beginning of the decline of Indian participation and the increase of white domination in the church.

In 1942, during the last years of Rev. Allen Wilcox's ministry, the closing of the Presbyterian church disturbed the racial division of labor between the two largest Protestant churches in Browning.[1] Mrs. Wilcox's description of the consequences of

---

[1] In official sources, the church was listed as vacant during 1942 and 1943. *Minutes*, Part I (1942), 696; *Minutes*, Part I (1943), 708.

this event illustrates clearly the important social factors involved:

> During our time the Presbyterian church died, and so the white people from there had to be ministered to also. This had its effect on the Indians who were ashamed because they did not have as good clothes as the whites. They still wore blankets and moccasins. So the adult Indians did not attend church as often as formerly.[2]

The social distance between the white members from the Presbyterian church and the full blood membership in the Methodist church apparently was too great to permit significant Blackfoot participation. After the full bloods withdrew, certain tendencies solidified in the Methodist church which strengthened the group —larger now— who wanted the church to mirror the needs and interests of the white population. The best way this goal could be accomplished was through cutting the church's ties with the national missions program. In 1945, there was just such a move toward autonomy.

During 1945, oil exploration on the reservation stimulated the imaginations of both Indians and whites. The non-Indian membership, who by this time controlled the church, saw themselves approaching a period of unbelievable wealth in the event that oil should be discovered on the church properties. Under the leadership of Rev. Stephen H. Smith, the Board of Trustees of the Browning church sought to end their relationship with the Board of Missions and to assume full control of their church policies and property.

The first step these local officials took was to return $300 to the national office.[3] This action was designed to demonstrate their church's attitude toward continued dependence upon the Board of Missions. In 1946, Smith was quite vocal in his approval of an autonomous, self-supporting church, independent of the national board. His reasons for taking this position are illuminating.

> My feeling right along since I came here is that this work has been misrepresented to your board. *The local Protestants*

2 Mrs. Allen C. Wilcox, personal correspondence.

3 Stephen H. Smith to H. C. Leonard, February 20, 1945. Official files of the Division of National Missions of the Board of Missions of the Methodist Church (hereafter cited as DNM), Philadelphia, Pa.

are mostly whites . . . The Indians are at least 80% Catholic and we have little chance in making any more progress with them than we have in the past. *The continued acceptance of gifts for Indian work does not meet with my personal approval.*[4]

Smith was realistic enough to know that some decision had to be made concerning the identity of the local church, and he saw three possible alternatives. First, the Methodists could turn the mission over to some other Protestant body and withdraw from the reservation completely. Second, the Browning church could be redefined as a white church and dropped as a special mission project. Third, a minister especially trained for Indian missions could be placed in Browning and the mission toward the Blackfeet expanded.[5] Smith actually preferred the first alternative because he was convinced that no real progress could be made in the face of the massive Catholic power on the reservation. Concerning this point, he was quite blunt and uncompromising: "My own feeling is that mission money should be spent in areas where progress can be made. This is one area where money can be better spent elsewhere."[6]

Smith also saw that the Methodists would probably refuse to exercise his first option and would instead choose to remain as they were. Thus, he advised consideration of his second option, that the church become self-supporting: "I feel very strongly that the local group could shoulder all expenses, or nearly all if they were made to. A sudden jolt makes the going hard at first, but it will make for a finer work in the future."[7] Smith seemed to feel that only radical surgery would cure the identity problem of the Browning church. His sharp realism produced such consternation in the Montana Conference that a study of the entire situation was recommended. By this means, church officials hoped to set a new "policy governing the inter-racial relationships and services."[8]

The issue, as stated by Smith, was too simplified to be manage-

[4] Stephen H. Smith to H. C. Leonard, January 11, 1946 (DNM). My emphasis.
[5] Stephen H. Smith to H. C. Leonard, January 22, 1946 (DNM).
[6] *Ibid.*
[7] *Ibid.*
[8] *Proceedings*, 1947, 444 (CHC).

able by the Methodist church. The Board of Missions could not arbitrarily break off a relationship which was now over a half-century old.[9] And Smith's radical perspective made rational consideration of policy impossible. Furthermore, even though many white members apparently agreed with Smith, there is evidence that his truculence finally alienated some of his most powerful white supporters.[10] In such an intolerable situation, the pastor's leadership was ineffective. Therefore, he left the mission after only two years and was replaced in 1947 by Rev. Edgar B. Smith. During Edgar Smith's appointment, there was a brief moratorium on the conflicts that had convulsed the Browning church.

Even during the short and stormy tenure of Stephen Smith, Methodist philanthropy to the Blackfeet continued as tons of used clothing were distributed on the reservation.[11] Also, a program of Christian education under the leadership of a Mohawk Indian, Miss Bernice Jackson, had some limited success. Participation by adult Indians in the Browning church, however, was virtually nonexistent.[12] With the arrival of Edgar Smith, continuities with the past became more obvious. In addition to philanthropy, sporadic attempts were made to involve adult Blackfeet in the church programs. In 1952, there was a movement to stimulate home crafts among the Blackfoot women, and as a consequence, a few women became interested in quilting. The church acquired three sewing machines in an attempt to expand this program; however, the new interest faded very quickly and soon died altogether.[13] Programs of Christian education were continued in the public schools after regular school hours, an effort which was an extension of earlier attempts to Christianize the Blackfeet.[14] Annual Christmas programs, the basic form of which

[9] In 1959 one church official said that over $60,000 had been spent to supplement the pastor's salary and to maintain the church. J. B. Harris to Oscar L. Doane, April 17, 1959 (BMC).

[10] "Blackfeet Mission History, 1874–1947" (mimeographed), (BMC).

[11] A decade later philanthropy was still a booming activity on the reservation. Rev. George S. Ritchey, personal interview, January, 1964.

[12] "Blackfeet Mission History" (BMC).

[13] Edgar B. Smith, "A Report to the Annual Conference in its 75th Year," June, 1952 (mimeographed), (BMC).

[14] Miss Ary Shough, Deaconess, "Fall Report, 1953" (mimeographed), (BMC).

had not changed appreciably since 1876, remained popular. However, one big difference between Agent Young's first Christmas and those of the mid-1950's was size. A deaconess working on the reservation reported that in 1953 some five hundred children and ninety adults attended Christmas programs held at fourteen places on the reservation.[15] These numbers do not indicate consistent participation, however. Furthermore, the majority of these Blackfeet were Roman Catholics, a fact which produced continuing tension between Protestant ministers and Catholic priests on the reservation.

About two years after Edgar Smith arrived in Browning, discussions at the conference level in the Methodist church produced some conclusions. Apparently these talks had revolved about the issues of the identity of the church (white church or Indian mission), and the role of the pastor (minister to the town population or Indian missionary). Concerning the basic identity of the Browning church and the role of the minister, the conference was very clear: "The discussion of the purpose of the Mission resolved in the decision that the first responsibility was to serve the Indians on the field."[16] In order to implement this decision, church officials recommended a return to the principle of institutional parallelism:

> It was recommended that the Sunday morning worship be continued as a formal worship service . . . and that an informal service be held in the evening with emphasis upon Indian participation, but open for attendance by whites also.[17]

Even though Edgar Smith and church officials at the national and regional levels attempted to curb the church's evolution toward white domination, their efforts were ultimately unsuccessful. And with the arrival of a new minister, Rev. George Ritchey, the evolution continued. While Edgar Smith evidently felt that he was primarily a missionary,[18] Ritchey seemed to see his position as simply one job in an itinerant series. Even though Ritchey

15 "Blackfeet Mission Newsletter," Winter, 1953–54 (mimeographed), (BMC).
16 *Proceedings*, 1949, 214 (CHC).
17 *Ibid.*
18 Smith made it a practice to attend meetings of the National Fellowship of Indian Workers.

remained at Browning only two years, white domination in the local church increased perceptibly. The increase was associated with a building program made possible after the Browning church treasury received a windfall.

When the Presbyterian church closed, the Methodists acquired the property which the Presbyterians had vacated.[19] In April, 1955, the property was sold by the Browning church for the tidy sum of $4,660.[20] Ritchey reported that the "money which was received for the property was re-invested in materials for the building of the educational-social unit erected on the east side of the church in 1955, and also to help remodel the interior of the church building itself."[21] The enthusiasm of the white membership ran high and led to increased participation in the church as well as improvement of the physical facilities:

> Since the arrival of the Ritcheys, there has been a 300% increase in regular church attendance at Browning, and a ⅓ increase in Sunday School attendance. Financial gains reflect the same general increase in interest and enthusiasm. Membership Training Classes are now being conducted. The Indian Committee of the Conference has purchased $812.50 worth of new furniture, and the Browning Woman's Society of Christian Service has added $325.00 in new furniture and upkeep.[22]

While white enthusiasm was high, the Blackfeet perceived the Methodist church as a white institution, serving white interests and dominated by white power. For example, Ritchey said of the Indian response to the building program, "The Indian membership . . . had very little interest in putting out physical and financial support for a project for the white [membership]."[23] In contrast, he thought the building program was a "very worthwhile project in the sight of the white people and it was very well supported by all of our white members."[24] Even nonmembers in the white population supported the Methodist

19 "Blackfeet Mission History" (BMC).
20 The record of this sale is in the mission files.
21 Ritchey, interview.
22 *Proceedings*, 1955, 497 (CHC).
23 Ritchey, interview.
24 *Ibid.*

building program because, according to the pastor, the "remodeling and improvements were looked upon as something the town needed, and the town helped with it."[25]

The building program served as an important catalyst for white aspirations and strengthened the cohesion of the white population in Browning. With a new sense of identity, born of common purpose and civic pride, the white Protestants eagerly turned to the task of remodeling "their" church. Some leading white members still recall with sentiment the golden age of the 1950's when the pastor oriented his ministry primarily toward Browning and the white population. Then—in the opinion of two powerful laymen—the pastor did not "waste his time out on the reservation."[26] For the white membership, the way the pastor had solved his role problem and the way the church had solved its identity problem marked the high point in Methodist history on the Blackfeet Reservation. The issue was by no means settled, however, and the conflict re-emerged when questions were raised concerning the administration of church property. As these questions were pressed, the ensuing conflict graphically illustrates the problems which remained unsolved in the Browning church.

The land where the Methodist mission had been established in 1893 remained in the possession of the church after the move into Browning in 1912. The acquisition of the original site on Willow Creek resulted from the government policy of setting aside reservation lands for educational and religious purposes. The effect of this policy on Protestant and Catholic missions on the Blackfeet Reservation was very clear by 1907:

> ... the Secretary of the Interior may reserve such lands as he may deem necessary for agency, school, and religious purposes, to remain reserved *so long as the agency, school, or religious institutions are maintained thereon for the benefit of the Indians,* not exceeding two hundred and twenty acres each to any one religious society: PROVIDED, That there is hereby granted three hundred and twenty acres each for

[25] *Ibid.*
[26] Sherburne, interview, and Donald Schmidt, personal interview, September, 1963. Both of these church members have substantial business interests in Browning.

the Holy Family Mission on Two Medicine Creek . . . and also to the mission of the Methodist Episcopal Church near Browning.[27]

The intent of the legislation is clear at this point for use of the land was limited solely to missionary functions. However, in 1909 authority was granted to issue fee patents to missionary organizations, and in 1918 a fee simple patent was issued to the Board of Home Missions and Church Extension, making this organization the legal owner of the property on Willow Creek.[28] By 1918, the Methodist church had moved its activities into Browning and had vacated the property on Willow Creek. Furthermore, the Browning church had received a fee patent for the land in the village by 1920.[29]

The vacated Willow Creek property, eventually known as the church ranch, was the scene of many experiments, most of which were failures. In addition to the plan for a Folk School proposed by Allen C. Wilcox, twenty years later Edgar Smith began experiments with truck farming, sheep raising, and dairying. None of these projects proved to be fruitful.[30] The policy which was eventually developed for the use of the church ranch was both simple and economically rewarding. The property was leased and the income used in the budget of the Browning church.[31] The contradiction implied in using these funds for the local church budget became serious in 1950, but by then the policy of local control over this money had become thoroughly entrenched. Whites were in their ascendancy, and Ritchey expressed their feelings in unambiguous language: "Money that came from the church ranch should be given to the church to be used as the church officials saw fit."[32] Even though the Board of Missions held title to the land, there is no evidence that national officials were aware of the implications of this ownership—espe-

27 Forrest R. Stone to Robert J. Hamilton, May 19, 1930 (BMC). My emphasis. Stone, the superintendent of the Blackfeet Agency, is quoting the Act of March 1, 1907 (34 Stats.), 1015–36.

28 This fee patent is preserved in the mission files.

29 This fee patent is preserved in the mission files.

30 Smith, "Report" (BMC).

31 Marian Lewis, personal interview, October, 1963.

32 Ritchey, interview.

cially since the local church was scarcely an Indian mission in 1950.

In 1959 the legal department of the Board of Missions "discovered" that it held title to the church ranch, even though in 1922 Henry Mecklenburg had shown his awareness of the title's status.[33] By this time, indications of the state of local affairs may have filtered up to the national level, for in January, the director of the Section of Church Extension received notification from the legal department that the lease contracted by the Browning church was invalid. Even if the moral issue remained clouded, the legal issues were very clear. Because the national board held title to the property, it was the only party that could legally enter into contracts concerning the church ranch. Furthermore, the legal department declared, *"Any payments made ... to the Methodist Church of Browning for the use of the real estate is not the monies of the Methodist Church of Browning but is the property of the Board of Home Missions."*[34]

Such sudden assumption of control of the land and funds by the national board naturally evoked strong reactions from local officials. The chairman of the Official Board in Browning wrote to the national board that the Indian community was quite disturbed by recent developments.[35] The implication was that the Indians actually wanted the local church to have the money, although at this time there were also reports from Indians who complained of discrimination in the Browning church.[36] Since so few Indians actually participated in the local church, it is rather difficult to see how the chairman determined the real feelings of the Indian community. The opinions he attributed to Indians were probably too close to those of the white membership to be taken as an accurate reading of Indian sentiment. Furthermore, the discussions of prejudice, discrimination, and segregation in the local church produced a recommendation from the Montana Conference in 1959. According to this resolu-

[33] H. C. Mecklenburg to W. J. Elliott, May 16, 1922 (PS). Mecklenburg had issued a five-year lease on the church ranch at a rent of $22.50 a month.

[34] Roger M. Whiteman to J. B. Harris, January 23, 1959 (BMC). My emphasis.

[35] Oscar L. Doane to J. B. Harris, n.d. (BMC).

[36] *Proceedings,* 1959, 464 (CHC).

tion, there would be "Constant effort to eliminate all discrimination in the church and its ministry."[37]

While the church was struggling with its moral problems, the director of the Section of Church Extension seemed more concerned with the question of legality. The legal situation was understandably disturbing to this official because the local church was using money derived from the church ranch to repay a loan contracted with the board itself. Since the board held title to the land, the situation was extremely embarrassing. The national official made a strong plea that the chairman of the Official Board work out some acceptable solution. "You can understand our desire," he said, "to 'regularize' this matter and to bring the proceeds of the lease on this property within the proper legal and bookkeeping regulations."[38]

The national office was prepared to issue a lease for the church ranch which would legalize the situation. According to their proposal, the money would no longer go into the Browning treasury but instead would be forwarded to the national office:

> The funds will then be used for Indian work, at the discretion of the Executive Committee of the Board of Home Missions and Church Extension of the Methodist Episcopal Church. It is possible . . . that some of these funds will be returned to the Browning Church, although the approval of the Executive Committee would have to be secured for such use of the funds.[39]

Evidently, some of the national officials were determined not only to legalize the situation but also to deal with the moral questions involved. However, in the face of a storm of local protest the national board finally bent to the will of the Browning church. It was agreed that the money would be sent to the board but then would be applied to the debt contracted by the Browning church. With the national board issuing the lease, the legal situation was clarified. The ethical problem of pretending to serve the Indian community without actually doing so was left undisturbed.

37 *Ibid.*
38 J. B. Harris to Oscar L. Doane, April 17, 1959 (BMC).
39 J. B. Harris to Donald E. Watson, January 30, 1959 (BMC).

Unable to formulate a strong national policy concerning Indian missions, the Methodist church remained dependent upon ministers who often capitulated to the parochial interests of the white community. The church failed to support the missionary role of the pastor against the role expectations held by the white membership, and thus what began as an Indian mission became a segregated church. White church members drew the institution around themselves and shaped it according to their own desires.

PART IV

*The Shape
of the Present*

XI

A Question of Social Justice

Race and poverty are two of the social issues that dominated the 1960's. Not only in the United States but throughout the world, these two problems have puzzled governments, convulsed societies, and given rise to some of the most aggressive social movements in recent history. The civil rights struggle and a passing concern with poverty in this country find their counterparts in movements in many other societies.

Profound moral implications accompany the economic and political dimensions of these movements. In fact, the recent concern for race and poverty can be interpreted ethically as a struggle to achieve greater social justice. Social justice, in relation to poverty, means an equitable distribution of wealth, opportunity, and other social resources to all groups within the society. And in relation to race, social justice means eliminating prejudice and discrimination against those who differ racially or culturally from the dominant majority.

The fate of Indians in American society is significantly illuminated when it is measured against the criteria of social justice. As national institutions and national life have developed, Indians have been dispossessed of their tribal institutions and their tribal lives. Deprived of their land and unable to participate in the wider society because their cultures failed to conform to the dominant national culture, Indians lapsed into poverty; and because they differed racially, Indians faced prejudice and discrimination.

During the nineteenth century, especially in programs of forced acculturation, government policy combined prejudice against Indian culture with the power of the state. Since the turn of the century, government policy has changed; but the Indians' poverty and the effects of prejudice and discrimination remain.

The change in government policy began when the Meriam Report, a document which ultimately produced a new Indian policy, was published in 1928. The report argued that plural groups could coexist in American society without the necessity of total assimilation,[1] a conclusion which ran directly counter to the policy of forced acculturation. According to this point of view, Indians could be assisted in formulating and achieving their own goals—whether those goals took the form of total assimilation, cultural pluralism, or preservation of traditional culture. The implication was that the choice of cultural pluralism or traditionalism would not result in economic deprivation or prejudice and discrimination, as it had in the past. The Roosevelt administration gave further impetus to the movement begun by the Meriam Report, and as a result, by 1934 the ethnocentrism which motivated forced acculturation was publicly rejected. Commissioner John Collier stated his views in unambiguous language: "No interference with Indian religious life or ceremonial expression will hereafter be tolerated. The cultural liberty of Indians is in all respects to be considered equal to that of any non-Indian group."[2]

Even though the new policy sought greater social justice, the destructive results of nineteenth century practices could not be completely reversed. Neither poverty nor prejudice was eliminated by a change in government policy. Although the condition of the present Indian population is improving, the group as a whole remains among the most deprived in the society. In 1964,

[1] See Lewis Meriam et al., *The Problem of Indian Administration*, 87–88.

[2] "Editorials by John Collier, Commissioner of Indian Affairs," 15; see also John Collier, Circular No. 2970, "Indian Religious Freedom and Indian Culture," January, 1934 (JA).

Indians had an average family income of about $1,500; their edu-
cational level was half the national average; their unemployment
rate stood as high as eight times the national average; and their
average age at death was forty-two years.[3] Moreover, Indians are
still the victims of discrimination that excludes them from economic participation in society and that compounds their poverty.
Even though the number of Indians is small in relation to the
total population of the country, the question of economic and
racial justice applies with peculiar force to their present condition.

The Blackfeet have shared the problems of Indians in general,
although in some ways they are in a worse state than are other
tribes. A discussion of their condition in the early 1960's and an
analysis of subsequent changes in that condition will prepare
the ground for an evaluation of the recent responses by Protestant and Catholic churches to the Blackfeet.

Although the Blackfeet had been poor since the disappearance
of the buffalo, at the beginning of the decade their condition
was desperate. In 1962, a Blackfoot family's median cash income
was estimated at about $500;[4] and in huts all over the reserva-
tion, disease was common and people were hungry. In 1958,
some 50 per cent of the tribe's work force were unemployed, and
by 1962 this figure had risen to 75 per cent.[5] During the seventy-
nine years since the starvation winter, the Blackfeet had experienced some brief periods of relative prosperity,[6] but by 1962
they had come almost full circle.

In Browning itself Blackfoot poverty was dramatically visible.
Although the town lies within sight of the magnificent peaks of

---

[3] U.S. Senate, Committee on Labor and Public Welfare, *Hearings Before the
Select Committee on Poverty*, 1937.

[4] U.S. House of Representatives, 88 Cong., 1 sess., Committee on Interior and
Insular Affairs, *Indian Unemployment Survey*, 128. This figure is very difficult to
interpret because it estimates *earned* income; it corresponds with a high unemployment rate, but it is not an accurate statistical measure. Since most of the
statistics reported from the reservation are based upon informed estimates, this
is a common interpretive problem. Regardless of the statistical difficulties, the
visual evidence of poverty was overwhelming in 1963.

[5] *Ibid.*

[6] Some Blackfeet were relatively prosperous during World War I, for example,
when their cattle herds were large and the price of beef was high. Ewers, *Blackfeet*, 319.

Blackfeet Reservation, showing approximate locations of past and present mission sites, Protestant and Catholic.

the Rocky Mountains, its physical and social ugliness was unmitigated by natural beauty. Its unpaved streets created gales of dust in dry weather and a sea of mud during occasional rains. Many of the 1,622 Indians who lived in Browning in 1960[7] were huddled together in a miserable rural slum picturesquely known as Moccasin Flats. The 389 white residents were better fed, better

[7] U.S. Bureau of the Census, *United States Census of Population: 1960*, Pt. 28, "Montana," 39. In 1960, Browning had a total population of 2,011. The present Indian population on the reservation is difficult to determine, although it was estimated that the total number was 5,430 in 1968. In the same year the total tribal membership, which includes all Blackfeet on and off the reservation, was estimated at 10,000. "Profile Blackfeet Tribe of the Blackfeet Reservation, Montana" (hereafter cited as "Profile"), (August 28, 1968), 6 (mimeographed).

housed, and more affluent because they controlled the economic resources of the town. The relationship between whites and Indians in Browning was a significant measure of conditions on the reservation as a whole.[8]

In addition to their poverty, the Blackfeet also suffered prejudice and discrimination. Prejudice was rooted in a stereotype of the Indian as drunken, sexually promiscuous, ignorant, and lazy. Like all stereotypes, this one bore some resemblance to reality. Drinking was one of the most serious problems on the reservation; there was widespread promiscuity; children did drop out of school; and many Indians refused to work. However, distortion and selective interpretation of the facts also contributed to the creation of such a stereotype. Prejudice did its job well in justifying patterns of discrimination and in communicating a negative self-image to Indians, but it failed to account for many of the causes of the observed behavior.

Thus, while drinking was a massive human problem at the beginning of the 1960's,[9] it was often interpreted moralistically rather than against the backdrop of what had happened to the Blackfeet as a people. The moralistic view tended to attribute drinking to some inherent flaw in Indian character. It is more probable, however, that the Blackfeet still suffered the deep frustrations of being divorced from their traditional culture while tragically being unable to find a meaningful relationship with the surrounding society. Faced with such a problem, many Blackfeet, like their ancestors, turned to "white man's water." Moralistic condemnation of drinking may have justified the continuation of discrimination, but it did very little to solve the problems of meaning which followed the loss of Blackfoot dignity.

As they did with drinking, many whites interpreted Blackfoot sexual behavior moralistically. To them, promiscuity and illegitimacy were simply signs of Indian immorality. And since the Blackfeet were bad, they could righteously be excluded from major social institutions. In contrast with this view, some Cath-

---

[8] These generalizations, as well as many others in this chapter, are interpretations based upon personal interviews with residents and observations made in Browning during 1963 and 1969.

[9] This consensus emerged in formal interviews and informal discussions. See also *Indian Unemployment Survey*, 129.

olic priests attributed Blackfoot behavior to a deep fear of permanence in marriage.[10] Although both explanations are too facile, the Catholic view was free from some of the grosser aspects of moralism. However, neither view took into account the Blackfoot past, with its heritage of polygamy and its resistance to white attempts to destroy traditional marriage. Furthermore, Blackfoot promiscuity was complicated by the fact that while programs of forced acculturation successfully undermined polygamy, they did not force the assimilation of monogamy. Thus, the stark moral evil seen by many whites was actually much more complex, and moral condemnation was too simplistic to modify the situation significantly.[11]

White attitudes toward drinking and sex also extended to education. For most middle-class whites, education was an unquestioned social value. Those who rejected education deserved to live with their consequent ignorance. Historically, the Blackfeet had developed their own methods and institutions for training the young. They resisted white education long after conquest, and even at the beginning of the 1960's some resistance still remained. In 1963, the total Indian enrollment in both elementary and high schools was 1,637. Of this total, 1,385 were in elementary schools and 252 were in high school.[12] High school dropouts for the 1961–62 school year totaled 46, with the majority leaving school before the eleventh grade. In 1962–63, dropouts had risen to 59.[13] Perhaps even more significant, the small percentage of elementary school students who went on to high school indicated a large dropout rate before and after the eighth grade. It was easy for whites to find evidence for Blackfoot "ignorance" in low levels of achievement, in frequent dropouts, and in parental disinterest. But the stereotype failed to expose the causes of the Blackfoot behavior; and it certainly could not recognize that, despite the traumas of the past, the Blackfoot family still retained some of its traditional cultural wisdom. The fact that

10 Father A. M. D. Gillen, personal interview, September, 1963.

11 Very little guilt is expressed by the Blackfeet themselves in reference to sexual behavior. For instance, Browning is a community that customarily gives showers for unwed mothers.

12 "Report of Indian Education in Montana, 1962–1963," 18 (mimeographed).

13 *Ibid.*, 19.

such wisdom was not marketable in the American economy did not diminish its continuing reality.

In addition to the problems of drinking, promiscuity, and lack of education, Blackfoot resistance to work continued to strengthen white prejudices. Blackfeet who worked only long enough to earn sufficient money for the winter, preferring part time to full time employment,[14] naturally incurred moral condemnation by whites who reflected the work habits of the wider society. People who understood work as a prime virtue and laziness as a cardinal sin were ill prepared to see that in the attitude toward time reflected by these work habits, part of the Indian world continued. The words of a former Blackfoot high school student hold evidence that a traditional outlook on life persisted. "The Indian," he said, "lives mostly from day to day or from week to week with no goal in mind."[15] While this view was perhaps connected with the early economy and nomadic habits of the Blackfeet, it also became further evidence to goal-directed whites that Indians were lazy.

Thus, at the beginning of the 1960's Blackfeet were not only poor, but they also were burdened by the weight of their own past and by the pressures of white prejudice and discrimination. However, social changes introduced by the government as the result of a massive flood in 1964, and as part of the war on poverty, produced visible differences by 1969.

The flood of 1964 brought death, homelessness, and extensive property damage. The pressure of nearly eight inches of rain in a little over thirty-six hours caused both Two Medicine Dam and Swift Dam at the head of Birch Creek to break. Roads, fences, outbuildings, and people were swept away in the waters that inundated the area. Thirty people were killed, a thousand were left homeless, and approximately twenty thousand acres of land were severely damaged. The work of reconstruction brought more than five million dollars of federal money to the reservation for repair of the damage caused by the flood.[16]

In addition, the newly created Office of Economic Oppor-

14 *Indian Unemployment Survey*, 129.
15 *Glacier Reporter*, September 12, 1963.
16 See "The Blackfeet Flood," Department of the Interior, Bureau of Indian Affairs, Billings Area Office, 1964 (mimeographed).

tunity began to make its influence felt. Between 1965 and 1968 the total expenditure on such programs as the Neighborhood Youth Corps, Work Study Programs, Community Action, Headstart, and Vista was $1,389,817.[17] Whether these programs will ultimately mend the social damage caused by conquest and forced acculturation cannot yet be determined. But certainly new jobs are being created, new leadership is emerging, and new experiences are available for some Blackfeet. Expenditures for 1969 and plans for 1970 do not indicate that activity will diminish; indeed, there is expansion in some areas.[18]

Debilitating poverty remains on the reservation, and many Blackfeet still suffer from problems related to loss of their old cultural identity. But since 1960 there have been some economic improvements, and such signs are reason for limited hope. The superintendent's 1963 income estimate of $500 a family had risen in 1968 to $3,250.[19] However, this figure is still only an estimate, and because it is an average, it does not show the lowest level of income. In any case, $3,250 will not provide the essentials of life, even on an Indian reservation.

Unemployment has declined since 1963, although here again there is little evidence of significant changes in the quality of life on the reservation. Compared to an unemployment rate of 75 per cent in 1962, the rate had fallen to 49 per cent by March, 1965; by March, 1966, it had fallen to 44 per cent; and in March, 1967, the rate hovered at 38 per cent.[20] Even so, a 38 per cent unemployment figure is shockingly high in relation to the surrounding society. Furthermore, there is little hope that a majority of the Blackfeet will migrate off the reservation successfully. In the program of employment assistance, which encourages Indians to seek permanent employment off the reservation, there was a returnee rate for 1966 through 1968 of 51 per cent.[21]

17 "Profile," 10–11.
18 See ibid., 14–15.
19 Ibid., 20. Some of the difference may be attributed to the fact that in 1963 the superintendent did not include noncash supplements of various sorts in his estimate.
20 "Profile," 17. In September, 1967, unemployment fell to 13 per cent because of temporary jobs in fire fighting. Following the return of the men to the reservation, rates rose again to about 38 per cent.
21 Ibid., 34.

Housing on the reservation is one of the most visible improvements—although there are ambiguities here as well. In addition to the new housing provided for flood victims, there are developments associated with low rent and mutual help housing projects. In 1968, 50 low rent units had been built and 55 more were planned; in the same year, 27 mutual help units were built and occupied while 113 more were planned.[22] Even though the housing is often poorly maintained and deterioration sets in quickly, some Blackfoot families are better housed today than they were in 1960.

School enrollment has risen slightly since the beginning of the decade, but the dropout rate has remained about the same. In the 1966–67 school year, enrollment in the elementary schools was 1,683, and in the high school, 351. The pattern of wholesale dropouts between elementary school and high school apparently persists. Moreover, there were 56 high school dropouts, half of which occurred between the ninth and tenth grades.[23] Even though the schools continue to be one of the most impressive institutions on the reservation, there are signs that Blackfeet still resist education. Dropout rates are but one measure of this fact; continuing parental disinterest and evaluations made by teachers point to the same conclusion. While there has been progress, there is no justification for making hope in the next generation a panacea for Blackfoot problems.

One change among the young Blackfeet today is an increasing interest in their tribal culture. The civil rights movement and the general emergence of minority self-consciousness in the world apparently are making an impact upon the Blackfeet. Whether the interest in traditional culture will lead to vigorous or even violent attempts to achieve a new identity cannot yet be determined. But it is a movement which cannot be dismissed— if the experience of Blacks in American society is any analogue.

Even though there have been changes in levels of poverty, unemployment, housing, and education, perhaps the most spectacular change has come in the physical appearance of Browning. In addition to the new housing developments, streets are being

22 *Ibid.*, 9.
23 *Ibid.*, 27.

paved, curbing installed, gutters and storm sewers completed, and sidewalks built. A grant has been approved for the town to develop a comprehensive plan for future improvements.[24] Physical renewal has brought rising expectations on the part of businessmen. A new shopping area is but one concrete outcome of redevelopment and is a sign to the business community that Browning has a bright future.

But what is the future for the Blackfeet? Economic improvements in Browning are too closely associated with the booming tourism in Montana to be directly beneficial to the Indians. White businessmen seem certain to gain the most from the present developments. Measured against the norm of social justice, the results of the 1960's are ambiguous. Most discouraging of all are signs that drinking, promiscuity, and violence—with their concomitant white prejudices—have not significantly diminished. Suicides, especially among the young, are particularly distressing.[25] These conditions indicate that the Blackfeet as a people still suffer serious difficulties. It is interesting to imagine what tourists of the next decades will see. As they drive across the highways on the reservation, will they see a people who are recovering their dignity and their heritage? Or will they confront a people who are still not far from the prophetic description Father Giorda made in 1864: "They will like ghosts linger about the towns of the whites and tell our children to what wretched existence they had been reduced by the white man."[26]

24 *Ibid.*, 8–9.
25 See "Hope Has Little Meaning for Blackfoot Indians," *New York Times*, May 6, 1969. By contrast with the present, suicide was not a widespread phenomenon in traditional society.
26 Father Giorda to Agent Upson, January 22, 1864 (BAA).

XII

Protestant and Catholic Responses

A century is but a tiny segment in the recorded activities of men in their societies, but it is long enough for an entire people to change markedly or even to become extinct. Between 1860 and 1960, the Blackfeet experienced changes in their environment and in their relationships with other groups—changes that radically modified their lives and, for a time, actually threatened them with extinction. In 1860, despite the destructive events which lay directly before them, they possessed a positive cultural identity; in 1960, after a century of shifting government policies, coercive programs of cultural change, and varying degrees of exploitation at the hands of white society—combined with a few bright years—the Blackfeet possessed a negative cultural identity.

Because they have been poor and because they have suffered the effects of prejudice and discrimination, the question of social justice is of great significance for all of the institutions with which the Blackfeet have contact—the government agencies, the schools, and also the churches. In their respective histories, the Protestant and Catholic missions among the Blackfeet have been characterized by shifting priorities. Although the question of social justice has not been absent from this missionary history, it has not been a primary concern. But by 1960, as a result of growing pressures in the United States and in the world, social justice at last became an important item on the agenda of the churches. The mission among the Blackfeet in the 1960's can profitably be viewed against the background of a contemporary crisis in the church at large; for even though the mission churches are isolated, they are not unaffected by strong currents beyond the reservation.

Since the early 1960's, churches in the United States have desperately sought to define their relation to the questions of race and poverty. The conflicts engendered by these social problems have disturbed the churches, often dividing congregations and denominations into hostile camps. Should the churches participate in the struggle for racial justice? In what ways? To what extent? Should the churches organize themselves to address the question of economic justice? In what ways? To what extent? The answers to these queries range from approval of direct participation in movements for social justice to affirmations that the church should attend to man's soul and should leave other issues aside.

The response by any specific church to the issues of racial and economic justice is shaped not only by the wider ecclesiastical context but also by its peculiar local history. Thus, the Protestants and Catholics on the Blackfeet Reservation are conditioned not only by shifts in denominational emphasis and the effects of Vatican II but also by their particular traditions. The interaction between specific heritages and wider social changes in the churches has shaped both their responses to the question of social justice and their ability to understand this issue as important to them.

The heritage of Roman Catholic missions among the Blackfeet includes three factors which helped to shape the Catholic response to social justice. First, the Catholic church emphasized the religious functions of the priest, especially in relation to the sacraments. Second, the church participated with the government in programs of forced acculturation which undermined even further the Blackfeet social order remaining after white conquest. And finally, by reason of the nature of their institutions, there was a tendency to integrate Indians into the church, at least partially. In contrast is the Protestant heritage,[1] much shorter than that of Roman Catholic institutions yet containing significant implications for social justice. Three dimensions of this heritage are crucial—an emphasis upon personal relations rather than sacramentalism, the substitution of philanthropy for other forms of social action, and a tendency to repeat within the church the racial and cultural separations of the wider society. The present Roman Catholic and Protestant missionary forms can be illuminated by consideration of these six dimensions.

At the beginning of the 1960's, Roman Catholic missionary activity on the reservation was primarily sacramental. That is, the church was chiefly concerned with the transcendent or supernatural elements of human experience. Sacramental activities in the Catholic church are defined in accordance with canon law, but the two priests on the reservation varied considerably in their views of the priestly role in relation to the Blackfeet. It is especially in the area of nonsacramental functions that divergences between the two priests emerge most clearly.[2]

Father A. M. D. Gillen of Little Flower Church in Browning defined his role in terms of a distinction between sacramental and social activities.[3] While the sacramental role was primary for Gillen, he also expressed deep concern for the social problems of the Blackfeet. He actively sought to influence patterns of work and marriage, as well as to persuade Catholic families to value education more highly. Furthermore, he was interested in the question of employment, which is essential to any understanding of the economic aspects of social justice.

Father Gillen attempted to implement his concern for social justice by participating in community affairs. He was especially interested in the meetings of the tribal council, the major Blackfoot political body on the reservation.[4] His attitudes and be-

---

[1] In the 1960's there were four Protestant groups in addition to the Methodists on the reservation—the Assembly of God church, the Church of Jesus Christ of Latter-day Saints, the Baptist church, and the Full Gospel church. These churches are not included in the analysis both because their histories are brief and because they had an insignificant number of Indian participants.

[2] See Joseph H. Fichter, S.J., *Social Relations in the Urban Parish*, 124.

[3] Father A. M. D. Gillen, personal interview, September, 1963.

[4] *Ibid.*

havior represented fairly traditional political participation rather than reform or revolution. Even though Gillen was apparently aware of the importance of social justice, his perspective did not allow him to formulate an institutional plan by which the church could deploy its power to deal with the Indians' problems. The only evidence that he thought about new institutional forms was his plan to use some of the Holy Family Mission buildings for a children's home, an idea that never materialized. And even if it had, it would have done very little to end poverty and prejudice on the Blackfeet Reservation.

At St. Anne's Church in Heart Butte, the mission was shaped by the lively outlook of Father Egon Mallman, who has served at this station since 1935. Mallman placed primary emphasis upon the sacramental aspects of his role, claiming that the social problems of the Blackfeet were subordinate to religious considerations.[5] He acknowledged points of co-operation with other agencies but maintained that these points were determined by mutual self-interest. The function of political, economic, and educational institutions was to create a framework for minimal civic and personal morality while the function of the church was to relate to the spiritual life of man. In his view, therefore, there was no clear imperative for the church to involve itself in programs of economic development—except in so far as the interests of the church and a particular secular institution might coincide. While Mallman had deep concern for the Blackfeet, he did not feel that the role of the church lay in reform or revolution.

Father Mallman's activities had continuities with the Jesuit heritage on the reservation. Early in his ministry, he was involved in struggles with the Powers of Darkness dwelling in the vicinity of his parish. His opposition to traditional practices, while not so ethnocentric and hostile as Carroll's, was based upon his theological view of the world. Though he distinguished between medical and religious superstitions, he was firmly opposed to both these elements of traditional Blackfoot culture. Father Mallman's opposition to superstition was so strong that in his first years at Heart Butte, he often simply ignored the "pagans."[6]

[5] Father Egon Mallman, S.J., personal interview, September, 1963.

During these first years, there were three deaths in his parish that he attributed to the practice of Indian medicine. As late as 1942, a young boy in the parish died because his parents refused to seek aid at the hospital and relied instead on medicine ceremonies and traditional doctors. As a consequence, Father Mallman refused to bury the boy. The priest's rejection of medical superstitions, when it took this form, certainly did not endear him to some of the full bloods who were involved. In fact, several families were so alienated from the Catholic church that they turned to the medicine of Protestantism. In 1950, Father Mallman was involved in a conflict over a sun dance. Despite the priest's warnings, the ceremonies were held, and again some Indian participants either left the church or began to respond to the overtures of the Protestants.[7]

The alienation of Blackfeet from the Roman Catholic church might have been greater had it not been for a point of view that softened interpersonal conflicts and reduced their potential for causing disruption. This perspective, which both Gillen and Mallman shared, was a conception of the priest's role as being fatherly. That is, priests traditionally are expected to give aid to the "drunken husband, the delinquent boy, the unchaste wife, the girl in trouble."[8] Both priests exhibited an enormous commitment to the fatherly role. For Mallman, such behavior had deeply religious sources, for he believed that a priest's life should mirror the sufferings and life style of Christ.[9] The fatherly role brought the priests into deep personal relationships with Blackfeet which helped bind the Indians to the church. In contrast, the pattern of segregation in the Protestant church made identification with that institution much more difficult for the Indians.

By the end of the 1960's, there had been very little change in the shape of Catholic institutions. Blackfeet participated—sometimes marginally—in the sacramental life of the church, as well as in such social activities as bingo parties. A major part of the priest's time was spent in sacramental and fatherly min-

6 *Ibid.*
7 Some of these families subsequently formed the nucleus of Apistatoke Methodist Mission established near Heart Butte in 1962.
8 Fichter, *Social Relations*, 126.
9 Mallman, interview.

istrations. The only highly visible change was the building of Little Flower Center in 1967. One of the finest buildings in the community, Little Flower Center provides space for recreation and other activities. Beyond this change, Father Patrick Stimatz, who replaced Father Gillen in 1965, seems to follow a style of ministry which is, in a way, more continuous than discontinuous with the past.

The three elements of Catholic tradition—sacramentalism, some opposition to traditional culture, and Indian participation —have continued to characterize the 1960's. The church has performed a function among the Blackfeet which is basically conservative in nature, although there have been times when opposition to traditional culture has produced destructive tensions. The tendency of Roman Catholic missionary institutions has been to create a tradition that is as yet incapable of making any significant innovations. For this reason, the church was and still is unable to respond adequately to the question of social justice on the Blackfeet Reservation.

In contrast to the evolutionary continuity with the past apparent in Roman Catholic missionary structures, changes have taken place in both the shape and style of Protestant institutions. There is continuity with the past, to be sure, but new efforts on the reservation by the Methodist church represent an atmosphere of innovation which has not been present since the ministry of Allen C. Wilcox. The changes began in 1959 with the arrival of Rev. James E. Bell as missionary. In addition to Bell's fresh perspective, there were important discussions of missionary policy at the level of the Montana Conference and the National Board of Missions. Out of these discussions came decisions which, by the end of the decade, had significantly altered the shape of Methodist institutions on the reservation. An explication of these policy discussions and a detailed analysis of Bell's perspective will clarify the nature and direction of change.

Of the three historical elements in the Protestant tradition— personal ministry, philanthropy, and segregation—the policy discussions in the Methodist church dealt mainly with segregation. By 1960, there was awareness in the conference as well as in the national board that a root problem in the Browning church was

Holy Family Mission Band (1908). The Museum of the Plains Indian,
Browning, Montana.

Little Flower Church. Chancery Archives, Diocese of Helena.

Eugene S. Dutcher, the first Methodist missionary to the Blackfeet.
Montana Historical Society, Helena, Montana.

Epworth Piegan Methodist Mission, built by Dutcher west of Browning, as it appeared about 1895. Glacier Studio, Browning, Montana.

Epworth Piegan Methodist Mission as it appeared after the move into Browning. Glacier Studio, Browning, Montana.

The Church of the Little Sweet Pine. Glacier Studio, Browning, Montana.

Father Egon Mallman, the last Jesuit missionary on the Blackfeet Reservation. Glacier Studio, Browning, Montana.

Three Generations. Toge Fujihira, United Methodist Missions.

its exclusivism. The most powerful local church opinion still held that the Browning church should be primarily oriented toward the town—which meant the white population. Likewise, the missionary should focus his attention on this population.

By 1963, three options designed to deal with exclusivism had emerged in the Board of Missions of the Montana Conference.[10] The first option, supported by the chairman of the Board of Missions, was to make Browning simply another conference appointment with no special definition as an Indian mission. This policy would eliminate the contradiction plaguing the local church—being a white, middle-class church while at the same time projecting the appearance of an Indian mission. The integrity of the church could be regained, in the chairman's opinion, by simply dropping the image of an Indian mission. This plan did not mean that the minister in Browning would cease to work with Indians. Instead, the pastoral ministry of the church would include all groups in Browning but would not single out any special group for missionary emphasis.[11]

The district superintendent advocated a second policy, similar to the chairman's plan but with important differences. He agreed that the local church should become a regular conference appointment, but he thought that the missionary emphasis should be preserved by separating it from the work of the local church. This would naturally require the development of a new institution, distinct from the Browning church, within which the mission to the Blackfeet could be nurtured.[12]

A third position was taken by Bell, who argued that the Browning church should be a totally inclusive institution. He insisted that the church be called "The Methodist Blackfeet Mission" in order to symbolize its inclusive character. Furthermore, Bell thought that the local church should not only include Indians in every aspect of its institutional life but should also extend the Methodist mission to the reservation population outside Brown-

---

[10] Prior to 1961, activities at Browning were the administrative responsibility of the Indian Committee of the Montana Conference. In 1961, this committee was dissolved and its functions assumed by the Conference Board of Missions.

[11] Rev. Herbert J. Burdsall, personal interview, September, 1963.

[12] Rev. Gordon A. Patterson, personal interview, September, 1963.

ing.[13] His view came into sharp conflict with opinions held by some of the most powerful laymen in the Browning church.

While discussions were proceeding in the Conference Board of Missions, the national board was also involved in policy considerations. Two divergent opinions dominated the national board. The executive secretary of the Division of National Missions, who supported the first option, favored separating the Browning church from the mission to the Blackfeet.[14] In contrast, the executive secretary of Town and Country Work had deep misgivings about the policy of separation: "I cannot imagine the . . . church that removes itself from support of and action in the mission on its doorstep."[15]

The two views that emerged from these discussions as real possibilities for the Browning church were the policy of separation and the policy of inclusion. The policy of separation functionally reflected the desires of the local church and at the same time realistically acknowledged local power. However, the policy was in essence an admission that segregation had become too entrenched to be changed. Judged by the criterion of social justice, it was an admission of failure. The policy of inclusion, however, represented an attempt to reverse the history of segregation and to address the question of racial justice. As the 1960's matured, there was a fascinating shift from a policy of inclusion, implemented by Bell, to a policy of functional separation. Even within the complicated tangle of events, the curve of this development can be plotted and the two remaining elements of the Methodist tradition—personal ministry and philanthropy —can be exposed.

When James Bell arrived in Browning, his status was different from that of other clergymen in the history of the Methodist mission because he had been officially commissioned as a missionary to the Blackfeet. Such men as Dutcher, Riggin, and Wilcox understood themselves to be missionaries, but their subjective understanding was not officially recognized by the church. Thus, there was a tendency to see the ministry in Browning as

13 Rev. James E. Bell, personal interview, September, 1963.
14 Allen B. Rice, personal interview, January, 1964.
15 L. Cornelia Russell to James E. Bell, October 25, 1962 (BMC).

part of the itinerant syndrome of short-term appointments. This syndrome did not characterize the ministry of Allen Wilcox, which was almost twenty years in duration, nor did it characterize those of some early ministers. But after 1945, when white domination of the Browning church was evolving, the itinerant pattern of ministry became typical.

From 1945 to 1959, the Browning church had a total of five different ministers.[16] Browning increasingly was understood as a regular conference appointment—one of the least desirable appointments. Men who came to the church during this period accepted Browning as a necessary way station in a pattern of career mobility hopefully leading upward to a better church in a more attractive community. Such a view was congenial to the role expectations of a white-dominated congregation. With the arrival of Bell, the understanding of the ministry as itinerant was rejected by the missionary and symbolically by the wider church through the act of commissioning.

The steps Bell took in 1959 indicated the direction his ministry would take. Although he was given no special training for his task by the Methodist church, he made an effort to study the life and culture of the Blackfeet. "This preparation," he said, "helped us to understand the people and to begin our work."[17] After studying Blackfoot history, Bell next began "to visit all the people we possibly could. *Especially did we want to visit the Indian people.* At the Indian hospital, in the homes and on the streets and roads we have made 789 calls since July 1 [1959]."[18] Such activity was one of the most important factors in finally reversing the trend of segregation—at one level—and re-establishing the Methodist church among the Indian population.

Interestingly, Bell chose to overcome segregation by establishing churches outside the town of Browning. Even though his efforts were as significant as those of Wilcox, he ultimately was

16 In order, these ministers were S. H. Smith, E. B. Smith, G. S. Ritchey, G. P. Cox, and Mrs. Charlotte Bridges.

17 Rev. James E. Bell, "Preliminary Report, Methodist Blackfeet Mission, 1959–1960," 1 (BMC). The fact that Bell had to study on his own initiative is not surprising since there has never been any formal training for Indian missionaries in the Methodist church.

18 *Ibid.*, 2. My emphasis.

unable to make the Browning church inclusive. By establishing indigenous churches, however, Bell thought that he was attacking the racial dimension of social justice.

In July, 1959, Bell began holding services in a public school building in Babb and eventually constructed a church in that community. Completed in 1962, the church was consecrated as Christ Methodist Mission in September. In August, 1959, the missionary also began meeting for church services in an Indian home in the Heart Butte area. These meetings led to the establishment of Apistatoke Methodist Mission in July, 1962. In 1964, Bell's reflection upon his five years on the reservation revealed not only his progress outside Browning but also some changes in the Browning church itself.

> . . . during these past five years we have witnessed a turning of the tide. Slowly, but surely, Indian people are coming back to the Methodist Church. A look at the progress during the last five years reveals this trend; Baptisms 212, of whom 155 were Indian; Professions of Faith 201, of whom 113 were Indian . . . The gain in Indian membership is reflected in the membership of the Three Missions: Browning, 130 (59 Indian); Babb, 62 (38 Indian) and Heart Butte, 46 (44 Indian).[19]

Bell's figures required interpretation, especially in relation to the Browning church. The question was, of course, how the fifty-nine Indian members were actually related to the local church. A close observation of attendance at worship services, combined with an analysis of the power structure of the Browning church, revealed that most of these Indians were related more to Bell than to an inclusive fellowship in Browning. The power structure was not controlled by Indians, although they had some representation. Of forty-six church officers, only ten were Indian, none holding positions of real power. In contrast, only nine of the thirty-one officers in Christ Methodist Mission were non-Indian, and Apistatoke Methodist Mission had only one non-Indian officer out of a total of fourteen.[20] Bell had made progress, especially at Babb and Heart Butte; and even though

19 *Proceedings*, 1964, 66 (CHC).
20 Howard L. Harrod, Blackfoot Field Notes, 1963.

the results were more ambiguous at Browning, there had been some movement toward the goal of an inclusive church. Part of Bell's optimism was justified when he wrote in 1964:

Every day new doors are opening to us among the Indian people. The longer we stay, the more we learn about their life and culture, the more friends we make, the more we are convinced that Methodism is coming back to the Blackfeet Reservation.[21]

By 1964, developments pointed toward a reversal of segregation—one of the basic dimensions of the Methodist heritage among the Blackfeet. During this same period, Methodist philanthropy continued as it had in the past, and a center for the distribution of used clothing was established. The tendency to depend upon personal relationships with parishioners could clearly be observed in Bell's style of ministry, but a type of sacramentalism also developed.

James Bell's sacramentalism emerged in his understanding of the church. For him, the participation of members in the sacraments of the church was most important; here grace was to be found, and here individuals were powerfully influenced. "It is our belief," he said, "that the Sacraments have power to convert and we have witnessed this power. We would call our evangelism the Evangelism of the Sacraments."[22] The similarities of his view of the church with the Roman Catholic conception is obvious, and by wearing a clerical collar Bell strengthened the resemblance.

Focusing upon the sacraments tended to make the missionary de-emphasize social, cultural, racial, and economic differences. For Bell, such distinctions had no place in the church, for they were overcome by the equal participation of all members in the sacraments: "When the object and concern of the worship of the church is objective in sacrament and word . . . it doesn't really matter whether somebody has a hat on or not, or whether they

21 *Proceedings*, 1964, 66 (CHC).
22 Rev. James E. Bell, "Mid-Winter Report to the Indian Committee of the Montana Conference," February 20, 1961, 4 (BMC). With this understanding of the sacraments, Bell moved closer to the Roman Catholic tradition and away from the earlier Methodist views. See *ibid.*, 155.

are wearing levis or shorts or blue jeans or boots. They are there and they participate."[23] Up to this point, Bell's perspective dealt theologically with the questions of prejudice and discrimination, although his views led him into increasing conflict with many white members of the Browning church.

Despite the fact that the missionary's sacramentalism promoted racial and cultural inclusiveness in the church, his views tended to obscure the question of economic justice. In an interesting similarity to the Jesuit tradition, the Protestant missionary placed economic justice far down on the list of church priorities. However, this superficial similarity was rooted in a theological perspective quite different from Roman Catholicism. Even though James Bell shared the sacramentalism of the Catholic priests, his view of the church's major purpose was derived more from Methodist individualism than from a strong theology of the sacraments.

Many Methodists since John Wesley have interpreted social change in individualistic terms, believing essentially that only the transformed heart can issue in a transformed society. Bell's position, though curiously overlaid with a Protestant sacramentalism, basically fitted into this category. While he could say that the major function of the church was to make "Christ known in his redemptive power by every means, and especially by word and sacrament,"[24] his reasons for refusing to emphasize economic justice were revealing:

> Were it a hundred years from now, and God had had the opportunity and the chance to move and to do His redemption in the hearts of these people, then I think that we could begin talking about better homes, better living conditions, nicer clothing, and all the rest.[25]

Given Bell's obvious sensitivity toward segregation, his myopia concerning Blackfoot poverty was striking. And while the Methodist mission had taken several halting steps toward racial justice by the mid-1960's, it had made little progress in dealing creatively with the question of economic justice.

The flood of 1964 was both literally and figuratively a turning

23 Bell, interview.
24 *Ibid.*
25 *Ibid.*

point for reservation institutions, the church included. The responses by the Protestant church to this event led to a weakening of the indigenous churches on the reservation and to the reestablishment of the policy of separation in the Browning church. Even though the tangle of historical events is confusing, it is possible to see that by the end of the 1960's functional separation has not meant a complete return to white domination. It is even possible to see the emergence of a new inclusiveness, based not upon the social reality of indigenous churches but rather upon the concept of a renewed church.

Two consequences of the flood had important implications for the shape of Bell's ministry on the reservation. First, because they lost their homes, almost half the membership of Apistatoke Methodist Mission moved into Browning.[26] Since this church was an indigenous Indian institution—with such full-blood names on its rolls as After Buffalo, Mad Plume, Heavy Runner, Bear Leggins, and Swims Under—the heavy loss of membership was damaging to one dimension of Bell's approach. It was in this church that the missionary had experimented with forms of liturgy and worship which employed classical elements of Blackfoot culture.[27] Furthermore, the church was a center of social activity as well as the nucleus of the first indigenous Indian church since Little Sweet Pine. But the loss of membership, combined with a change in policy a few years later, led to its virtual extinction.

Second, when the rain began to fall on June 7, 1964, another tragedy destroyed an additional part of Bell's work. On the first day of the flood, Christ Methodist Mission at Babb burned to the ground. Even though this church was eventually rebuilt, its institutional strength never recovered. Furthermore, the change in policy that affected Apistatoke also undermined the wavering resources of this church.[28]

The policy change which damaged the indigenous churches

26 Thirty-one out of the sixty-nine members moved into Browning. "Membership Roll, Apistatoke Methodist Mission, May 13, 1964" (BMC).

27 Rev. James E. Bell, "Report to the Conference Board of Missions, February 18, 1966" (BMC).

28 *Proceedings*, 1964, 67–68 (CHC). By 1966, the average attendance at this mission church was six, with only ten at the church school. Rev. James E. Bell, "Report," February 18, 1966 (BMC).

and which finally led to a redefinition of the mission to the Blackfeet began with the separation of the Browning Methodist
Church from the missionary activity outside the town. The year
after the flood, the Methodist ministry was divided into two parts.
Bell became the missionary-at-large and was to tend the two
churches on the reservation as well as extend Protestant influence
to other points outside Browning. The Browning church received a new minister, Rev. Conrad Himmel, who was to focus
upon the town population and help the church became a self-
supporting institution.[29] As the two ministries became auton-
omous, institutional separations even deeper than those already
existing could have developed. This development also could
have accelerated the processes of exclusivism which had such a
long history in the Browning church. These consequences did
not occur, however, because of the departure of Bell in 1967 and
the articulation of a new policy by Himmel.

Bell's policy had been based upon an essentially traditional
view of missions. For him, missions meant the incorporation of
new members into the church. The establishment of Christ
Methodist Mission and Apistatoke were symbols of his policy.
In contrast, Himmel's view of the church and missions involved
not only a commitment to inclusive institutional forms but also
a deep concern for economic justice on the reservation.

After Himmel had been in Browning for a few months, he
was speaking openly about the fragmented character of the town.
He perceived the socioeconomic and cultural divisions between
such groups as businessmen, ranchers, agency employees, assimilated Blackfeet, and the population of Moccasin Flats. He
formulated the task of the Browning church in terms of healing
these basic divisions in the social order. But before the church
could perform its task, according to Himmel, it had to heal itself: "Browning Methodist Church, upon examination, is just
as broken as the totality of its surrounding."[30] This meant, first,
that the Browning church had to overcome its exclusivism and,
second, that the Browning church had to come to a new self-
understanding.

29 *Proceedings*, 1965, 220 (CHC).
30 Conrad Himmel, "Mid-Winter Report, 1966" (BMC).

To Himmel, a new self-understanding involved both an individual and an institutional level. Individually, each member had to conceive of himself as a minister in the community. Traditionally, the layman had seen himself as the passive recipient of a professional clergyman's ministry. Himmel was committed to a fundamental change in this self-understanding: "Our basic striving is to help every Christian understand himself as a minister in his vocational role."[31] If this goal could be accomplished, then the church would be an army of disciplined persons who could promote social justice on the reservation.

If the problem of individual self-understanding could be solved, then Himmel hoped that a new institutional self-understanding would emerge.

> As to things not yet conceived by this local church, one of the greatest is its role as a servant within the whole community. It is becoming obvious, if not accepted, that the church must involve itself in the social, economic, and political phases of community life, and break the old institutional image that has dominated so many years.[32]

Himmel believed that by conforming itself to the servant image, the Browning church could become an innovative force in the life of the reservation.

Obviously, with such an understanding of the church and its membership, Himmel's view of missions was quite different from Bell's. Most notably, Himmel was not interested in incorporating new members into the church. He did not spend time and energy seeking to revive the churches at Babb and Heart Butte, which are now virtually dead. While his positive understanding of missions is not yet fully articulated, it clearly involves his assessment of what the Blackfeet most deeply need. Apparently, they do not necessarily need to be incorporated into the church, since church membership does not seem to affect their poverty and powerlessness. What the Blackfeet really need, according to Himmel, is a new self-understanding, a new identity.

The way to meet their needs is not entirely clear. One attempt

---

31 *Ibid.*
32 "Pastor's Report, Fourth Quarterly Conference," May 21, 1967 (BMC).

is the program of a new Day Care Center, which opened October 15, 1968, under Methodist sponsorship. While attention is given to the physical care of each child, the basic purpose of the school is to deal with the child's self-image. According to the present conception of the staff, self-image involves two dimensions. First, there is the dimension of identification with the past. It was discovered that Indian children had difficulty seeing themselves in relation to their own heritage. When they were taken to the Museum of the Plains Indian in Browning, many wanted to know who the people in the funny clothes were. An emphasis upon cultural heritage in the center seeks to enable children to identify themselves with traditional Blackfoot culture and not merely the marginal limbo of the reservation. Second, there is the dimension of the future. Here, the attempt is to mold a self-image which will one day help the child regain his past, live productively in the present, and creatively shape his future.[33]

These are high goals toward which the Browning Day Care Center aspires. It will be years before anyone can see how well the center has succeeded with the twenty-five children who were enrolled in 1969. Nor have Himmel's aspirations for the emergence of a servant church and laity clearly become fact. These goals are realities largely in the mind of the minister, although they deeply shape his action on the reservation. Only the future can tell whether they will issue in new structures that foster social justice on the Blackfeet Reservation.

In the present, however, one thing is clear; neither the Catholics nor the Protestants have historical traditions which nurture new movements toward social justice. For the Catholics, the temptation is to do business as usual, incorporating Blackfeet into the church but never really dealing with the deeper questions of prejudice and poverty. For the Protestants, the temptation is to capitulate to exclusivism—especially if the present minister is moved to another church. Historically, the itinerant pattern of ministry has prevented Protestants from pursuing any single policy over a long period of time and has made the church susceptible to local pressures toward white domination. The real danger is that the new life represented by the Browning Day

[33] Mrs. Conrad Himmel, "The Browning Day Care Center," July, 1969 (BMC).

Care Center will join the heap of idealistic, yet long-forgotten programs which litter the Methodist past on the Blackfeet Reservation.

CONCLUSION

The Two Heritages Compared

More than a century and a quarter has passed since Father De Smet baptized the first Blackfeet and over three-quarters of a century since Rev. Dutcher established the first permanent Methodist mission on Willow Creek. Looking back over the history of Catholic and Protestant missions, important lines of convergence as well as differences stand out sharply. Placing both similarities and differences in a broader comparative pattern will make explicit some of the facts which, up to this point, have been only implicit in the historical data.

At a very general level, affinities between Protestant and Catholic missions are visible at three points—both share the Christian religion as a common heritage, both are not only religious institutions but also bearers of Western civilization, and both came among the Blackfeet for the purpose of converting them to the Christian faith. However, a moment's reflection transforms apparent similarities into important contrasts. While both missionary movements were expressions of Christianity, they are quite different in their structure and ethos. While these missionary institutions are rooted in a common culture, there are also distinctions between them both in cultural content and in the modes of its expression. And while both Protestants and Catholics had missionary motives for coming among the Blackfeet, their intentions were not unmixed, and their actions have had important nonreligious consequences. These three broader categories suggest certain specific variations between the groups that shed further light upon the historical development of the two churches.

One of the clearest disparities is that Roman Catholic institutions had a greater diffusion than did Protestant institutions. The reasons for this contrast lie both in the nature of the two religious structures and in the Blackfoot culture which missionaries sought to influence. In the first instance, historical priority played an important role. The simple fact that Catholic missionaries came among the Blackfeet earlier and stayed longer partly explains why their missionary forms rooted more deeply than those of the Protestant church.

Second, institutional resources committed to the task were always greater among Catholics than among Protestants. Both sides had shortages of personnel and money, but the Catholics sent the Jesuits, and that made all the difference. While Protestant missions to the Indians suffered because of the attractiveness of missions outside the United States, Jesuits ironically were being lured from Europe to save the Indians' souls. Thus, in a strange way, two equally strong romantic missionary movements had quite different results. Furthermore, since the Jesuits operated in groups, Holy Family Mission had a large staff and a functioning institution. In contrast, there was only a lone Methodist minister and his wife on the reservation during this period.

Third, differences in the structure of the Catholic ministry are important for understanding the accomplishments of the Catholic church. Their success depends not only upon historical accident but also upon celibacy. The celibate religious order was a tight cadre of men whose common life reinforced their personal life styles. They were able to create their own social world which, in turn, protected them from the dangers of absorption into the vital Indian world and at the same time provided a strong base from which they could work. They were able to follow Blackfeet on the hunt, to remain at an isolated post, to disband or regroup on command—in short, to be mobile, flexible, and disciplined enough to meet diverse situations on the missionary frontier. The fact that their wider organization operated through a vertical chain of command made the deployment of resources even easier. In contrast, the Protestant minister, with responsibilities for wife and family, was often unable to penetrate the Indian world or to remain long at his post to await the arrival of civilization and its supports. Furthermore, the organization the minister served was more loosely structured than the Jesuit order and often had insufficiently focused energy to fulfill its purposes.

Fourth, there were important distinctions between the theological perspectives of the two groups. The priests' sacramentalism gave them a sense of identity and a role to sustain them in difficult circumstances. The Protestant minister, while he could relate to whites, often had real difficulty confronting a people so different racially and culturally from himself. His problems derived in part from the fact that his basic identity was racially and culturally rather than sacramentally defined. Catholic sacramentalism not only tended to increase the priest's sense of purpose and support his self-understanding, but it also enabled him to transcend human differences and incorporate more Indians into the church. With his role so dependent upon a common racial and cultural heritage, the Protestant minister had identity problems as a missionary. As a result, the Protestants eventually excluded the Blackfeet from the church.

Fifth, differences in quality of preparation and general education produced variations in the missionary outcome. The Roman Catholic missionaries were usually well-educated men gifted with many talents, including linguistic abilities. Predictably, the activities of a group of versatile, talented priests were more effective than the activities of isolated Protestant pastors— some ill prepared for their tasks and none specifically trained by the church.

In addition to the heterogeneity in white missionary institutions, factors in Blackfoot culture also influenced missionary action and often determined the way missionary forms would be accepted by the Indians. First, Blackfoot autonomy was perhaps the most important element. As long as the Blackfeet were independent people, with their own social world, they were not motivated to change their religion. They did selectively accept those parts of the white man's medicine which seemed superior to their own. But even then, there was a tendency for ideas or practices of the two religions to remain side by side rather than for Christianity to displace tribal ways. Christian prayers did not drive out traditional prayers in the same way that the iron pot eclipsed the clay pot in Blackfoot life. With the loss of Blackfoot autonomy through the destruction of their social world, there was greater opportunity for the missionaries to convince Indians to accept Christianity, though there was considerable resistance even then.

Second, it is probably true that the Black Robes and their religion, with its rich symbolism and intricate liturgical expressions, seemed closer to Blackfoot religion than did the faith of the Short Coats. Blackfoot responses to De Smet, Point, and later Prando show how readily they identified the Black Robe with the medicine man. It must have been easy for Indians to see the cross, the saints, and the prayers of the Black Robe as at least similar to the charms and bundles, the spirits and prayers of their traditional religion. It was perhaps less difficult for Blackfeet to harmonize the Catholic expression of Christianity with their past than to be converted to a Protestantism that was limited in liturgy and symbolism, though rich in passion.

Any just comparison of Roman Catholic and Protestant missions must not only account for their differing degrees of institutional development but must also account for the negative impact of the missions. At the very moment when the Blackfeet were being undermined by the cumulative pressures of white contact, the Catholic missionary movement was often a force which further robbed Indians of life rather than a force for renewal of life. At just the appropriate time in history, missionaries joined their belief that Blackfoot culture was depraved with government ethnocentrism and power; and with their combined strength, they further emasculated the Indian life forms that had survived conquest. In this sense, Catholic attacks upon Blackfoot polygamy and religion diminished the Indian's inner world at a time when his outer world was disappearing. When the missionaries and the government failed to transform Indians into white men, the destructive consequences of their action remained.

In this history, it is easy to see how closely missionary institutions reflected the cultural motifs of the nineteenth century. Although the priests were mostly recent immigrants from Europe, they quickly assumed the ideology of forced acculturation. It was natural for a working relationship between church and state to develop—despite the separation affirmed by the Founding Fathers. This co-operation was reinforced by the fact that priests often came from countries with a Catholic establishment, where such a relationship was normal.

While the association of the Catholic church with forced acculturation had its destructive effects, these consequences were softened by the church's success in incorporating the Blackfeet, especially the children, into the institution. People who were in danger of losing all order and identity were given a chance to achieve a sense of order and an alternate identity. The Protestants also had the early tendency to reflect the ideology of forced acculturation, but they had neither the institutional resources nor the power to implement these ideas. While Protestants were not often culpable of coercion, they were guilty of exclusivism. Their rejection of the Blackfeet undermined any constructive role which they might have had as an institution and is responsible for the fact that they remain largely marginal to Indian life on the Blackfeet Reservation.

At its broadest level, the history of Blackfoot missions demonstrates how fallible the churches were and that the consequences of their actions were mixtures of good and evil. While many factors frustrated missionary intentions, missionaries were not wholly the captives of historical powers beyond their control. Thus, history can be instructive—rather than being simply the revelation of predetermined patterns. By looking back upon the ambiguity of missionary action in a specific situation, churchmen can perhaps learn to assess the consequences of their acts a bit better. Without hoping to eliminate evil in history or to control the future, they can at least mitigate some of the more destructive aspects of their activity.

In the final analysis, two matters remain shrouded in mystery. First, none of the data surveyed reveals anything about the religious significance of Christian missions to individual Blackfeet. It is impossible to determine how many Indians discovered new meaning for life in the medicine of the white man. Second, it is impossible fully to project the future. Therefore, the question remains unanswered whether the Christian churches and Americans in general can find the imagination and the resources to further social justice among the Blackfeet in reparation for a bloody past. No one knows for sure. But even though institutional evolution will probably have certain continuities with the past, the future remains partially open. Both men and institutions have limited historical freedom. The question is whether that freedom can be so employed that the Blackfeet will be enabled to walk into a more human future.

Appendix:
"To the Indians, Heart Butte"

The following sermon is the only surviving example of Jesuit preaching emanating from Holy Family Mission that I have been able to discover. It was preached by Father Aloysius Soer, a Dutch Jesuit, to a congregation at Heart Butte on the first Sunday in Lent, 1904. Father Soer made regular trips to Heart Butte from Holy Family between 1905 and 1932, and under his leadership the little church, St. Peter Claver, was completed in 1911.

The sermon, reproduced from a greatly revised cursive manuscript exactly as it was written, contains one of the fullest examples of Jesuit methods of implanting their theological ideas; of their use of scripture; of their dualism, rooted in a division of the world between God and Satan; of the theological contradictions in their perspective; and of indirect information about Blackfoot attitudes which appear in Soer's opposition to certain interpretations of the priest's role. Toward the end of the sermon is a reference which indicates that Soer was at this time already planting the idea of building a church at Heart Butte.

TO THE INDIANS, HEART BUTTE
Instructions for the First Sunday in Lent, 1904
Father Aloysius Soer

Text: "Thou shalt not tempt the Lord, thy God." (Matt. 4: 7)

Today the holy book says that we must not try the power of God. We must not make fun of the power of God. Jesus said these words to the devil: "Thou shalt not tempt the Lord thy God." You must not make fun of God.

Today the holy book (the Gospel) tells us that Jesus went into the desert & staid alone there for 40 days. 40 days he fasted; for 40 days he did not eat; & then he was hungry. The devil, the bad spirit, was watching him all the time. He thought that he was the Son of God, but he was not sure. He saw that he had not eaten for a long time, & he knew that he was hungry. So he came up and said to Jesus: "If you are the Son of God, change these stones into bread." Jesus answered & said: "It is written, not in bread alone doth man live, but in every word that proceedeth from the mouth of God." God says that bread alone can't make a man happy; but the words of God can make a man happy. If we hear the words of God, if we believe in God & keep His commandments, God will help us in this world, & when we die, He will bring us to everlasting happiness in heaven. We have but a short time to live in this world. We have not here a lasting abode. This world is not our home. We are just stopping here for a little while. Heaven is our true home. We all have to die; some young, some old. It is a short time. Those who are good & follow the ways of God in this world shall live forever in heaven in everlasting happiness. But those who are bad shall be separated from God forever. They shall go to the devil, they shall go down into the earth, into hell, there they shall burn forever in fire hotter than any fire upon this earth; there they shall cry & curse forever; there children will hate their parents & forever curse them. Oh! Parents, be good & take care of your children now that you may never see them there. Now teach them to pray, to go to church on Sundays & how to be good! . . .

There are two great spirits working in this world, the good

Spirit & the bad Spirit; the Good Spirit is God, the bad Spirit is the devil. God is our true Father. He made us, & He made all things that are made. He made us out of love; He made us to be forever happy in heaven. All the good things that we have in this world come from Him. For us He has made the Sun, the moon, & the stars—for us He has made the earth, the mountains, the snow, the rain, the creeks & all the waters upon the earth; For us He has made the grass, the flowers, the trees, & all the birds that fly in the air. We are better than all these things. God made all these things for us. He made them to Help us to be good & to go to heaven. Man is better than all the other things that we see in the world; man is closer to the heart of God than all these things.

Hence it is, that God has commanded us not to pray to the sun & to the other things which He has made for us, because they cannot help us. God has commanded us to pray to Him alone, & to love him for all the good things that He has given us. God made all the other things which we see to serve man, but he made man to serve Himself here in this world. We are created to love God here in this world & to love Him forever in heaven.

God is the good Spirit. He has lived always without beginning, & He shall have no end. He is infinitely happy—He is infinitely great. His goodness is infinite—His power is infinite; He can do all things. He made all things. The greatest things & the small-est things He made. He made the highest mountain & the smallest fly that moves upon the earth. All things belong to Him. There is only one God. God is only one great Spirit; He is only One in nature, One in life, One in goodness & in power; but He is three in person & the Three persons in God are called the Father the Son and the Holy Ghost. God is our true Father, the Good Spirit.

But who is the devil? He is the bad spirit. He is God's enemy. God made the devil. He made him before He made the first man, about 6000 years ago. He made him an angel, good & happy; at the same time He made many thousands of other angels; He placed them all in a part of heaven; and He put them all on trial. He wanted them to show that they loved Him. Two thirds of the Angels obeyed His command. Them God took into heaven to be forever happy with Him. Now they are happy in heaven.

But the devil saw that he was very beautiful, full of light, & shining like the sun. So he became proud; he would not obey God; but he fought against God; he tried to place himself above God; ⅓ part of the angels followed the devil; they disobeyed God & fought against Him. In one moment God changed them all into ugly devils; He created hell in one moment in the lower part of the earth; & He cast all those bad angels with the devil at their head into hell to burn in fire forever. They are now the bad spirits. And the devil is their chief. They hate God; & they hate us, because God made us to take their places in heaven which they lost by sin. Now God lets them travel over this earth to try the strength of man. The devil & all those bad spirits go about this earth like mad lions, seeking whom they may devour. They work against God. They are trying to bring all men down to hell. They work in the minds & hearts of men to make them think what is wrong, to believe what is false, & to desire what is bad.

The devil is a liar, & the father of lies. By a lie he led our first father & mother into sin. Long ago he entered in a snake, wrapped himself around the apple tree of which God had told our 1st parents not to eat; & he told them if they would eat they would not die. But God had said that [they] would, if they eat that fruit. So by a lie he made our first parents unhappy; he brought sin into the world. Because our first father & mother listened to the devil & disobeyed God, God condemn[ed] them with all their children to death. That is why we all have to die; that is why there is sickness & so many miseries in the world. That [is] why [there is] ignorance. Sin has brought misery [and] death into the world. That same wicked spirit by his lies tried to lead the Son of God into sin; But he could not. Jesus has shown us how to conquer the devil & not to mind his lies.

That same wicked spirit today tells lies to the minds & hearts of men. He says that the same God did not make all men. He says that the White people's God did not make the Indians. He says the Indians have one father, & the White people another. That is a big lie. The devil knows that all the people on this earth; White people & Indians, negroes & Chinese, have come from the same father & mother. All people are brothers.

But why does the devil tell a lie? Because he is proud, & hates

God. He wants to draw people away from God; he wants to make himself the father of people; he gives some little help to foolish people in this world, so that he can fool them & bring them to hell. So those people who do not love God & work not for Him, who do not go to church on Sunday, who do not mind the priest, take the devil for their father, & they work for the devil.

Now who is the priest? The priest is the minister of God. The priest works for God & he fights against the devil. God has given the priest power to break the chains of the devil & to set people free from his grasp. He has given to the priest the Keys of heaven, so that he can open heaven to all those who wish to leave the devil. The devil hates the priest, & he gets some people to say bad things about him. Same say that it is all foolishness to believe the priest. The priest goes to see sick people & prays over them, & the sick people die; he prays for people to die & keeps people from living to be old. That is a big lie coming from the heart of the devil. The priest never does pray for anybody to die, he never made anybody die sooner. God fixes the time for each one to die. God did not make [the] priest to cure people from sickness. He made doctors for that. Sometimes when sick people have strong faith, & strongly believe in God, God cures them by prayer & by the help of the priest. But the priest's business is not to cure the sick; but he does not make people die soon. Often people die young because they do not mind God, because they do not mind the priest. But the priest never makes anybody die; prayer never makes anybody die. The devil tells that lie; he tries to make people afraid of the priest to keep them away from him, to keep them out of heaven & to bring them to hell.

Some people get mad with God when their children die, they stop praying. They do not love God; they do not fear God. They make fun of God; they despise Him. God is the Lord & He takes children when He sees best. God often punishes very hard those people who stop praying & who don't go to church because they lose a child, or a relation. God often takes away from them one child after another by death.

A long time ago theye was a holy man named Job. He was very rich. He prayed very much. He had many cattle & sheep; & he had 7 sons & 3 daughters. One day God let the devil take away all that Job had. One day some people at war took away all of his cattle, & his sheep were destroyed by fire, & the house in which his children were was blown down by the wind, & his 7 sons and 3 daughters were all killed. Job got all this bad news at one time. When he heard it he fell down & prayed to God; & he said: 'The Lord gave; and the Lord hath taken away; blessed be the name of the Lord.' Then God had mercy on Job and he helped him. Soon again Job had twice as many sheep & cattle as he had before; 7 more sons & 3 more daughters were born to him; & after this he lived 140 yrs., & he saw all of his children, grand children, & great grand children good & happy; & when he was a very old man he died a happy death.

There are two classes of people in the world; the good & the bad; those who belong to God & those who belong to the devil; those who are on the road to heaven & those who are on the road to hell.

Now who are those who wish to be on the side of God? The priest can help those who wish to work for God; but the priest can not help those who wish to work for the devil.

Those who are on the side of God, & who love God ought to do something for God. The Heart of God is the best of all Hearts. The Sacred Heart of Jesus is all good; that is the Heart that loves most of all. Now those who love God & our Lord Jesus Christ, for His Holy Heart ought to join together to build a Church here at Heart Butte. Build God a house, where He can live among you & pour out his good things more plentifully upon you & your children; where you & your children can come to pray to God & to learn the ways of God; the way to heaven.

Now this is the holy time of the year, called Lent. 40 days before Easter is the holy time. It is a time to pray much, to fast, & to do penance for sin. There are 40 days because Our Lord fasted 40 days in the desert. Good Friday, the day that Jesus died on the Cross for our sins, is coming. It will be two days before Easter. Let us now pray & be sorry for our sins, & try to atone for them, so that we may have part with Jesus in the joys of Easter & in His never ending happiness in heaven. Amen.

Bibliography

I. UNPUBLISHED MATERIALS

Blackfeet Agency Archives, Museum of the Plains Indian, Browning, Mont., containing letter-books, miscellaneous correspondence, and other manuscripts and microfilms relating to the administration of Indian affairs.

Browning Methodist Church Files, Browning, Mont., containing correspondence, legal documents, and miscellaneous papers relating to the Methodist mission among the Blackfeet.

Chancery Archives, Diocese of Helena, Helena, Mont., containing correspondence, official statistics, and newspaper files relating to the Catholic church in Montana.

Correspondence and documents relating to the Epworth Piegan Mission, 1922–34, from the records of the Board of Missions of the Methodist Church, now on file at Collins Memorial Library, University of Puget Sound, Tacoma, Wash.

Files of Little Flower Church, Browning, Mont., containing baptismal and marriage records, as well as general statistical information about the parish.

Harrod, Howard L., Blackfoot Field Notes, 1963; 1969.

Montana Conference Historical Collection, Paul M. Adams Memorial Library, Rocky Mountain College, Billings, Mont., containing the letters and papers of William Wesley Van Orsdel, as well as rare copies of early conference journals and other records.

Montana Historical Society, Helena, Mont., containing manuscripts and typescripts of documents relating to Indian affairs in Montana.

National Archives, Records of the Washington Superintendency of Indian Affairs, Washington, D.C.

Official Files of the Division of National Missions of the Board of Missions of the United Methodist Church, Philadelphia, Pa.

Oregon Province Archives of the Society of Jesus, Gonzaga University, Spokane, Wash., containing records, manuscripts, correspondence, and miscellaneous papers on Indian missions in Montana.

II. GOVERNMENT DOCUMENTS

"Blackfeet Flood, The," Department of the Interior, Bureau of Indian Affairs, Billings Area Office, 1964 (mimeographed).

Dominion of Canada. *Annual Reports of the Department of Indian Affairs*, 1880–1915.

Record of Engagements with Hostile Indians Within the Military Division of the Missouri from 1868 to 1882. Chicago, 1882.

"Report of Indian Education in Montana, 1962–1963" (mimeographed).

"Report to the Secretary of the Interior by the Task Force on Indian Affairs," July 10, 1961 (mimeographed).

U.S. Bureau of the Census. *United States Census of Population: 1960*. Vol. I, Part 28, Montana. Washington, D.C., 1963.

U.S. Congress. "Blackfeet Indian Reservation," Serial 2, *Hearings Before the Joint Commission of the Congress of the United States*. Washington, D.C., 1915.

U.S. *Congressional Record*. Vol. XI.

U. S. Department of Health, Education, and Welfare. *Indians on Federal Reservations in the United States: A Digest*. Public Health Service Publication No. 615. Washington, 1958.

U.S. Department of the Interior. *Annual Reports of the Commissioner of Indian Affairs*, 1859–1901.

————. "The Montana-Wyoming Indian." Billings, Mont., 1961 (mimeographed).

————. "United States Indian Population and Land." Washington, D.C., 1963 (mimeographed).

U.S. House of Representatives, Committee on Interior and Insular

Affairs. *Indian Unemployment Survey.* Committee Print No. 3, 88 Cong., 1 sess. (July, 1963).

U.S. Senate, Committee on Labor and Public Welfare. *Hearings Before the Select Committee on Poverty.* Washington, D.C., 1964.

III. BOOKS

Andrist, Ralph K. *The Long Death.* New York, 1964.

Bakeless, John, ed. *The Journals of Lewis and Clark.* New York, 1964.

Banton, Michael, ed. *Anthropological Approaches to the Study of Religion.* London, 1966.

Barclay, Wade Crawford. *History of Methodist Missions: The Methodist Episcopal Church, 1845–1939.* New York, 1957. Vol. III.

Beaver, Robert Pierce. *Church, State, and the American Indians.* St. Louis, 1966.

Berger, Peter L. *The Sacred Canopy.* New York, 1967.

Berger, Peter L., and Thomas Luckmann. *The Social Construction of Reality.* New York, 1967.

Berkhofer, Robert F., Jr. *Salvation and the Savage.* Lexington, 1965.

Bischoff, William N. *The Jesuits in Old Oregon.* Caldwell, Idaho, 1945.

Book of Discipline of the United Methodist Church, The. Nashville, 1968.

Brosnan, Cornelius J. *Jason Lee, Prophet of the New Oregon.* New York, 1932.

Brummitt, Stella W. *Brother Van.* New York, 1919.

Burns, Robert Ignatius, S.J. *The Jesuits and the Indian Wars of the Northwest.* New Haven, 1966.

Chittenden, Hiram Martin. *The American Fur Trade of the Far West.* 2 vols. New York, 1935.

Chittenden, Hiram Martin, and Alfred Talbot Richardson. *Life, Letters, and Travels of Father Pierre-Jean De Smet, S. J.* 4 vols. New York, 1905.

Collier, John. *Indians of the Americas.* New York, 1957.

Contributions to the Historical Society of Montana. Vol. III.

Corbishley, Thomas, S. J. *Roman Catholicism.* New York, 1964.

Curtis, Edward S. *The North American Indian.* 20 vols. Seattle and Cambridge, Mass., 1907–30.

Denig, Edwin Thompson. *Indian Tribes of the Upper Missouri.* Ed. by John C. Ewers. Norman, 1961.

Denny, Sir Cecil E. *The Law Marches West*. Ed. by W. B. Cameron. Toronto, 1939.

De Smet, Father Pierre Jean. *Oregon Missions and Travels over the Rocky Mountains in 1845–46*. New York, 1847.

———. *Western Missions and Missionaries*. New York, 1863.

Doctrines and Disciplines of the Methodist Church (1916, 1960, 1964).

Durkheim, Emile. *The Elementary Forms of the Religious Life*. Tr. by Joseph Ward Swain. New York, 1961.

Erikson, Erik H. *Childhood and Society*. 2d. ed. New York, 1963.

Ewers, John C. *The Blackfeet*. Norman, 1958.

Fichter, Joseph H., S.J. *Social Relations in the Urban Parish*. Chicago, 1954.

Garraghan, Gilbert J., S.J. *Chapters in Frontier History*. Milwaukee, 1934.

———. *The Jesuits of the Middle United States*. 3 vols. New York, 1938.

Gold, Douglas. *A Schoolmaster Among the Blackfeet Indians*. Caldwell, Idaho, 1963.

Goldfrank, Esther S. *Changing Configurations in the Social Organization of a Blackfoot Tribe During the Reserve Period: The Blood of Alberta, Canada*. Ed. by A. Irving Hallowell. New York, 1945.

Gordon, Milton M. *Assimilation in American Life*. New York, 1964.

Grinnell, George Bird. *Blackfoot Lodge Tales*. New York, 1892.

Gustafson, James M. *Treasure in Earthen Vessels: The Church as a Human Community*. New York, 1961.

Hagan, William T. *American Indians*. Chicago, 1961.

Hanks, Lucien M., and Jane R. Hanks. *Tribe Under Trust*. Toronto, 1950.

Henry, Alexander, and David Thompson. *New Light on the Early History of the Greater Northwest: The Manuscript Journals of Alexander Henry and David Thompson*. Ed. by Elliott Coues. 3 vols. New York, 1897.

Hughes, Katherine. *Father Lacombe: The Black-Robe Voyageur*. New York, 1911.

Innis, Harold A. *The Fur Trade in Canada*. New Haven, 1962.

Jung, A. M. *Jesuit Missions Among the American Tribes of the Rocky Mountain Indians*. Spokane, 1925.

Kroeber, A. L., and Clyde Kluckhohn. *Culture*. New York, 1963.

LaFarge, John, S.J. *A Report on the American Jesuits*. New York, 1956.

Lancaster, Richard. *Piegan*. New York, 1966.

Larpenteur, Charles. *Forty Years a Fur Trader on the Upper Missouri*. Ed. by Elliott Coues. 2 vols. New York, 1898.

Laveille, E., S.J. *The Life of Father De Smet, S.J.* Tr. by Marian Lindsay. New York, 1915.

Leeuw, Gerardus van der. *Religion in Essence and Manifestation*. Tr. by T. E. Turner. 2d ed. New York, 1963.

Leppert, Peter. *The Jesuits*. Tr. by John Murray. New York, 1958.

Lewis, Oscar. *The Effects of White Contact upon Blackfoot Culture*. Ed. by A. Irving Hallowell. New York, 1942.

Lind, Robert W. *From the Ground Up*. N.p., 1961.

Linton, Ralph, ed. *Acculturation in Seven American Indian Tribes*. New York, 1940.

Logan, George. *Histories of the North Montana Mission, Kalispell Mission and Montana Deaconess Hospital with some Biographical and Autobiographical Sketches*. N.p., n.d.

Loran, C. T., and T. F. McIlwraith, eds. *The North American Indian Today*. Toronto, 1943.

McBride, C. Angela. *Ursulines of the West*. Everett, Wash., 1936.

McClintock, Walter. *The Old North Trail*. London, 1910.

McDougall, John. *On Western Trails in the Early Seventies*. Toronto, 1911.

MacInnes, Charles M. *In the Shadow of the Rockies*. London, 1930.

Maclean, John. *Canadian Savage Folk*. Toronto, 1892.

Malinowski, Bronislaw. *Magic, Science, and Religion*. New York, 1948.

Mannheim, Karl. *Essays on the Sociology of Knowledge*. London, 1968.

———. *Ideology and Utopia*. New York, 1936.

Maximilian, Alexander Philip, Prince of Wied Neuwied. *Travels in the Interior of North America*. Tr. by H. Evans Lloyd. London, 1843.

Mead, George H. *Mind, Self, and Society*. Chicago, 1934.

Memorie Del P. Filippo Rappagliosi. Rome, 1879.

Meriam, Lewis, *et al. The Problem of Indian Administration*. Baltimore, 1928.

Merton, Robert K. *Social Theory and Social Structure*. Revised ed. Glencoe, Ill., 1957.

Mills, Edward L. *Plains, Peaks and Pioneers: Eighty Years of Methodism in Montana*. Portland, 1947.

Missionary Society of the Methodist Episcopal Church. *Annual Reports*. 1870–83.

Moberg, David O. *The Church as a Social Institution*. Englewood Cliffs, N.J., 1962.

Morice, A. G. *History of the Catholic Church in Western Canada*. 2 vols. Toronto, 1910.

Morison, Samuel Eliot. *The Oxford History of the American People*. New York, 1965.

Morris, Alexander. *The Treaties of Canada with the Indians of Manitoba and the North-West Territories*. Toronto, 1880.

Murdock, George P. *Ethnographic Bibliography of North America*. 3d ed. New Haven, 1960.

Niebuhr, H. Richard. *The Responsible Self*. New York, 1963.

———. *The Social Sources of Denominationalism*. New York, 1929.

Nix, James E. *Mission Among the Buffalo*. Toronto, 1960.

Olmstead, Clifton E. *History of Religion in the United States*. Englewood Cliffs, N.J., 1960.

Palladino, L. B., S.J. *Indian and White in the Northwest*. 2d ed. Lancaster, Pa., 1922.

Park, Robert Ezra. *Race and Culture*. Glencoe, Ill., 1950.

Pelikan, Jaroslav. *The Riddle of Roman Catholicism*. New York, 1959.

Platt, Ward, ed. *Methodism and the Republic*. Philadelphia, n.d.

Playter, George. *The History of Methodism in Canada*. Toronto, 1862.

Point, Nicolas, S.J. *Wilderness Kingdom*. Tr. by Joseph P. Donnelly, S.J. New York, 1967.

Price, A. Grenfell. *White Settlers and Native Peoples*. Cambridge, England, 1949.

Priest, Loring Benson. *Uncle Sam's Stepchildren*. New Brunswick, 1942.

Prucha, Francis Paul. *American Indian Policy in the Formative Years*. Cambridge, Mass., 1962.

Radin, Paul. *The Story of the American Indian*. New York, 1927.

Rahill, Peter J. *The Catholic Indian Missions and Grant's Peace Policy*. Washington, D.C., 1953.

Schapiro, Harry L., ed. *Man, Culture, and Society*. New York, 1960.

Schoenberg, Wilfred P., S.J. *A Chronicle of the Catholic History of the Pacific Northwest: 1743–1960*. Spokane, 1962.

———. *Jesuits in Montana, 1840–1960*. Portland, 1960.

————. *Jesuit Mission Presses in the Pacific Northwest.* Portland, 1957.

Schultz, James Willard. *Blackfeet and Buffalo.* Norman, 1962.

Schutz, Alfred. *Collected Papers.* Ed. by Maurice Natanson. 3 vols. The Hague, Netherlands, 1964, 1966, 1967.

Scott, Martin J., S.J. *Isaac Jogues Missioner and Martyr.* New York, 1927.

Simpson, George Eaton, and J. Milton Yinger. *Racial and Cultural Minorities.* New York, 1953.

Spicer, Edward H., ed. *Perspectives in American Indian Culture Change.* Chicago, 1961.

Stearn, E. Wagner, and Allan E. Stearn. *The Effect of Smallpox on the Destiny of the American Indian.* Boston, 1945.

Stonequist, Everett V. *The Marginal Man.* New York, 1937.

Thompson, David. *David Thompson's Narrative of His Explorations in Western America, 1784–1812.* Ed. by J. B. Tyrrell. Toronto, 1916.

Thwaites, Reuben Gold, ed. *Early Western Travels: 1748–1846.* 32 vols. Cleveland, 1904–1907.

Tims, John W. *Grammar and Dictionary of the Blackfoot Language in the Dominion of Canada.* London, 1889.

Wagley, Charles, and Marvin Harris. *Minorities in the New World.* New York, 1958.

Washburn, Wilcomb E., ed. *The Indian and the White Man.* New York, 1964.

Weber, Max. *The Protestant Ethic and the Spirit of Capitalism.* Tr. by Talcott Parsons. New York, 1958.

————. *The Sociology of Religion.* Tr. by Ephraim Fischoff. Boston, 1963.

Wissler, Clark. *Indians of the United States.* Garden City, 1940.

Work, John. *The Journal of John Work.* Ed. by William S. Lewis and Paul C. Phillips. Cleveland, 1923.

IV. PERIODICALS

Calumet, The. July, 1932.

Catalogus Vice Provinciae Missourianae, Societatis Jesu, 1841. Gandavi, 1841.

Collier, John. "A Reply to Mrs. Eastman," *The Christian Century,* Vol. LI (August 8, 1934), 1018–20.

Duignan, Peter. "Early Jesuit Missionaries: A Suggestion for Further Study," *American Anthropologist*, Vol. LX (1958), 725–32.

Eastman, Elaine Goodale. "Does Uncle Sam Foster Paganism?", *The Christian Century*, Vol. LI (August 8, 1934), 1016–18.

Ewers, John C. "The Horse in Blackfoot Indian Culture," Bureau of American Ethnology *Bulletin 159*. Washington, 1955.

————. "Identification and History of the Small Robes Band of the Piegan Indians," *Journal of the Washington Academy of Sciences*, Vol. XXXVI, No. 12 (1946), 397–401.

————. "The North West Trade Gun," *Alberta Historical Review*, Vol. IV, No. 2 (Spring, 1956), 3–9.

————. "Self-Torture in the Blood Indian Sun Dance," *Journal of the Washington Academy of Sciences*, Vol. XXXVIII, No. 5 (1948), 166–73.

Grinnell, George Bird. "Early Blackfoot History," *The American Anthropologist*, Vol. V (April, 1892), 153–64.

Heise, David R. "Prefatory Findings in the Sociology of Missions," *Journal for the Scientific Study of Religion*, Vol. VI, No. 1 (April, 1967), 49–58.

Indian Sentinel, The. First Series, 1903–14.

————. Second Series, 1920–33.

Jeffreys, M. D. W. "Some Rules of Directed Culture Change Under Roman Catholicism," *American Anthropologist*, Vol. LVIII (1956), 721–31.

Klett, Guy S. "Missionary Endeavors of the Presbyterian Church Among the Blackfeet Indians in the 1850's," *Journal of the Department of History of the Presbyterian Church in the U.S.A.*, Vol. XIX, No. 8 (December, 1941), 327–54.

Lowie, Robert H. "Plains Indian Age-Societies: Historical and Comparative Summary," *Anthropological Papers of the American Museum of Natural History*, Vol. XI, Part 13 (1916).

Maclean, John. "Social Organization of the Blackfoot Indians," *Transactions, Canadian Institute*, Vol. IV (1892–93).

Mallett, Major Edmond. "The Origin of the Flathead Mission of the Rocky Mountains," *Records of the American Catholic Historical Society of Philadelphia*, Vol. II (1886–88), 174–205.

Minutes of the General Assembly of the Presbyterian Church in the U.S.A. (1924, 1926, 1942, 1943).

Montana Christian Advocate. First Series, 1895–99.

Point, Nicolas. "A Journey in a Barge on the Missouri River from the Fort of the Blackfeet [Lewis] to that of the Assiniboine

[Union], 1847," tr. by Paul A. Barrette, *Mid-America*, Vol. XIII, No. 3 (January, 1931).

Proceedings of the Montana Conference of the Methodist Church, 1893–1969.

Riggin, F. A. "Recollections of Methodism in Montana From the Early Seventies," *The Messenger*, Vol. VII, No. 2 (Feb. 1, 1911), 6–7.

Schaeffer, Claude. "The First Jesuit Mission to the Flathead, 1840–1850: A Study in Culture Conflicts," *The Pacific Northwest Quarterly*, Vol. XXVIII, No. 3 (July, 1937), 227–50.

Simpson, George E., and J. Milton Yinger, eds. "American Indians and American Life," *The Annals of the American Academy of Political and Social Science*, Vol. CCCXI (May, 1957).

West, Helen B. "Starvation Winter of the Blackfeet," *Montana*, Vol. IX, No. 1 (January, 1959), 2–19.

Wissler, Clark. "Ceremonial Bundles of the Blackfoot Indians," *Anthropological Papers of the American Museum of Natural History*, Vol. VII, Part 2 (1912).

———. "The Social Life of the Blackfoot Indians," *Anthropological Papers of the American Museum of Natural History*, Vol. VII, Part 1, (1911).

———. "Societies and Dance Associations of the Blackfoot Indians," *Anthropological Papers of the American Museum of Natural History*, Vol. XI, Part 4 (1913).

———. "The Sun Dance of the Blackfoot Indians," *Anthropological Papers of the American Museum of Natural History*, Vol. XVI, Part 3 (1918).

Wissler, Clark, and D. C. Duvall. "Mythology of the Blackfoot Indians," *Anthropological Papers of the American Museum of Natural History*, Vol. II, Part 1 (1908).

Woodstock Letters, Vol. X, No. 2 (1881); Vol. XII, No. 1 (1883); Vol. XII, No. 3 (1883).

V. NEWSPAPERS

Glacier Reporter (Browning, Mont.), September 12, 1963.

New York Times, May 6, 1969.

VI. THESES AND DISSERTATIONS

Black, Hugh M. "The History of the Holy Family Mission, Family,

Montana, From 1890 to 1935," master's thesis, Saint Paul Seminary.

Harrod, Howard L. "Mission Among the Blackfeet: An Evaluation of Protestant and Catholic Missions among the Blackfeet Indians," doctoral dissertation, Yale University, 1965.

Whitner, R. L. "The Methodist Episcopal Church and Grant's Peace Policy: A Study of the Methodist Agencies, 1870–1882," doctoral dissertation, University of Minnesota, 1959.

VII. FORMAL INTERVIEWS AND CORRESPONDENCE

Bell, Rev. James E., former pastor, Methodist Blackfeet Mission, Browning, Mont. Personal interview. September, 1963 (tape recorded).

Bentley, Rev. C. A., former pastor, Baptist Mission on the Crow Reservation, Lodge Grass, Mont. Personal interview. September, 1963.

Burdsall, Rev. Herbert J., former chairman, Montana Conference Board of Missions. Personal interview. September, 1963 (tape recorded).

Fortier, Father G., principal, Blood Roman Catholic Indian Residential School, Blood Indian Reserve, Cardston, Alberta. Personal interview. October, 1963.

Gillen, Father A. M. D., former priest at Little Flower Church, Browning, Mont. Personal interview. September, 1963.

Gillette, Gerald W., research historian, Presbyterian Historical Society. Personal correspondence. February, 1965.

Halligan, Monsignor M. J., former priest at Little Flower Church. Personal interview. July, 1969.

Himmel, Rev. Conrad, pastor, Browning Methodist Church. Personal interview. July, 1969.

Lamb, Rev. O. H., principal, St. Paul's Anglican Indian Residential School, Blood Indian Reserve, Cardston, Alberta. Personal interview. October, 1963.

Lewis, Marian, former deaconess, Epworth Piegan Mission, Browning, Mont. Personal interview. October, 1963.

McDonald, Daniel D., employment assistance officer, Blackfeet Agency, Browning, Mont. Personal interview. September, 1963.

Mallman, Father Egon, S.J., priest at St. Anne's Church, Heart Butte, Mont. Personal interview. September, 1963.

Mecklenburg, Rev. Henry, former pastor, Epworth Piegan Mission,

Browning, Mont. Personal interview. October, 1963 (tape recorded).

Merchant, Mrs. John, Piegan. Personal interview. September, 1963.

Neal, Robert C., former member of the Montana Conference Board of Missions. Personal interview. September, 1963 (tape recorded).

Patterson, Rev. Gordon A., former superintendent, Glacier District of the Montana Conference. Personal interview. September, 1963 (tape recorded).

Rice, Allen B., executive secretary, Section of Home Missions, Division of National Missions of the Methodist Church. Personal interview. January, 1964 (tape recorded).

Ritchey, Rev. George S., former pastor, Browning Methodist Church. Personal interview. January, 1964.

Schmidt, Donald, member of the Browning Methodist Church. Personal interview. September, 1963; July, 1969.

Sherburne, Mrs. Frank, member of the Browning Methodist Church. Personal interview. September, 1963.

Ward, Philip A., Jr., superintendent, Browning Public Schools. Personal interview. September, 1963.

Wilcox, Mrs. Allen C., wife of former pastor, Epworth Piegan Mission, Browning, Mont. Personal correspondence. April, 1964.

Williamson, Mrs. Mae, Piegan. Personal interview. September, 1963 (tape recorded).

Index

THE CIVILIZATION OF THE AMERICAN INDIAN SERIES
of which *Mission Among the Blackfeet* is the 112th volume, was inaugurated in 1932 by the University of Oklahoma Press, and has as its purpose the reconstruction of American Indian civilization by presenting aboriginal, historical, and contemporary Indian life. The following list is complete as of the date of publication of this volume.

1. *Forgotten Frontiers:* A Study of the Spanish Indian Policy of Don Juan Bautista de Anza, Governor of New Mexico, *1777–1787.* Translated and edited by Alfred Barnaby Thomas.
2. Grant Foreman. *Indian Removal:* The Emigration of the Five Civilized Tribes of Indians.
3. John Joseph Mathews. *Wah'Kon-Tah:* The Osage and the White Man's Road.
4. Grant Foreman. *Advancing the Frontier, 1830–1860.*
5. John H. Seger. *Early Days Among the Cheyenne and Arapahoe Indians.* Edited by Stanley Vestal. Out of print.
6. Angie Debo. *The Rise and Fall of the Choctaw Republic.*
7. Stanley Vestal. *New Sources of Indian History, 1850–1891:* A Miscellany. Out of print.
8. Grant Foreman. *The Five Civilized Tribes.*
9. *After Coronado:* Spanish Exploration Northeast of New Mexico, 1696–1727. Translated and edited by Alfred Barnaby Thomas.
10. Frank G. Speck. *Naskapi:* The Savage Hunters of the Labrador Peninsula. Out of print.
11. Elaine Goodale Eastman. *Pratt:* The Red Man's Moses. Out of print.
12. Althea Bass. *Cherokee Messenger.* (A Life of Samuel Austin Worcester.)
13. Thomas Wildcat Alford. *Civilization.* As told to Florence Drake. Out of print.
14. Grant Foreman. *Indians and Pioneers:* The Story of the American Southwest Before 1830.
15. George E. Hyde. *Red Cloud's Folk:* A History of the Oglala Sioux Indians.
16. Grant Foreman. *Sequoyah.*
17. Morris L. Wardell. *A Political History of the Cherokee Nation, 1838–1907.* Out of print.
18. John Walton Caughey. *McGillivray of the Creeks.*
19. Edward Everett Dale and Gaston Litton. *Cherokee Cavaliers:* Forty Years of Cherokee History as Told in the Correspondence of the Ridge-Watie-Boudinot Family.
20. Ralph Henry Gabriel. *Elias Boudinot, Cherokee, and His America.* Out of print.
21. Karl N. Llewellyn and E. Adamson Hoebel. *The Cheyenne Way:* Conflict and Case Law in Primitive Jurisprudence.
22. Angie Debo. *The Road to Disappearance.*
23. Oliver La Farge and others. *The Changing Indian.* Out of print.
24. Carolyn Thomas Foreman. *Indians Abroad.* Out of print.
25. John Adair. *The Navajo and Pueblo Silversmiths.*
26. Alice Marriott. *The Ten Grandmothers.*
27. Alice Marriott. *Maria:* The Potter of San Ildefonso.

28. Edward Everett Dale. *The Indians of the Southwest:* A Century of Development Under the United States. Out of print.

29. *Popol Vuh:* The Sacred Book of the Ancient Quiché Maya. English version by Delia Goetz and Sylvanus G. Morley from the translation of Adrián Recinos.

30. Walter Collins O'Kane. *Sun in the Sky.*

31. Stanley A. Stubbs. *Bird's-Eye View of the Pueblos.* Out of print.

32. Katharine C. Turner. *Red Men Calling on the Great White Father.*

33. Muriel H. Wright. *A Guide to the Indian Tribes of Oklahoma.*

34. Ernest Wallace and E. Adamson Hoebel. *The Comanches:* Lords of the South Plains.

35. Walter Collins O'Kane. *The Hopis:* Portrait of a Desert People.

36. *The Sacred Pipe:* Black Elk's Account of the Seven Rites of the Oglala Sioux. Edited by Joseph Epes Brown.

37. *The Annals of the Cakchiquels,* translated from the Cakchiquel Maya by Adrián Recinos and Delia Goetz, with *Title of the Lords of Totonicapán,* translated from the Quiché text into Spanish by Dionisio José Chonay, English version by Delia Goetz.

38. R. S. Cotterill. *The Southern Indians:* The Story of the Civilized Tribes Before Removal.

39. J. Eric S. Thompson. *The Rise and Fall of Maya Civilization.* (Revised Edition.)

40. Robert Emmitt. *The Last War Trail:* The Utes and the Settlement of Colorado. Out of print.

41. Frank Gilbert Roe. *The Indian and the Horse.*

42. Francis Haines. *The Nez Percés:* Tribesmen of the Columbia Plateau. Out of print.

43. Ruth M. Underhill. *The Navajos.*

44. George Bird Grinnell. *The Fighting Cheyennes.*

45. George E. Hyde. *A Sioux Chronicle.* Out of print.

46. Stanley Vestal. *Sitting Bull, Champion of the Sioux:* A Biography.

47. Edwin C. McReynolds. *The Seminoles.*

48. William T. Hagan. *The Sac and Fox Indians.*

49. John C. Ewers. *The Blackfeet:* Raiders on the Northwestern Plains.

50. Alfonso Caso. *The Aztecs:* People of the Sun. Translated by Lowell Dunham.

51. C. L. Sonnichsen. *The Mescalero Apaches.*

52. Keith A. Murray. *The Modocs and Their War.*

53. *The Incas of Pedro de Cieza de León.* Edited by Victor Wolfgang von Hagen and translated by Harriet de Onis.

54. George E. Hyde. *Indians of the High Plains:* From the Prehistoric Period to the Coming of Europeans.

55. *George Catlin:* Episodes from "Life Among the Indians" and "Last Rambles." Edited by Marvin C. Ross.

56. J. Eric S. Thompson. *Maya Hieroglyphic Writing:* An Introduction.

57. George E. Hyde. *Spotted Tail's Folk:* A History of the Brulé Sioux.

58. James Larpenteur Long. *The Assiniboines:* From the Accounts of the Old Ones Told to First Boy (James Larpenteur Long). Edited and with an introduction by Michael Stephen Kennedy. Out of print.

59. Edwin Thompson Denig. *Five Indian Tribes of the Upper Missouri:* Sioux,

Arickaras, Assiniboines, Crees, Crows. Edited and with an introduction by John C. Ewers.

60. John Joseph Mathews. *The Osages:* Children of the Middle Waters.
61. Mary Elizabeth Young. *Redskins, Ruffleshirts, and Rednecks:* Indian Allotments in Alabama and Mississippi, *1830–1860.*
62. J. Eric S. Thompson. *A Catalog of Maya Hieroglyphs.*
63. Mildred P. Mayhall. *The Kiowas.*
64. George E. Hyde. *Indians of the Woodlands:* From Prehistoric Times to 1725.
65. Grace Steele Woodward. *The Cherokees.*
66. Donald J. Berthrong. *The Southern Cheyennes.*
67. Miguel León-Portilla. *Aztec Thought and Culture:* A Study of the Ancient Nahuatl Mind. Translated by Jack Emory Davis.
68. T. D. Allen. *Navahos Have Five Fingers.*
69. Burr Cartwright Brundage. *Empire of the Inca.*
70. A. M. Gibson. *The Kickapoos:* Lords of the Middle Border.
71. Hamilton A. Tyler. *Pueblo Gods and Myths.*
72. Royal B. Hassrick. *The Sioux:* Life and Customs of a Warrior Society.
73. Franc Johnson Newcomb. *Hosteen Klah:* Navaho Medicine Man and Sand Painter.
74. Virginia Cole Trenholm and Maurine Carley. *The Shoshonis:* Sentinels of the Rockies.
75. Cohoe. *A Cheyenne Sketchbook.* Commentary by E. Adamson Hoebel and Karen Daniels Petersen.
76. Jack D. Forbes. *Warriors of the Colorado:* The Yumas of the Quechan Nation and Their Neighbors.
77. *Ritual of the Bacabs.* Translated and edited by Ralph L. Roys.
78. Lillian Estelle Fisher. *The Last Inca Revolt, 1780–1783.*
79. Lilly de Jongh Osborne. *Indian Crafts of Guatemala and El Salvador.*
80. Robert H. Ruby and John A. Brown. *Half-Sun on the Columbia:* A Biography of Chief Moses.
81. *The Shadow of Sequoyah:* Social Documents of the Cherokees. Translated and edited by Jack Frederick and Anna Gritts Kilpatrick.
82. Ella E. Clark. *Indian Legends from the Northern Rockies.*
83. *The Indian:* America's Unfinished Business. Compiled by William A. Brophy and Sophie D. Aberle, M.D.
84. M. Inez Hilger, with Margaret A. Mondloch. *Huenun Ñamku:* An Araucanian Indian of the Andes Remembers the Past.
85. Ronald Spores. *The Mixtec Kings and Their People.*
86. David H. Corkran. *The Creek Frontier, 1540–1783.*
87. *The Book of Chilam Balam of Chumayel.* Translated and edited by Ralph L. Roys.
88. Burr Cartwright Brundage. *Lords of Cuzco:* A History and Description of the Inca People in Their Final Days.
89. John C. Ewers. *Indian Life on the Upper Missouri.*
90. Max L. Moorhead. *The Apache Frontier:* Jacobo Ugarte and Spanish-Indian Relations in Northern New Spain, *1769–1791.*
91. France Scholes and Ralph L. Roys. *The Maya Chontal Indians of Acalan-Tixchel.*

92. Miguel León-Portilla. *Pre-Columbian Literatures of Mexico*. Translated from the Spanish by Grace Lobanov and the Author.

93. Grace Steele Woodward. *Pocahontas*.

94. Gottfried Hotz. *Eighteenth-Century Skin Paintings*. Translated by Johannes Malthaner.

95. Virgil J. Vogel. *American Indian Medicine*.

96. Bill Vaudrin. *Tanaina Tales from Alaska*. With an introduction by Joan Broom Townsend.

97. Georgiana C. Nammack. *Fraud, Politics, and Dispossession of the Indians:* The Iroquois Land Frontier in the Colonial Period.

98. *The Chronicles of Michoacán*. Translated and edited by Eugene R. Craine and Reginald C. Reindrop.

99. J. Eric S. Thompson. *Maya History and Religion*.

100. Peter J. Powell. *Sweet Medicine:* The Continuing Role of the Sacred Arrows, the Sun Dance, and the Sacred Buffalo Hat in Northern Cheyenne History.

101. Karen Daniels Petersen. *Plains Indian Art from Fort Marion*.

102. Fray Diego Durán. *Book of the Gods and Rites* and *The Ancient Calendar*. Translated and edited by Fernando Horcasitas and Doris Heyden. Foreword by Miguel León-Portilla.

103. Bert Anson. *The Miami Indians:* Sovereigns of the Wabash-Maumee.

104. Robert H. Ruby and John A. Brown. *The Spokane Indians:* Children of the Sun. Foreword by Robert L. Bennett.

105. Virginia Cole Trenholm. *The Arapahoes, Our People*.

106. Angie Debo. *A History of the Indians of the United States*.

107. Herman Grey. *Tales from the Mohaves*.

108. Stephen Dow Beckham. *Requiem for a People:* The Rogue Indians and the Frontiersmen.

109. Arrell M. Gibson. *The Chickasaws*.

110. *Indian Oratory:* A Collection of Famous Speeches by Noted Indian Chieftains. Compiled by W. C. Vanderwerth.

111. *The Sioux of the Rosebud:* A History in Pictures. Photographs by John A. Anderson, text by Henry W. Hamilton and Jean Tyree Hamilton.

112. Howard L. Harrod. *Mission Among the Blackfeet*.